David K. Wyatt, Translator & Editor

The Nan Chronicle

Studies on Southeast Asia

SEAP

Southeast Asia Program
Cornell University, Ithaca, New York
1994

Studies on Southeast Asia No. 16

ISBN 0-87727-715-X

TABLE OF CONTENTS

ILLUSTRATIONS

PREFACE

Long ago, probably in June of 1963, Professor R. B. Jones of Cornell received from Alexander Griswold a translation of the chronicle of the old principality of Nan which Prasœt Churatana had done for him. At the time, I was conducting dissertation research in Bangkok and buying books for the Cornell University Libraries; and Jones and the library passed on to me an urgent request that I find a copy of the original printed edition of this chronicle so that the translation might be checked before publication by Cornell's Southeast Asia Program. I found the 1918 publication and sent it off to Cornell. A year later, as I was leaving Ithaca to take up my first teaching position in England, Jones told me there were some problems with the translation, and that he would appreciate my taking on the job of editing it. And so I spent many odd moments during the 1964/65 academic year working on the Nan Chronicle, changing many parts of the translation and meeting Griswold's requests for a more systematic romanization of Thai names and words. The resulting slim volume was published by the Southeast Asia Program in 1966 as number 59 in its Data Papers series. There the matter might have ended, though I did return to it at one point with corrections to the dates.[1]

It was only on visiting the north of Thailand for the first time in 1976 that I began to become aware of the enormous wealth of the literary and historical traditions of that region. Then and on subsequent visits in 1980 and 1984 I purchased primers that promised to teach me to read the northern Thai alphabet, but with the press of various distractions I never managed to get around to working seriously on them.

Finally, in 1987 I obtained a whole year's leave after a period of service as department chair; and with children now grown and few distractions to nail me to Ithaca, I decided, quite offhandedly and on the spur of the moment, to spend my leave in Chiang Mai. As my fiftieth birthday approached, I decided that it was now or never for learning to read Northern Thai. One morning in September 1987 I paid a visit to Dr. Udom Roongruangsri in the Department of Thai at Chiang Mai University. He averred as how I might teach myself to read Northern Thai by working methodically through a book he had written which had Northern Thai and standard Central Thai on facing pages. I spent a few weeks faithfully trying to understand the poetry of Maha Phrom, and decided that I would rather be expending my efforts on "real" history, namely a palm-leaf historical manuscript.

I therefore went to the Social Research Institute in Chiang Mai in search of a proper manuscript to read. But what text to choose from among hundreds of histories there preserved on microfilm? I browsed through their catalogue. It

---

[1]David K. Wyatt, "The Chronology of Nan History, A.D. 1320-1598," *Journal of the Siam Society* 64:2 (July 1976), 202-206.

might have made sense to choose a Chiang Mai history, of which there must have been sixty; but which one would be best to start with? Then I noticed "Nan" in the catalogue. There were not many historical manuscripts from Nan—perhaps a dozen or so—and these ranged from short texts to long ones. Because of my work on the Prasœt Churatana translation twenty years earlier, I decided on Nan, and chose a short manuscript of only nine pages, figuring that it would be best to start where I might quickly be in sight of the sense of accomplishment that comes from "completing" a task; and then I moved to ever longer texts. In the process, I discovered that the history of Nan was just as interesting now as it had been a quarter-century earlier. The adventure thus begun became ever more complex, as more and more texts came to light.

The volume that now results from that work is very different from "The Nan Chronicle" of a quarter-century ago. The most important difference is that this current work is a translation from the original palm-leaf manuscript in Northern Thai, rather than Prasœt Churatana's translation from a Central Thai translation. The difference is not trivial: the 1966 translation repeats the mistakes of the printed Central Thai edition, and where Prasœt skipped difficult words and passages the current edition grapples with them. Finally, the extensive footnotes and introduction to this edition make extensive references to what can safely be called the whole of the Nan historical-manuscript tradition, enabling one to begin to develop an appreciation for the historiographic skills of the original author, *Sænluang* Ratchasomphan. Like the 1966 edition, the current edition treats only the explicitly-Nan portion of the chronicle.

In the course of this long journey, I have benefited from the helpful assistance and advice of many. Here I must particularly thank Dr. Udom Roongruangsri, who gave me a start towards learning Northern Thai; Dr. M.R.W. Bhansoon Ladavalya, then director of the Social Research Institute; and Miss Phanphen Khruathai of the Institute's staff who helped me get started. Work continued especially during two subsequent visits to Chiang Mai and Nan in 1991 and 1992, on the latter occasion aided by a Fulbright-Hays Faculty Research Fellowship. I am deeply grateful to the Fulbright authorities in Bangkok for their generous assistance, especially Apiram Sowaprux, Doris Wibunsin, and Dr. Patamaka Sukontamarn; and to the staff of the Social Research Institute, especially Dr. Chayan Vaddhanaphuti, now director, Balee Buddharaksa, and Paithun Dokbuakæo. For a great deal of help and advice along the way I am grateful to Dr. Harald Hundius of the Department of Thai, Chiang Mai University, who helped with a few difficult passages and persuaded me that romanization can be a very political business; to Somchet Vimolkasem, of the Satri Sri Nan Girls' School and the Provincial Cultural Commission in Nan, for local knowledge; to the staff of the public works department of the municipality of Nan, who provided me with a fine, detailed map of the city; and especially to Aroonrut Wichienkeeo, who found additional manuscripts, helped with difficult words, and spent countless hours helping me through the most difficult passages in the manuscript. None of them should be held accountable for the numerous errors and infelicities that surely remain in this work.

DAVID K. WYATT

Ithaca
December 1993

ABBREVIATIONS

Jkm. ....Ratanapañña Thera, *The Sheaf of Garlands of the Epochs of the Conqueror, being a translation of* Jinakâlamâlîpakaranam, tr. N. A. Jayawickrama. London: Luzac for the Pali Text Society, 1968.

McCMap ....James McCarthy, *Surveying and Exploring in Siam*. London: John Murray, 1900. "Triangulation Chart" on page 1; "Map of the Kingdom of Siam and its Dependencies," in pocket at end.

MNBPS ....*Müang Nan: borankhadi prawatsat læ sinlapa*. Bangkok: Fine Arts Dept., 1987.

MS.1 ....Phün wongsa mahakasat tang lai tangtæ Paña Samantalat phon ma læ phün wongsa caonai ton sawœi latcasombat nai müang Pua læ müang Nan. MS. Wat Panet, *tambon* Wiang Nüa, *amphœ* Müang, Nan; SRI 82.107.05.043, 240 ff°.

MS.2 ....Phün wongsa caonai ton sawœi latcasombat nai müang Pua læ müang Nan. MS. Wat Dòn Kæo, *tambon* Nai Wiang, *amphœ* Müang, Nan; SRI 82.107.05.044, 130 ff°.

PMN&TY ....Prawat müang Nan læ Tamlâ yâ. MS. Wat Muang Tüt, *tambon* Muang Tüt, *amphœ* Müang, Nan; SRI 82.107.05.047, 39 ff°.

PNMN ....Phün na müang Nan læ khâo thâng müang Nan, ed. Aroonrut Wichienkeeo. Chiang Mai: Sûn Watthanatham Cangwat Chiang Mai, Witthayâlai Khru Chiang Mai, 1985 ('Ekkasan lamdap thi 9). MS., SRI 82.107.05.049, 42 ff°

PTMN ....Prawat tang müang Nan. MS., SRI 82.107.05.045, 182 ff°. Transcription: SRI, by "Buntha— Caran" and checked by Buntha Sriphimchai; dated 19 November 2525 (1982).

T15RW ....Tamnan sip ha ratchawong. 3 v. Chiang Mai: Social Research Institute, 1981-1990.

TCH ....*See* TCH/SF.

TCH (1931) ....Tamnan Phrathat Chæ Hæng. Bangkok: crem. Cao Mahaphrom Surathada (Mahaphrom na Nan), 1931.

TCH/MT ....Tamnan Pathat Cao Cæ Hæng. MS. Wat Muang Tüt, Nan, dated BE 2481 [AD 1938]. 13 double pages. Davis Ms. fl-?; Lanna Thai Manuscripts from the Richard Davis Collection, Australian National University; Microfiche #8.

TCH/PP ....Tamnan Pathat Cæ Hæng. MS. Wat Phaya Phu, Nan, dated 1928; copied by *nân* Kua Lüalit, 1972. Davis fl-38; Lanna Thai Manuscripts from the Richard Davis Collection, Australian National University; Microfiche #3.

TCH/SF ....Tamnan Cæ Hæng. MS. Wat Sæn Fang, *tambon* Chang Mòi, *amphœ* Müang, Chiang Mai; SRI 78.020.01L.038; 19 ff°.

TCH/TC ....Tamnan Pathat Cæ Hæng. MS. Wat Tan Cum, undated. 21p. Davis Ms. fl-49; Lanna Thai Manuscripts from the Richard Davis Collection, Australian National University; Microfiche #12.

TCRM......................Takun cao latcawong Mahapom. MS. Wat Mongkhon, *tambon* Nai Wiang *khet* 2, *amphœ* Müang, Nan; SRI 82.107.05.052, 9 ff°; originally dated 1850; copy dated 1879.

TMN.........................Tamnan müang Nan. MS. Wat Tan Cum, Nan; copied by Nòi Inta Müangpom, 1972. Davis fl-47. Lanna Thai Manuscripts from the Richard Davis Collection, Australian National University; Microfiche #24.

TPMCM ....Tamnan phün müang Chiang Mai, ed. Sanguan Chotisukkharat. Bangkok: Samnak Nayok Ratthamontri, 1971.

Udom ....Udom Roongruangsri, *Photcanânukrom Lân Nâ-Thai, chabap Mæfâ Luang*. 2 vols. Chiang Mai and Bangkok: Mûnnithi Mæfâ Luang and Thanâkhân Thai Phânit, 1991.

vV ....Vliet, Jeremias van. *The Short History of the Kings of Siam*, tr. Leonard Andaya. Bangkok: The Siam Society, 1975.

INTRODUCTION

Nan is little known and seldom remembered. Compared with other towns of bustling modern Thailand, Nan does not amount to much: the town has a population of only 25,000, and the entire province only about 400,000. The traders and tourists whose trucks and buses roar through Phræ and Lampang, Lamphun and Chiang Mai, Phayao and Chiang Rai, do not go to Nan, which lies on the way to nowhere important. Nan is tucked away in the eastern corner of the North of Thailand, in the headwaters of the Nan River. It is surrounded on the west, north, and east by mountains; and the way south now is blocked by the massive Sirikit Dam, which has inundated the old water route to the south. The railroad never got closer to Nan than Den Chai in Phræ province, some 75 miles (125 km.) to the southwest and, until the modern road was constructed in the 1960s, it was a rough ride over the mountains. In the world of the 1990s, Nan is a backwater, whose name conjures up images of a woebegone, dilapidated rusticity.

Just a century ago, however, the ancient principality of Nan was at the peak of its power. It was covered by lush teak forests, just beginning to be worked by foreign logging firms. (Nan today still has nearly half its area covered with forests, though most of the larger trees are gone.) It sat astride major trade routes that linked Luang Prabang and northern Laos to the mighty rivers of the central Siam plains.[1] Nan was ruled by a line of energetic and effective kings, dating back to the eighteenth century, who had given their people almost a century of peace, as well as unprecedented wealth and power. Their efforts had been rewarded by their suzerains in Bangkok, the Cakri monarchs, who bestowed upon them status as kings, and held them responsible for an enormous territory encompassing all of what is now northwestern Laos and neighboring portions of China, in addition to the present province of Nan. Nan in 1890 was more extensive, and probably more populous, than the much better known Lao kingdom of Luang Prabang, which enjoyed a similar status. When the Irish surveyor James McCarthy traversed northern Laos in the 1880s and 1890s, mapping the frontiers of Siam for the king in Bangkok, he did so with an escort from the king of Nan, not from the king of Luang Prabang.[2]

And then, suddenly, in 1893 the domains of the king of Nan were shrunk back to their fifteenth-century extent, the headwaters of the Nan River alone: after the Paknam Crisis of that year, Siam was forced to yield most of its Laos domains to the French. The kings of Nan lasted for nearly another forty years, apparently in some prosperity. When the last king of Nan died in 1931, however, the powers of the old ruling house were abolished, and Nan thereafter was administratively and politically like any other province of Thailand, with only the new palace that had been under construction in 1931 standing to remind Nan

---

[1]Christian Taillard, *Le Laos: stratégies d'un Etat-tampon* (Montpellier, 1989).

[2]James McCarthy, *Surveying and Exploring in Siam* (1900), and his *An Englishman's Siamese Journals, 1890-1893* (Bangkok, 1983). The latter is not explicitly attributed to him, but it is clearly an earlier and fuller version of the 1900 book.

people of their special history. The palace no longer was the focus for public life that it once had been, and it gradually was overgrown, to be rescued for service as a fine museum only in 1987.[3]

It was in the immediate aftermath of the 1893 crisis—felt at least as sorely in Nan as in Bangkok—that *Sænluang* Ratchasomphan, a high-ranking official of the Nan king, composed a lengthy chronicle of the history of the principality in 1894. The Nan Chronicle, as we will call it, came to be particularly well known because it was published in 1918 as the tenth volume in the distinguished collection of chronicles published by the National Library in Bangkok,[4] and because, alone of the northern chronicles, it was translated into English almost thirty years ago.[5] It might appear, therefore, that Nan historiography is especially noteworthy. This is not the case. True, Phræ has no chronicle, and Phayao has few; but Chiang Mai, Lampang, Lamphun, Chiang Rai, and Fang have many, including the extraordinary chronicles written in Pali in Chiang Mai in the fifteenth and sixteenth centuries. At least on the face of things, there is nothing about the Nan Chronicle that should single it out for special distinction. It is, after all, very late: it is closer in time to the *Phongsawadan Yonok* (1898) of the Bangkok official Phraya Prachakitkòracak (Chæm Bunnag) than to the traditional chronicles of most of the rest of the north. There are two things about it that make it peculiarly interesting: the time when it was written, and the fact that we appear to have most of the materials upon which *Sænluang* Ratchasomphan based his compilation.

We will have occasion later to remark upon the significance of when the Nan Chronicle was written. Let us for the moment consider its sources.

THE NAN CHRONICLE AND ITS SOURCES

1. MAIN MANUSCRIPT (MS.1)

Sænluang Ratchasomphan's 1894 Nan Chronicle is a palm-leaf manuscript of 240 pages (that is, both sides of 120 leaves), with five lines to the folio, dated 1 November 1894. In the left margin of both sides of the first leaf is inscribed a title: "Story of the Lineage of All the Kings from Phraya Samantaraja Onwards, and Story of the Lineage of Princes Who Have Enjoyed the Sovereignty of Pua and Nan."[6] There probably are numerous copies of this manuscript in various places, including the National Library and the library of the Siam Society in Bangkok. The National Library copy was that used in preparing the 1918 published edition. I have used a microfilm copy in the Social Research Institute of Chiang Mai University which comes from Wat Phranet in Nan.

---

[3]A good quick survey of Nan's history is given in Richard B. Davis, *Muang Metaphysics* (Bangkok: Pandora, 1984), pp. 27-37.

[4]*Sænluang* Râtchasomphan, *Râtchawongpakòn phongsâwadân müang Nan* (Bangkok?: Crem. Phracao Suriyaphongphrittadet, 1918).

[5]*The Nan Chronicle,* tr. Prasœt Churatana (Ithaca: Southeast Asia Program, 1966; Data Paper, no. 59).

[6]*Pün wongsâ mahâkrasat tang lai tang tæ Pañা Samantarâja pon ma, læ Pün wongsâ caonâi ton sawœi lâtcasombat nai müang Pua læ müang Nan.* MS. Wat Phranet, tambon Wiang Nüa, amphœ Müang, Nan; SRI 82.107.05.043, 240 ff°. In all references to the manuscripts, the first number given is the folio; the second, after the diagonal slash, the line.

The very title of our Main Manuscript (MS.1) indicates that it is a composite text, for the title is really two titles, connected with a conjunction. The first third of the text (ff° 1-81) has nothing to do with Nan in particular, but is instead a history of human kingship from legendary times in India down to the early seventeenth century, concentrating especially on the rulers of Lan Na (Chiang Mai) and their predecessors. Because the last ruling dynasty of Nan came from Chiang Mai in the eighteenth century, this section functions to legitimize the Nan kings by placing them in a loose lineage that goes back to the Buddha; but I have not translated it here.

That the division of MS.1 into two parts is not arbitrary is confirmed both by a major division within the manuscript after f° 81 (where there is a blank leaf at f° 82, and then a separate marginal title for the remainder of the manuscript),[7] and by the existence of a second palm-leaf manuscript (see **2** below) that includes just the explicitly Nan portion; i.e., beginning with f° 83 of the Main Manuscript, and with the same title as the last half of the title of MS.1.[8]

MS.1 has been published three times: (1) as part 10 of the series *Prachum phongsawadan* (PP), on the occasion of the cremation of the Nan ruler King Suriyaphongpharittadet in 1918; (2) in volume 4 of the complete reprint of PP by Samnakphim Kaona in 1964; and (3) in volumes 9 and 10 of the Teachers' Institute (Khurusapha) reprint of PP in 1964. The Teachers' Institute edition is somewhat carelessly done, and should be used with caution.[9]

The main printed editions are, on the whole, competently done, but I have discovered numerous mistakes by comparison with the manuscript (and a few instances where the printed edition, presumably reflecting another manuscript, includes words and phrases missing from the Wat Phranet manuscript).

The Wat Phranet manuscript includes additional material at the end, comprising the last eleven folios of the manuscript. This manuscript appears to fall into several sections. First is simply a continuation of the story begun in the last paragraph of the printed text, which I am persuaded was simply omitted by the person who transcribed the text in Bangkok. There is a sharp break in the text, and then another section, a story of pious works, begins. This section includes dates in the RS era (RS + 1781 = AD), running from 1904 to 1918, and appears to be an addendum to the original manuscript done by, or at the behest of, a titled official, Cao Uttarâkânkoson. There is a lengthy duplication here: with but minor differences, ff° 233-236 are duplicated on ff° 237-240, with the exception of the final paragraph, which occurs only at the very end of the text. In these two cases, both sides of two palm leaves are involved.

---

[7]*Pün wongsâ caonâi / ton sawœi lâtcasombat / nai müang Pua læ / müang Nân tînî kòn læ (Chronicle of the Line of Rulers who have Enjoyed the Sovereignty of Pua and Nan)*; f° 83, left margin.

[8]There is also a manuscript in the Social Research Institute in Chiang Mai (SRI 82-107-05-051) from Wat Muang Tüt in Nan, labeled *Nangsü pün müang Nân pûk tî 2 (Chronicle of Nan, bundle 2)*, which, when I read it in 1988, I decided was identical to bundle 2 of the well-known *Tamnân 15 râtchawong*, a chronicle of Chiang Mai. Only now [1991] do I realize that it could formerly have been deliberately inserted into a version of the Nan Chronicle. There is nothing in the original manuscript, however, to indicate that it has anything to do with Nan.

[9]Compare the stories of the boys born from eggs in the Khurusapha and Kaona editions.

2. SHORTER VERSION (MS.2)

The second manuscript (MS.2) is titled "Story of the Lineage of Princes Who Have Enjoyed the Sovereignty of Pua and Nan." It runs to 130 pages (i.e., 65 leaves, written on both sides), and has only four lines to the folio. It clearly is incomplete: it breaks off in mid-sentence on f° 130, just as it is starting to give a date. The last full date mentioned seems to be in CS 1157 (AD 1795/96). Because of its length, I have not fully studied this manuscript. It is possible, but not likely, that it is much earlier than *Sænluang* Ratchasomphan's chronicle, and might have served as his chief source. There are, however, numerous other manuscripts that can fit that description, and it is to those that we now turn.

3. RELIQUARY CHRONICLES

Among the chief of these sources, and surely among the earliest to have been written, are what might be called the "reliquary chronicles" of Nan; specifically the chronicles of the great reliquary shrine that came to be the focal point of Buddhism in Nan and, indeed, the symbol of Nan's identity. This shrine is the Chæ Hæng reliquary (Wat Phra That Chæ Hæng), on the hill called Phu Phiang, a few kilometers east of the Nan River opposite the modern city of Nan.

We know little about how such religious chronicles came to be written, but we are surely safe in assuming that they were written and then subsequently copied and recopied by monks.[10] There is one revealing episode in the Nan Chronicle, as well as in the reliquary chronicles and related sources, that suggests that one function served by reliquary histories was to persuade rulers to support the religious institutions.[11]

There are five Chæ Hæng chronicles that I have consulted in working on the Nan Chronicle, and there are strong indications that *Sænluang* Ratchasomphan had access, either directly or indirectly, to the information contained in them. (And there are other versions extant, suggesting that the text was fairly widespread.)

The first, and apparently the oldest, is a manuscript entitled "Chronicle of Chæ Hæng" (TCH/SF), comprising 19 folios.[12] This text comes from Wat Sæn Fang in downtown Chiang Mai. The latest date included in this text is the 4th waning of the month of Caitra, a *kat pao* day, in the CS year 947, equivalent to Wednesday, 17 April AD 1585.[13]

A second copy of the manuscript comes from Wat Muang Tüt in Nan (TCH/MT). The original from which our copy comes may have been copied in 1864, but it surely dates ultimately to some time shortly after CS 1066 (AD 1704). In that year, it is said that the reliquary—and many similar shrines in the

---

[10]David K. Wyatt, "Chronicle Traditions in Thai Historiography," in *Southeast Asian History and Historiography: Essays Presented to D. G. E. Hall*, ed. C. D. Cowan and O. W. Wolters (Ithaca: Cornell University Press, 1976), pp. 107-22. On copying, see particularly Harald Hundius, "The Colophons of Thirty Pâli Manuscripts from Northern Thailand," *Journal of the Pali Text Society* XIV (1990): 1-173.

[11]See the early paragraphs of Chapter Three and the sources cited there.

[12]*Tamnan Cæ Hæng*. MS. Wat Sæn Fang, tambon Chang Moi, amphœ Müang, Chiang Mai; SRI 78.020.01L.038; 19 ff°. Aroonrut Wichienkeeo was kind enough to obtain a copy of this text for me from the Social Research Institute.

[13]For the date conversion, see Appendix 3.

northern hills—toppled, due both to the failure of people to heed accepted morality and the failure of the rulers properly to maintain and repair the reliquary.[14] It was copied for the anthropologist Richard Davis in October 1972.

A third manuscript comes from Wat Phaya Phu in the city of Nan. It was written in 1928, and also was copied for Richard Davis in 1972. Its title is given as the "Chronicle of the Holy Reliquary of Chæ Hæng" (TCH/PP).[15] The last full date given in the text—which appears to be the occasion for which the text was originally written—is the 14th waxing of the 12th month in the *kap san* year, CS 1066, equivalent to Friday, 12 September, AD 1704.

A fourth manuscript comes from Wat Than Chum in Nan (TCH/TC), and was copied for Davis in 1972.[16] It is much like the texts previously mentioned, but at its conclusion it gives a brief summary of reigns down to AD 1835, which might be considered as the date of the manuscript.

The final such text bears a similar title, "Chronicle of the Holy Reliquary of Chæ Hæng" [TCH(1931)]. Its coverage extends fully only down to CS 1066, like the second and third texts, of which it must be another copy. It comes from a manuscript of Wat Phra Singharam in Chiang Rai dated Wednesday the 3rd waning of the 5th month in CS 1262, equivalent to Wednesday, 7 February AD 1901. It was published for the cremation of the king of Nan, Cao Maha Phrom Surathada, in 1931.[17]

What is particularly distinctive about these five texts is that most of their dates, and especially the earlier dates, are given only in the decimal and duodecimal cycles (e.g., the northern Thai equivalent of "Year of the Cock, Tenth of the Decade"), without years expressed numerically in the CS era. Because later texts clearly borrowing from the reliquary chronicles frequently add CS-era year numbers, it is reasonable to conclude that texts without CS dates are earlier. [CS + 638 = AD.]

There are other Chæ Hæng reliquary chronicles that I have not used. One comes from Wat Huai So in the remote eastern district of Mæ Carim in Nan. It is titled "Chronicle of the Chæ Hæng Reliquary," and runs to twenty-one folios, four lines to the folio.[18] Despite repeated attempts, I have found it simply too difficult to read.[19]

---

[14]*Tamnan Pathat Cao Cæ Hæng;* MS. Wat Muang Tüt, Nan, dated BE 2481 [AD 1938]; 13 double pages; Davis Ms. fl-?; Lanna Thai Manuscripts from the Richard Davis Collection, Australian National University; Microfiche #8. This manuscript seems more frequently to omit CS numbers and give simply cyclical names for years than the copies of the TCH listed below.

[15]*Tamnan Pathat Cæ Hæng;* MS. Wat Phaya Phu, Nan, dated 1928; copied by *nân* Kua Lüalit, 1972; Davis fl-38; 25 pp.; Lanna Thai Manuscripts from the Richard Davis Collection, Australian National University; Microfiche #3.

[16]*Tamnan Pathat Cæ Hæng;* MS. Wat Tan Cum, undated; 21p. Davis Ms. fl-49; Lanna Thai Manuscripts from the Richard Davis Collection, Australian National University; Microfiche #12.

[17]*Tamnan Phrathat Cæ Hæng*. Bangkok: crem. Cao Mahaphrom Surathada (Mahaphrom na Nan), 1931.

[18]*Tamnan Pathat Cæ Hæng,* MS. Wat Huai So, tambon Mo Müang, amphœ Mæ Carim, Nan; SRI 88.161.01L.048; 21 ff°. Aroonrut Wichienkeeo was kind enough to obtain a copy of this text for me from the Social Research Institute. There are also two additional Cæ Hæng chronicles in the Davis Collection, but I have not yet had the opportunity to consult these.

[19]There are also other published versions; one published in Northern Thai script, *Tamnân Pathât Cao Pû Piang Cæ Hæng* (Chiang Mai, 1923); and a new edition recently published in Nan,

As a working hypothesis, let us assume that the compiler of the Nan Chronicle had at hand at least one version of the Chæ Hæng reliquary chronicle, and used it liberally to fill in the names, dates, and sequence of rulers, and major religious activities in the principality, often word-for-word from the reliquary chronicle.

4. THE "HISTORY OF THE FOUNDING OF NAN"

Of all the sources presumably available to the author of the Nan Chronicle, none is as interesting, nor as perplexing, as a long manuscript from Wat Phra Kœt, *tambon* Wiang Nüa, *amphœ* Müang, Nan province. In 1982, this manuscript was borrowed by staff of the Social Research Institute, Chiang Mai University, and taken to Chiang Mai. There it was microfilmed for the collection of the institute and the original was returned to Nan. The manuscript consists of 91 palm leaves, with four lines of writing on each side of each leaf, making a total of 182 "pages."[20]

In the course of filming, the manuscript was given a title, "Prawat tang müang Nan," which might be roughly translated as "A History of the Founding of Nan." The title is hardly exact, for the manuscript is actually a compendium of many different texts, all related, and all perhaps copied around the same time. The contents are so interesting that it is desirable to give a full description of the manuscript here. Bear in mind, however, that the division of the manuscript into parts reflects this investigator's personal judgment rather than any explicit divisions within the text itself.

The first leaf of the manuscript (unnumbered by the microfilm team) consists simply of two astrological diagrams representing the dates of the foundations of the cities of Pua and Nan. (Pua was the first seat of the kingdom of Nan, today located some 50 km. north of the modern city of Nan.)

The first diagram, a square form of what Thai astrologers call a *duang*, is labeled "The year 730 of the [Culasakarat] Era, a *pœk san* year, the foundation of this first city." Below the label appears the first of the two diagrams redrawn below, the numbers representing the positions of the planets in the heavens on the given date The second diagram, which appears on the right-hand side of the page and is given on the right below, is labeled "The year 787 of the [Culasakarat] Era, a *dap sai* year, the first foundation of the present city of Nan."

The full date of the first foundation of the city is given elsewhere in the text as a Tuesday, the 6th day of the waxing moon of the 12th month, equivalent to 19 August 1368. The planetary positions for that day come fairly close to

---

Tamnân Phrathât Cæ Hæng, chabap Phrasamuha Phrom læ wannakam khamson Khrao Ham, ed. Somcet Wimonkasem (Nan: Sun Watthanatham Cangwat Nan, 1983) which is based on the Chiang Mai edition. These show no major variations from the manuscripts I have used.

[20]In the microfilm collection of the Social Research Institute, the manuscript has the number SRI 82.107.05.045, indicating that it was filmed in 1982, it is on reel #107, the subject is history (05), and it is the 45th item on the reel. In this case I worked with a transcription of the text. The transcription was done by "Buntha — Caran" and the work was checked by Buntha Sriphimchai. The transcription is dated 19 November 2525 (1982). I have much confidence in the quality of the transcription especially because it is more exact than any other transcriptions I have seen, indicating even Northern Thai abbreviations and subscripts.

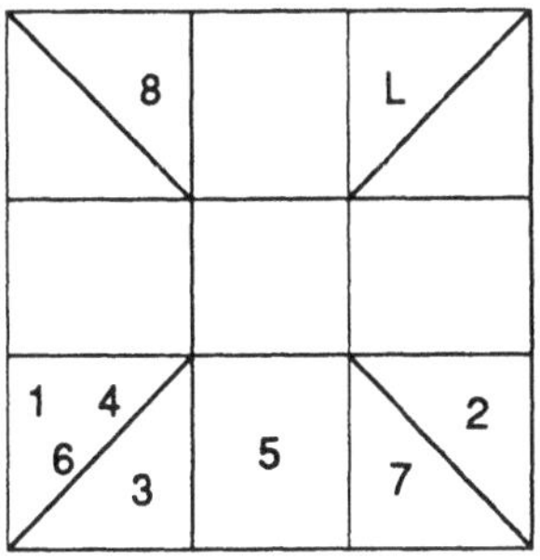

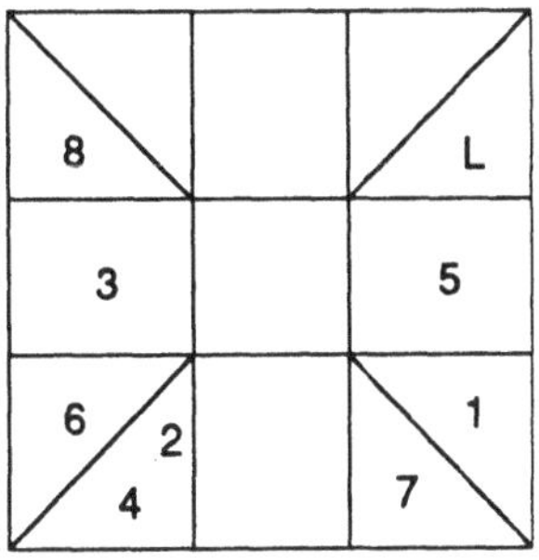

checking out. The second date is equivalent to 20 September 1425.[21] Beginning a historical manuscript in this fashion does not appear to be common in northern Thailand.

A. Immediate Background

The first section of the manuscript proper (ff° 1-22) establishes what we might consider to be an immediate context for the compilation of the text. It consists of a relatively detailed account of the major actions of the King of Nan, Sumanathewarat, from his accession to the throne of Nan in 1810 until 1821.

This section is a chronicle in the strict sense; that is, all information is in strict chronological order, and there is at least one entry for each year. All events are dated to the day, and sometimes even to the day of the week of the lunar calendar. A brief review of these events may prove useful in establishing the logical threads that hold the manuscript as a whole together.

This chronicle section begins by outlining the circumstances that began the reign, when Cao Attawalapanño went to Bangkok to attend the funeral obsequies for King Rama I (who died in 1809) and died there. Cao Sumanathewarat was named to succeed him as ruler at the end of that year (early in 1811). After a trip to Bangkok to be invested as ruler of Nan, Sumana returned home, and, early in 1812, led troops into what is now northern Laos to attack and take Müang La and Müang Pong. At the conclusion of the expedition, early in 1813 the ruler built a religious building in Nan and then took 6,000 families from the newly conquered territories (from La, Phong, Chiang Khœng [Müang Sing?], and Müang Luang Phukha) to Bangkok. The next year featured more of the same, with the Lao (Tai Nüa?) rulers accompanying Sumana to Bangkok in late 1813. In 1814 and 1815, the ruler was using his newly acquired surplus manpower to expand considerably the irrigation works immediately to the south and west of the modern city of Nan.

Sumana then had what his contemporaries would have considered the exceptional good fortune to have his subjects capture two auspicious elephants—a white elephant in 1816 and a red elephant in 1817, both of which were escorted to Bangkok with great pomp and circumstance, and both of which brought the Nan rulers unusually generous presents from the King of Siam. As if to thank the heavenly powers for his great good fortune, Sumana had a spirit house (*hò thewada*) built where the elephants were found. In 1818 and 1819, after severe

[21]Date worked out by Dr. J. C. Eade; undated letter, June 1991.

flooding nearly leveled his capital, Sumana had Nan moved to slightly higher ground, apparently where the city sits today. The ruler then set about reorganizing his officials, establishing a new city pillar, and repairing religious foundations. His last major act reported here was to appoint a *sangharaja* (a head of the Buddhist Sangha) in mid-1821.

The first two-thirds of this section of our manuscript are thus taken up with relatively straightforward accounts of the doings of the ruler, written in a fashion very similar to that in which the doings of the earlier rulers of his dynasty are written up in the Nan Chronicle. There is, however, an unusual tone and content to the last third of this section. If this section is read as a coherent text, with a logical subtext that structures it, the argument of the section builds to the ordering or reordering of the polity of Nan between the time of the capture of the elephants in 1816-17 and the appointment of the *sangharaja* in 1821: the city was moved, old religious shrines were renovated, officials (and the Buddhist monkhood) were properly organized, and the irrigation works were repaired. Once this physical and human (and ecclesiastical) world is placed in proper order, the text (by f° 13) moves to another level. The last third of this section is concerned with a moral universe that is both Buddhist and non-Buddhist. The early folios of this portion speak of the Buddhist Sangha and the duties of the ruler, the teachings of the Buddha concerning morality, and the various Buddhist texts in which that morality is expressed. It goes on to warn that deities (*devaputra* and *devata*) kill or otherwise discomfit those who do not tread the path of righteousness;[22] and all the supernatural forces are brought into play—rivers, lakes, streams, various kinds of spirits, and so forth. The last portion of this subsection (f° 21) amounts to a curse directed against those who stray from the path of righteousness, meaning especially conformity with the order imposed by the ruler.[23]

We might say, then, that the opening portion of the manuscript is concerned both with the present moment and with the eternal. The unspoken logic of what follows would seem to demonstrate both how the present evolved out of the past and the ineluctable workings of eternal principles through the past experience of the people of the Nan valley.

B. Legendary Origins

The second major portion of the manuscript (ff°22-38) consists of a very old-fashioned, traditional account of the origins and early history of the Nan River valley, told in a manner very reminiscent of Chapter 1 of the Nan Chronicle. The very first line of this section sets the tone by stating that what follows is according to the "ancient tales" (*tâm phün burân;* f° 22/2).[24]

These "ancient tales" appear to be based at least on a list of dates, and more likely on an indeterminate number of other manuscripts, including especially the *Tamnan Müang Nan* discussed below. After recounting the legendary beginnings of the first ruling house of Pua and Nan with the birth of two princes

---

[22]The phrase used repeatedly in the text is *nai khlòng rajasacca.*

[23]There must be a better way of translating this. *Kòng* is Lao *khòng*, as in *hit 12 khòng 14.*

[24]The word *pün* once puzzled me immensely. Its usual contexts suggest a meaning like that given for the word in Marc Reinhorn, *Dictionnaire laotien-français* (Paris, 1970), p. 1566: "le récit, l'histoire, le sujet."

hatched from eggs, and of the relations of their descendents with the house of Ngam Müang, ruler of Phayao, a handful of relatively full dates is provided in this section:

(1) Prince Sai Yok became king of Pua with the name of Pha Kòng in the *ka kai* year, 214 [sic] of the Era;

(2) Pha Kòng ruled from the *ka sai* year, 714 of the Era, for five years, until the *kap sanga* year;

(3) in the *rawai san* year, 718 of the Era, King Kan Müang came to rule;

(4) in the *ka mao* year, 715 of the Era, Pha Kòng became ruler;[25] and

(5) a white-robed ascetic, *phakhao* Nantha, of Wat Dòn Khrai, recommended a better site for the city, and Nan was built there in the *pœk san* year, 730 of the Era, on Tuesday, the 3rd day of the waxing moon of the 12th month.[26]

From this point onward, there are no year numerals in this section of the text: all major events are dated, but only the year names are given, in the sixty-year animal/decimal cycle, plus, in many instances, the day and the month (rarely the weekday, and then usually in sixty-day animal/decimal cycle form). Here, clearly, is the source of the chronological problems in the 1894 Nan Chronicle: the chronicler added year numbers in the Culasakarat Era, but computed them erroneously.[27] These chronological problems are dealt with in the footnotes to the Chronicle.

The text of this section of our manuscript is unexceptional. The language is straightforward, and close to the language of the Chronicle. The story of the birth of Cao Pha Kòng, for example (§1.11-12), is very close to the version given in the PTMN (ff° 26-27): quoted speech is virtually unchanged; while some other passages are word-for-word transcriptions, some are abridged, and others are changed to reflect late nineteenth-century idioms.

At the conclusion of this section there is a short passage which credits its information to the "chronicle of the müang" and the "chronicle of the Reliquary"—apparently the Great Reliquary of Phuphiang Chæ Hæng. It also mentions a date: Monday, the 8th day of the waxing moon of the 7th month of the *müang mao* year, 1049 of the Era (1687).[28]

Taking this section as a discrete text, we might conclude that this section on the earliest history of Nan might date back to the seventeenth century.

---

[25]There is obviously some confusion here: see (1) above!

[26]The month is given in Keng Tung style: equivalent to 18 July 1368, which was a Tuesday.

[27]See David K. Wyatt, "The Chronology of Nan History, A.D. 1320-1598," *Journal of the Siam Society* 64:2 (July 1976), 202-206.

[28]The date does not work. The closest would be to regard the month as Keng Tung style, Saturday 19 April 1687. In both this and in the case in CS 1123 cited below, the day is off by two days. Both cases are supposed to be lunar leap years (years with two eighth months). It is possible that chronologists in Nan followed a different formula for placing lunar leap years, the result of which would be to throw the year off by two days.

C. The Origin of Müang Khwang

The third section of the manuscript (ff° 38-39) is very brief, and tells the following story. There was a certain Yi Ba, an ascetic, who lived in a cave and came to Phraya Sai Yok at Pua to tell him that he knew of a good place to found a city. Sai Yok had Cao Am Pòm take people there and founded a city, named Müang Khwang. Am Pòm became its ruler until he later fled to Phayao, where he died. His spirit (*arak*) returned to dwell in Müang Khwang. This information is not repeated in the Nan Chronicle.

D. Genealogy of the First Ruling House

The fourth section of the manuscript (ff° 40-42) centers on the interesting and important point that only the first eleven rulers of Nan are of the line descended from the two boys hatched from eggs. The full genealogy of this family is given. The section concludes by explaining that King Kan Müang built a hall at Pua dedicated to the guardian spirits (*arak*) of the müang, which all the rulers of Nan had to reverence; and all eleven rulers descended from Sai Yok did so, and so preserved the *pan na* of Nan.

Now, *pan na* is a very problematic term, best known from its occurrence in the formal name of the Sipsong Panna of southern Yunnan. It literally means "a thousand rice fields," but it would seem wise not to use such a literal meaning here. In the PNMN, discussed below, the political geography of Nan is described in great detail, various numbers of *na* being listed for each of the administrative units of the principality, ranging from 200 to 4000 *khao* per unit.[29] The total for all of Nan is 115,800. We might think of *pan na,* at least in the context of Nan, as "administrative units" or "chiefdoms," it being understood that the population as a whole is grouped into these units.

E. The Origins of the Salt Wells

The next section (ff° 42-44) tells an amusing tale that accounts for the names of the four major salt wells in the east-central portion of the principality, in the headwaters of the Nan and Wa rivers. The story is brief enough to be summarized here.

Of the two brothers born from eggs, the younger became the ruler and founder of Nan, while the elder, Thao Nun, became ruler of Candapuri, that is, Vientiane in present-day Laos. Thao Nun had a daughter named *nang* Khamlæn. An official of the king of Siam visited the court, admired her beauty, and told his master about her. He requested her hand in marriage and she went to the southern capital. She was so unhappy that she regularly cried as she cooked for the king, and her tears fell into her curries. The king grew angry at the salty taste, and imprisoned her. She escaped, and sought her father—for some reason, in the territory between Nan and the Mekong River to the east. Four times the king of the South sent envoys seeking her return, and her replies on these four occasions form the names of the four salt wells, each of which is salty because of her continuing tears. The four wells are Bò Wa, Bò Næ, Bò Mang, and Bò Phak. Everywhere she cried, salt wells are to be found; and in local lore she is known as "Mistress Salt" (*nang klüa*). This section of the manuscript concludes with a

[29]PNMN, pp. 1-3.

statement to the effect that "this is the legend of Mistress Salt" (*tamnân nâng klüa*).

The four wells are to be found in the extreme east of Nan province, in the long valley formed by the headwaters of the Nan and Wa rivers bordering Laos, the most productive area apparently being that due east of Pua. The salt wells are described by James McCarthy, who went through the area around 1890:

> Near the source of the Nam Nan, and in the vicinity of the main watershed, are several salt-wells, from which an excellent supply of salt is obtained. These wells are jealously guarded, and the fears of the people are excited by stories of the punishments inflicted by the spirits on those using them wrongfully. Certain people have the privilege of working them, paying one rupee for four *muns*, about 530 lbs. The wells are from 30 to 40 feet deep, and it was said that three buckets of water produced one and a half of salt. In the rainy season they are constantly worked, but in the dry season they run dry, and work ceases. There is nothing to show how the presence of salt was discovered or what suggested the sinking of the wells; the people say they are very ancient.[30]

Though the legend recounted here is not referred to in the Nan Chronicle, the salt itself is: it figures in the origins of Chiang Mai's control over Nan in the fifteenth century.

F. Rituals and Customs of Pua

The next section of the manuscript (ff° 44-56) seems to detail the customs and ceremonies of the Nan principality dating back to Pua times. The language of this section is exceedingly obscure, and it defies all attempts at translation. The local guardian spirits (*arak*) are frequently mentioned, together with an indication of the old boundaries within which they operate (ff° 46/4-47/1). There are mentions of various crafts practiced in the *müang*, and information on processions by water (f° 50/2-3) and the court music (f° 50/4). There is no reflection of this material in the Nan Chronicle.

G. The Spirit Halls of Pua

Section G (ff° 56-59) begins with an explicit introductory statement: "Here we will tell about the lumber for the spirit halls, according to the old writings" (f° 56/3). What follows is a straight listing of various localities in the region and the particular architectural timbers which they were responsible for providing whenever the spirit halls at Pua had to be rebuilt. Five such halls are directly mentioned: Rong Arak, Rong Chai, Rong Phat [for music?], Rong Luang, and Rong Chang. The places listed would appear to be the following:

---

[30]*Surveying and Exploring in Siam* (London, 1900), pp. 80-81. Exactly the same passage appears in *An Englishman's Siamese Journals 1890-1893* (Bangkok, 1983), p. 72. For an illustration of a salt well, and of offerings being made to the spirits to whom McCarthy refers, see *Muang Nan* (Bangkok, 1987), p. 16.

In June 1992 I visited one of the salt wells, which I took to be Bò Mang, at the eastern end of the highway that climbs over Mount Phukha, and found it substantially as McCarthy describes, including the shrines to the spirits.

Müang Pua	Khuan	Phon Ngop
Müang Khwang	Chiang Muan	Chama
Müang Ngim	Müang Lim	Chiang Klang
Phong Uan	Müang Ngæng	Müang Pong
Yang Yom	Sakhün	Müang Phüa
Bò Mang	Sakhœn	Müang Læ
Ban Khæm	Saphang	Sa-iap

(This list is much less than certain: because of the way in which the list is constructed, and the obscurity of the architectural terms included in it, it is possible that place names and architectural terms have been confused.)

H. The Lineage of King Mangrai

"Here we shall speak of the lineage of King Mangrai," begins the next section, which extends from f° 59/4 to f° 67/2. This and the following section read continuously, and they would be combined here were it not for the fact that the manuscript explicitly delimits them: "The progression of monarchs who enjoyed the sovereignty of the City on the Ping [River] ends here" (f° 67/2), comes at the end of this section.

The story begins in Müang Ngœn Yang Tha Sai, when the people went to the "king of the Lawa" (*cao Lawa*) and asked him to be their ruler. He had three sons—Lao Khom, Lao Chang, and Lao Klao—and when he became elderly (120 years old!), Lao Klao succeeded him as ruler at Ngœn Yang. He in turn taught his son, Lao Khong, the customs (*hit khòng*) and legends (*tamnan bulan*). The succession of rulers moves very quickly, probably with interruptions, down to Mangrai, who succeeded his father at the age of twenty, went to war with Chiang Rai and Fang, and sent Ai Fa to subvert Phraya Ba of Haripuñjaya (who fled to Lopburi). In a highly abbreviated version of the well-known stories, Mangrai took Lamphun, built Chiang Mai, and after a reign of eight years [*sic*] died at the age of 73 in the *ruang pao* year 723 (1361!). A very bare list of rulers and major events follows, extending down to the mid-sixteenth century when the Burmese came. The last year mentioned in this section is 993 (AD 1631/32). This section ends with the statement quoted above.

An indication of the density of this section is the fact that there is about one year per written line. The various Chiang Mai chronicles might be searched for a source for this account. Because the Nan line ruling in the early nineteenth century originated in Chiang Mai, it would not be unreasonable to attribute our manuscript's account to a Chiang Mai written source.

I. More Chiang Mai History

The section that follows (ff° 67-69) provides another version of events in the history of Lan Na Thai during the period from about 1589 to the 1630s, overlapping with the previous sections. This section includes a few more references to Nan than the previous section, but still not very many. The section concludes with the statement that "The progression of monarchs who enjoyed the sovereignty of Lan Na is finished here" (f° 69/3). We should note, of course, that the concluding date is still early, which might suggest a seventeenth-century source, or a copy of a seventeenth-century manuscript.

J. Customs of the Müang

Just as the next section (ff° 69-81) begins, a detailed date is provided: Monday, the 11th day of the waning moon of the 7th month, in the year 1122 of the Era (AD 1760/61).[31] Then follows a statement that seems to indicate that a certain *nai sæn* Sutthawong and *phò kæo* Pa Tit were interrogated as to the customs (*hit khòng*) of the *müang*, particularly as to the "eating utensils" (*khüang kin*) of the tutelary spirits (*arak*) of the *müang* (f° 69/4).

What follows seems to be two separate lists of these utensils, interrupted at f° 71/3 stating that the list is complete. Perhaps the second list, which continues to f° 78/1, itemizes not utensils but rather other paraphernalia associated with the cult of the tutelary spirits. The language is sufficiently esoteric as to require a specialist to decipher it.

Finally, towards the end of the section is yet another date, Saturday the last day of the 8th month of the year 1123 of the Era (AD 1761/62),[32] followed by more details of the paraphernalia of the spirits.

K. Moral Maxims

The section that follows (ff° 81-90) is one of the most delightful parts of the manuscript. It begins with the statement that "We will consider the ten royal duties (*dasarâjadhamma*), as follows" (f° 81/1). The ten duties of the ruler, well known in the political literature of Buddhist Southeast Asia, are then enumerated, in a somewhat folksy style. But the section does not stop with these. The *Seven Aparihâniyadhamma* are also listed. These include such rules as "He who rules should convene his officials three times daily, without fail, to consider all matters, good or ill, in his own country and in the countries of other rulers" (f° 82/1). Finally, beginning at f° 85/2 are what seem like supplementary rules for the conduct of rulers. At f° 85/3 these are called *bayutti* and *kodhabayutti*.

L. The Power of the Spirits

Three subsections follow which logically belong together, though the chronicler implicitly separates them by titling each at its conclusion.

The first subsection (ff° 90-96) ends with the phrase "The History of Resistance to Yunnanese Tribute Demands here concludes" (*tamnân tit suai Hò læo thao ni*) (f° 96/1). This subsection tells how the ruler of Yunnan (Phraya Hò Lum Fâ) requested tribute of King Kü Na of Lan Na in the *dap sai* year 727 (AD 1365). Lan Na's successful resistance is attributed to the assistance of the local spirits (*arak*).

A second subsection (ff° 96-100) is similar. It deals with the period from 751 to 767 (AD 1389-1405). In this episode, the spirits are reverenced and a fierce storm arises to frighten away invading Chinese armies. This subsection concludes with the statement that the "History of the Defeat of the Yunnanese owing to the power of the guardian spirits of the *müang* is this" (f° 100/2).[33]

---

[31] Again, the closest I can come to converting this date is Saturday, 11 May 1760—another case of the day being off by two days in what should be a lunar leap year.

[32] This day does not work out at all: either Tuesday 2 June 1761 or Wednesday 1 July 1761, the latter case assuming that the month is expressed in Keng Tung style.

[33] This section needs to be checked carefully against the Chiang Mai chronicles. There appears to be a comparable passage which ends with the phrase "tamnan Hò ma tok sük mi

The third subsection (ff° 100-110) tells yet another similar story, but with different villains. It consists of a series of episodes. First, in the 770s (the second decade of the fifteenth century) the guardian spirits are invoked by both Lan Na Thai and Ayudhya in warfare in which the Lan Na forces fail to take advantage of a good horoscope and the Ayudhya monarch takes such good care of his *müang*'s guardian spirits that Ayudhya is spared. The second episode carries the story forward into the reign of King Tilok of Lan Na (1441-87). At that time, the Vietnamese (Kæo) attack Lan Sang (Laos) and Lan Na comes to Lan Sang's defense, whereupon the king of Vietnam invades Lan Na as well, thrusting first towards Nan. The Lan Na people pay elaborate respects to their own guardian deities, and move a very powerful Buddha image from Phayao to Nan. This combination of magical powers raises a storm so powerful that the Vietnamese forces flee in fright. This subsection, again, ends with a title: the "history of how the Vietnamese invaded but had to flee, owing to the power of the *devata* and *arak*, is like this" (f° 109/1).[34]

Finally, the section concludes by briefly mentioning how the spirits killed two rulers who did not pay proper attention to them. The section as a whole ends with the statement that "the history of how the Hò requested tribute and the Vietnamese were defeated is completed here" (f° 110/3).

M. The "Old History"

The next and final section is very long (ff° 110-183), and is much more properly a *tamnan* history than most of the sections that have preceded it.[35]

It begins with a very general statement that "we will relate the ancient legends" (*cak klâo tamnân borân*), and proceeds to tell the story of Nan from the time the Buddha visited Nan—"müang Nandapurî Phûphiang Cæ Hæng"—and prophesied the future of the place. We might note the list of places through which the Buddha is said to have travelled to reach Nan: Kusinârâi, Khû Lâo, Müang Kæo [Vietnam], Müang Langkâ [Sri Lanka], Müang Suan Tân [?], China, Müang Hò [Yunnan], Müang Li [i.e., Lü, Sipsong Panna], Müang Khœn [Keng Tung], Müang Phayâk, Müang Chiang Sæn, Chiang Râi, Doi Duan Phrayâo [Phayao], Còm Wæ, Lamphlâng Nakhon Wiang Wong [Lampang], Phræ, and Müang Nantha [Nan], where He went to bathe in the Huai Khrai stream (ff° 112/1-2). Nan was left with a hair relic of the Buddha, which was enshrined at Phu Phiang Chæ Hæng and guarded with a powerful *yantra*. The cetiya built over the hair relic was later rebuilt in BE 80 and BE 218.

The chronicle here gives some information on various changes in the counting of the eras, and then skips down to a time when Khrân Müang (i.e., Kân

---

dang ni læ" ["the attack of the Hò was like this"] in the *Tamnan phün müang Chiang Mai* (Bangkok, 1971), p. 48; cf. Notton, III, p. 102.

[34]There is a war with the Vietnamese (Kæo) in the Chiang Mai chronicles in which Nan figures prominently, and Thao Kha Kan; but there it is dated in C.S. 841. Cf. *Tamnan phün müang Chiang Mai* (Bangkok, 1971), pp. 136-37; *Tamnan sip ha ratchawong* (Chiang Mai, 1981-1990), II, p. 52 (= phuk 5, f° 16); Sanguan Chotisukkharat, *Nangsü phün müang Chiang Mai* (Chiang Mai, 1972), pp. 80-81; and Phraya Prachakitkòracak, *Phongsawadan Yonok* (Bangkok: Phræ Phitthaya, 1973), p. 345.

[35]On "tamnan history" as a genre, see Wyatt, "Chronicle Traditions in Thai Historiography"; and Charnvit Kasetsiri, *The Rise of Ayudhya: A History of Siam in the Fourteenth and Fifteenth Centuries* (Kuala Lumpur, 1976), pp. 1-7.

Müang) was ruling Nan, in CS 718, a *lwai san* year (f° 123/1). The history then becomes quite detailed, continuously covering events down to CS 1170 [AD 1808], when the text ends in the middle of a folio.

It would appear that this section has served as one of the chief sources for our chronicle. The language is similar, if not identical, to *Sænluang* Ratchasomphan's Nan Chronicle. The coverage is closely similar: there are few events in this portion of the PTMN that do not appear in the Nan Chronicle, though there are numerous additions.

Taking the PTMN as a whole, it seems reasonable to conclude that it was compiled in mid-1821, as part of the "housekeeping" which Sumanathewarat undertook on reorganizing his state. It seems to have been based upon a wide variety of earlier manuscripts, including treatises on kingship and animistic practices. It became then something like part of the regalia of the kings of Nan, an item which all "real" kings had to have in order to be worthy of the name.

5. The "Old Chronicle"

Long after that text was studied, the results incorporated into the notes, and the preceding section written, a very curious text came to light that bears the title "Chronicle of Nan" *(Tamnân müang Nân,* TMN).[36] The chronicle is included among the large body of texts that Richard Davis had local assistants copy in Nan in the early 1970s. On the basis of parallels in other northern Thai principalities, one might have expected a text with such a title to exist, yet it had not previously been found. It almost exactly duplicates sections **B** through **F** as listed above.

The text runs to eighteen pages, and has a concluding date equivalent to AD 1952. However, the context suggests a date of composition of AD 1688 (f° 10), with additional information added from other sources.

This is a most curious text. In some ways it is like the reliquary chronicles, for it usually gives year dates only by reference to their cyclical names, without numbers. However, it lacks virtually all the references to religious activities of the kings that are found in the other chronicles. It seems to have a very strong non-Buddhist quality: it opens and closes with references to the ceremonies conducted for the guardian spirits at Pua.

Moreover, unlike virtually all of the rest of the chronicles, it does not attribute the relics enshrined in the Chæ Hæng reliquary to a gift from the king of Sukhothai, but insists that they were dug up on the spot. On the whole, its chronology is messier than the other versions (as the footnotes will attest), and its details often are at variance with the other versions. After working with it, I have the feeling that it was used by the writers of the reliquary chronicle *and* by the writer(s) of the "Founding" chronicle.

6. The "Royal Genealogy"

A late addition to the "regalia" of the kings of Nan was a royal genealogy, a manuscript titled "The Family of Mahaphrom, the Cao Ratchawong" (*Takun cao*

---

[36]*Tamnan müang Nan.* MS. Wat Tan Cum, Nan; copied by Noi Inta Müangphom, 1972. Davis fl-47. Lanna Thai Manuscripts from the Richard Davis Collection, Australian National University; Microfiche #24.

lâtcawong Mahâpom, TCRM).[37] This manuscript consists of just nine pages (five palm leaves, written on both sides, with five lines per leaf). The microfilm copy in the Social Research Institute in Chiang Mai comes from Wat Mongkhon, *tambon* Nai Wiang Khet 2, *amphœ* Müang, in Nan province. It bears a date in the left margin of the first palm-leaf, CS 1212, equivalent to AD 1850/51; and a phrase at the very end of the text indicates that it was "written" by a certain *nai* Chiawong[38] on Friday, the full-moon day of the eleventh month in the *kat mao* year, CS 1241, equivalent to Friday, 23 August 1850.

The bulk of the TCRM gives a genealogy of the ruling family of Nan from the founder of the last dynasty, Cao Luang Tin Mahawong of Chiang Mai. Because it uses the pre-regnal title (f° 6/1) of a man who became ruler in 1857, we can be confident that the 1850 date for the manuscript is correct and the writing date in 1879 is simply a copying date.

The TCRM begins by recounting the curious story of how the man who was responsible for inviting Cao Luang Tin to Nan had second thoughts about his action, and committed suicide (ff° 1/1-3/4). The remainder of the manuscript consists of a simple listing of all the descendents of Cao Luang Tin, down to about the middle of the nineteenth century AD.

Virtually all of the material in the TCRM is included in MS.1, though there it is somewhat rearranged and clarified. The most telling feature of the TCRM, however, is that it *has* to be *Sænluang* Ratchasomphan's source. The key passages are §5.24 of the Nan Chronicle and f° 7/5 of the TCRM: both give the same information and leave blank exactly the same proper names. There could be no more conclusive evidence that the Nan Chronicle is based upon the TCRM for the genealogical information contained in what we have termed Chapter Five.

7. The "History of Nan and Treatise on Medicine"

One very interesting text is a *Prawat müang Nan læ Tamra ya (History of Nan and Treatise on Medicine).*[39] It treats in some detail the last half of the eighteenth century, from CS 1113 to CS 1155 (AD 1751-1793) in the first twenty-two folios, and then, very suddenly, becomes a treatise on medicine.

This manuscript is very clearly fragmentary. The historical portion, which is written five lines to the folio, ends very abruptly in mid-sentence at the end of folio 22, and a medical text just as plainly begins in mid-sentence at the top of folio 23. The two texts are written in very different hands. One has to conclude that some anonymous librarian either deliberately or accidentally placed the leaves of the two texts together, later to be found and microfilmed together. The historical portion is very close in substance, if not in wording, to Chapter Six and to §§7.1-14 of Chapter Seven.

This text is relatively fuller and seemingly more accurate than PTMN, and it seems likely that the author(s) of the "History of the Founding of Nan" used this particular text, or a copy of it, when writing in the 1820s. This conclusion is strengthened by a reference in the text to a character still living who had been a

[37]SRI 82.107.05.052.

[38]*Nai* Chiawong is not listed among the descendants of the Nan rulers in Chapter Five of MS.1.

[39]Wat Muang Tüt, *tambon* Muang Tüt, *amphœ* Müang, Nan; SRI 82.107.05.047, 39 ff°

powerful official in the 1770s, which would suggest that the text cannot be more than forty or fifty years later (at the most) than 1775.

8. MISCELLANEOUS MANUSCRIPTS

There are several other extremely interesting early documents from Nan which, although it is doubtful the compiler of the Nan Chronicle used them, still deserve notice.

The first is a Nan manuscript[40] composed of three parts, the first of which details the taxable units of all of Nan. The term used is *na*, literally wet-rice fields; but it would appear that a rather more abstract or artificial unit is intended. These are listed as appertaining to localities, officials, and functions. The language of this manuscript is extremely archaic and almost impossible to translate. A second portion appears to deal with taxes and expenditures, and is even more resistant to translation than the first part. There are a number of dates given in this section, the latest of which (f° 15/1) is the 5th waning of the second month in CS 1079, a *müang rao* year—equivalent to 23 November AD 1717. The third section of the manuscript details the routes from Nan to various provincial and district towns and villages, and to distant places, giving usually distances and the locations of overnight stays. Because a new ruler had just been appointed after a particularly difficult period (see the last paragraphs of Chapter Four), it is tempting to imagine that this text might have been intended to give a new governor coming to the principality for the first time an understanding of how the area traditionally had been governed.

The second manuscript is a code of laws written in CS 1202 (AD 1840/41). This is the "Laws of the Kings of Nan," of unknown provenance.[41] It details civil and criminal offenses and offers guidance for judges. It appears to be relatively late, with portions added perhaps even as late as the 1850s. It would repay careful study, for it includes much detail about the lives of ordinary people in earlier times.[42]

Finally, we should simply take note of a manuscript, the title of which promised consideration of the history of Nan, but which did not prove to be of use in this study.

In the microfilm collections of the Social Research Institute in Chiang Mai there is a text titled *Nangsü pün müang Nan, puk thi 2 (Book of the History of Nan,*

---

[40]*Phün na müang Nan læ khâo thâng müang Nan*, ed. Aroonrut Wichienkeeo. Chiang Mai: Sûn Watthanatham Cangwat Chiang Mai, Witthayâlai Khru Chiang Mai, 1985 ('Ekkasan lamdap thi 9). MS., Wat Hua Khuang, *tambon* Nai Wiang, *amphœ* Müang, Nan; 42 ff°; SRI 82.107.05.049.

[41]"Kotmâi phracao Nan," transcribed by Singkha Wannasai; in *Kotmai phracao Nan, Tamnân Phracao Hai* (Chiang Mai: Sûn Songsœm læ Süksa Watthanatham Lân Nâ Thai, Witthayâlai Khru Chiang Mai, 1980; 'Ekkasan lamdap thi 4).

[42]Note that later visitors, including the British Consul who visited Nan in 1886, commented very favorably on the strictness of judicial administration in Nan. *Report by Mr. C. E. W. Stringer of a Journey to the Laos State of Nan, Siam* (London, 1888; *Parliament. Papers by Command*, C.-5321), pp. 6-7. Note also, especially, Reginald le May, *An Asian Arcady: The Land and People of Northern Siam* (Cambridge, 1926), pp. 92-93, where there are statistics for the early 1920s.

A number of the laws of Nan have been published. See Aroonrut Wichienkeeo, "Phraratchakatha müang Nan R.S. 111," *Ruam botkhwam prawattisat* 2 (January 1981), 34-49; and, especially, "Anacak lak kham (kotmai müang Nan)," in Saratsawadi Ongsakun, *Lakthan prawattisat Lan Na* (Chiang Mai, 1991), pp. 56-100 and photocopy of text in appendix.

bundle 2). This is not about Nan at all: it proves to be bundle (*phûk*) 2 of the well-known and published Chronicle of the Fifteen Dynasties (*Tamnân 15 râtchawong*) of Chiang Mai.[43] It could be that this "second bundle" of the Chronicle of the Fifteen Dynasties did in fact form the "second bundle" of *Sænluang* Ratchasomphan's Nan Chronicle, for that early section of the Fifteen Dynasties chronicle is very like the early sections of the Nan Chronicle. However, since the current study does not cover the early portion of the Nan Chronicle, the question of this text's relevance to Nan history will have to await future consideration.

THE LINEAGE OF THE TEXTS

We have, then, four different groups of texts that have some bearing on how *Saenluang* Ratchasomphan's 1894 history might have been composed. It remains here to consider their relationships to each other and to the 1894 compilation.

The oldest group of texts appear to be those we have termed the "reliquary chronicles." They can be considered to be the oldest because they are the only texts that render many dates in a patently archaic fashion, giving years only their cyclic names and not their numbers in any era. Many other texts, including *Saenluang* Ratchasomphan's history, which seem to have been based on these reliquary chronicles have added year numbers, often erroneously. It has been suggested above that the oldest of these texts may date from late in the sixteenth century. There are many different copies of the reliquary chronicles, and it is not possible to judge which copy or version *Saenluang* Ratchasomphan might have used.

The next oldest manuscript is what we have called the "old chronicle" (section 5 above). It appears to have been written using, and expanding upon, the reliquary chronicle, and also perhaps building upon some earlier but undiscovered chronicle of the principality.

The third major source for the history of Nan that might have been available to *Saenluang* Ratchasomphan is the ca. 1821 compilation called the "History of the Founding of Nan." This lengthy and complex work, fully summarized above, seems to have been compiled on the basis of both a representative of the reliquary chronicle tradition, and a representative of the "old chronicle" tradition, as well as a number of other sources which are mentioned by name. That this work is clearly a patchwork of material gathered from other sources is demonstrated by the duplication of material within the text. (It is worth mentioning that duplicated passages rarely contradict each other, which suggests that the corpus of sources retained a certain integrity.) It would have been possible for *Saenluang* Ratchasomphan to compile the earlier portions of his chronicle (down to 1821) using this source exclusively, though his treatment of dates suggests his familiarity with the reliquary chronicle tradition.

---

[43]Wat Muang Tüt, *tambon* Muang Tüt, *amphœ* Müang, Nan; SRI 82.107.05.051, 44 ff°.

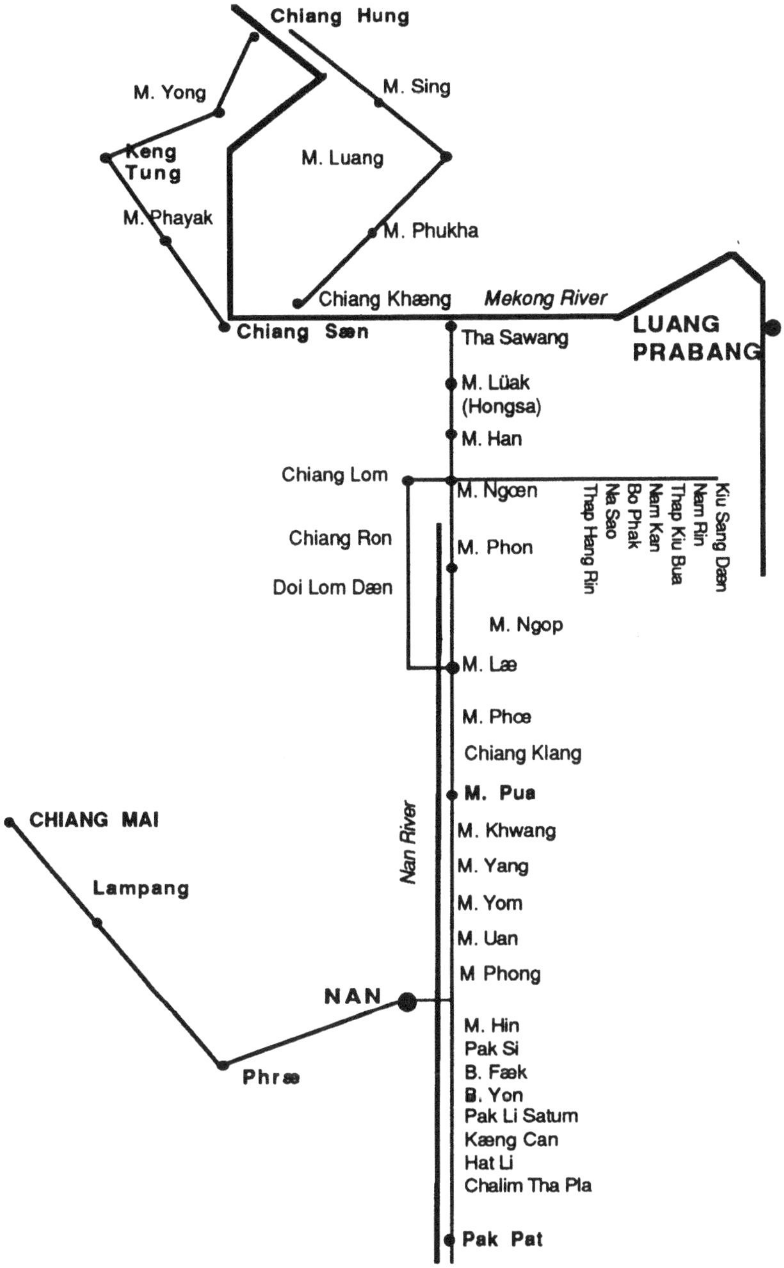

Figure 1. Schematic map of routes within Nan and linking Nan to the outside world, according to the Phün na müang Nan læ khâo thâng müang Nan, *ed. Aroonrut Wichienkeeo (Chiang Mai: Sûn Watthanatham Cangwat Chiang Mai, Witthayâlai Khru Chiang Mai, 1985). (Not to scale.)*

The final written source that we know *Saenluang* Ratchasomphan used is the "Royal Genealogy" (6 above), which dates from 1850 and is known to us through a copy from 1879. We can be certain that Ratchasomphan used this text, for reasons outlined above. It comprises what we have denoted "Chapter 5" in the translation.

We simply do not know what sources *Saenluang* Ratchasomphan might have used in writing the history of Nan after 1821—roughly one-fourth of his whole text. We must assume that he had written sources to work from, for the most part, because the dates are too detailed to have been passed on by oral transmission. The uneven flow of the narrative between the secular and religious activities of the kings of Nan suggests that he had both court and temple records to work with here. At least the final portion of the manuscript may have been informed by the author's own experience and recollection.

Considering only that portion of the Nan Chronicle for which we have older sources, can we conclude anything about *Saenluang* Ratchasomphan's use of his sources? We can say that he was a relatively critical historian. He usually did not include the more fanciful and legendary material that is to be found in some of his sources. He omitted the earlier portions of the reliquary chronicles dealing with the supposed earlier visit of the Buddha to the land that ultimately would become Nan; and he omitted almost all references to the non-Buddhist religious practices that are so prominent a feature of the 1821 history. He was, therefore, clearly a man of his own, late-nineteenth century time, a period when orthodox Buddhism had come officially to exclude non-Buddhist beliefs and practices. He was a loyal servant of the king of Nan, but also a subject of the king of Siam. He seems to have accepted, in a matter-of-fact way, the administrative reforms being pushed on Siam's dependencies by the regime in Bangkok, though his failure to say much about them raises the question of how he perceived them.

We have argued that *Saenluang* Ratchasomphan drew from a range of local written sources when writing his history in 1894, and in the process we have noted that his sources were themselves compilations from earlier sources. We are left to inquire as to just what the nature of the chronicles might be. Are we to draw some arbitrary line between earlier sources that are "primary" and later sources that are "secondary"? Just where might that line fall? Can we ever be certain that we have gone all the way back to the earliest sources? And to what extent might we consider that later sources accurately convey what the earlier sources have to say? There do not seem to be any ready answers to such questions in the traditions represented in, and intertwined with, the Nan Chronicle. But before we dismiss *Saenluang* Ratchasomphan's work as "secondary" and consider Rattanapañña's *Jinakalamali* as "primary," we should bear in mind that even the early sixteenth-century *Jinakalamali* might be just as "secondary" as the Nan Chronicle; that is, it may be just as far removed from its original sources as the Nan Chronicle is. We should, I think, be concerned less here with such arbitrary labels than with the integrity, the accuracy, and the coherence of such works, and try to appreciate the work of local historians on their merits.

THE LANGUAGE OF THE TEXTS

The language of MS.1. is for the most part unexceptional. It should stand as a good example of late Northern Thai expository prose, clear, terse, and relatively colloquial in style. There are several features of the text which call for special notice.

First, the text betrays a certain amount of confusion in its use of the R/L consonants. This phenomenon is a reflection of the phonetics of Northern Thai, in which R and L usually are not distinguished in speech, though they are written differently. The manuscript also similarly, but inconsistently, miswrites initial consonant clusters in which R or L is the second element, for the same reason, or because of a mistaken sense of "proper" written style.

Second, the manuscript indulges in a good deal of what the linguists call hypercorrection; that is, bowing to an unreal or imaginary standard. The best example of this usage is the consistent writing (in this and other manuscripts) of | *mlâ* | where | *mâ* |, "horse," is meant.

The biggest surprise for me was to discover how close written Northern Thai is to standard written Central Thai. There is a good deal of specialized vocabulary, to be sure, but not so much as to render access to the manuscript(s) impossible for the non-expert.

EDITING PROCEDURES

It remains to mention here the process by which this edition was prepared, as a number of innovations had to be made to accommodate the peculiar problems of the text.

In working on the manuscript(s), I began with mechanical prints from the microfilms at the Social Research Institute in Chiang Mai. These I took to a local copy center and had them re-copied on the largest paper available, 11 x 17 inches. I then transcribed the manuscript from these second-generation enlarged copies, and typed the transcription in Northern Thai script using a specially designed alphabet on an Apple Macintosh computer.[44]

The next step in the process was to automatically convert the Northern Thai chapters into standard Thai, using a computer program specially written for the purpose. This is a straightforward mechanical process, with two major exceptions: subscripts and special letters are marked with a subscript dot under the preceding letter; and -R- clusters, which are typed with the R first in Northern Thai, are inverted to the correct order in standard Thai (KR, TR, KHR, etc., instead of RK, RT, and RKH, etc.)

I began the process of translation by printing the standard Thai on the left-hand column of pages, with the 1966 Prasœt Churat translation (which I then edited and substantially revised) in the right-hand column. I revised and corrected the translation, and extended it to include the final portion of MS1. I did some substantial re-division of the text into paragraphs and chapters, and

---

[44]The computer files of the various chapters of this manuscript were typed with spaces separating each "word," facilitating the production of complete word lists. Spaces and line breaks in the original were preserved. Separate computer programs "unspace" the files and dump words to a database file for dictionary-building purposes.

numbered the paragraphs to facilitate easy comparison among the various versions. Where readings were unclear, I compared the transcription with the published versions of the text.

The final stage of editing and annotating the translation was done with references to other manuscripts and printed texts from Nan, which are indicated in the footnotes.

I had originally planned to publish the new edition of the Nan Chronicle in two parallel columns, standard Thai transcription and translation; but this seemed to be much more than most readers will require. I have therefore put both the Thai transcription and a printed copy of the Northern Thai version in the Cornell University Library's John M. Echols Collection on Southeast Asia.

ROMANIZATION

Early drafts of this volume all showed all Northern Thai names and terms rendered into roman script as if they had been written in standard, Central Thai. It took a strong negative reaction from one reader to bring home to me the political implications of what I had been doing: that is, rendering Northern Thai names as if they were Central Thai denies to the North and its people their distinctive identity.

This left me with two alternatives: either to put Northern Thai names in a form which reflects their actual spelling, or to put them in a form which reflects their pronunciation. The former course would lead to utter chaos, as the manuscripts spell very unsystematically and haphazardly, even within the same palm leaf. The latter course, however, presented one very serious problem: although I feel that I can *read* Northern Thai relatively well by now, I have no notion of how it was and is pronounced. I have therefore used Harald Hundius's admirable phonetic description of Northern Thai, and followed his rules.[45]

There are two things about the language of the text that those accustomed to standard Central Thai will find strange. First, almost all R initial consonants appear as L initials; and, though they are "correctly" written, many initial consonant clusters (PR, KR) have collapsed to their initials (P, K). Second, Northern Thai has at least one initial consonant cluster, LW (as in the name of one year in the decimal cycle, *lwai*, which I previously read as *rawai*), which seems very strange.

POSSIBLE FUTURE DIRECTIONS

It will become obvious to the reader that the Nan Chronicle is a very complex text, consisting as it does of portions, passages, and information from a variety of different sources. It seems that the chronicle certainly is susceptible of offering the scholar more than just corroboration of dates and events, which is the function to which it has been relegated in the past, as important and useful as that function may be. Because we have some idea of the sources used by

---

[45]Harald Hundius, *Phonologie und Schrift des Nordthai* (Abhandlungen für die Kunde des Morgenlandes, XLVIII, 3; Stuttgart: Franz Steiner, 1990), esp. pp. 222-45. Note, however, that I have used his phonetics, but not his transcription system, which I found to be far too complex for a work of this sort.

Sænluang Ratchasomphan in 1894, we have here a rare opportunity to examine processes of intellectual, cultural, and political change in the pre-modern Tai world.

Let us begin with the assumption that we have in this corpus of material six separate texts or groups of texts, each arising out of particular social and political circumstances: (1) the very old reliquary histories, or *tamnân*, dating back to well before the eighteenth century, written by Buddhist monks; (2) the "old chronicle," the *tamnân müang Nân;* (3) the fragments of political history and administration dating back to the seventeenth century; (4) the group of texts represented particularly by the "History of the Founding of Nan" and the "History of Nan and Treatise on Medicine," deriving from the court of a newly resurgent Nan in the early nineteenth century; and (5) the "Royal Genealogy" dating from the middle of the nineteenth century; all of which are drawn upon, to greater or lesser extent, in (6) the 1894+ Nan Chronicle.

Each of these six groups of texts suggests themes or questions that might fruitfully be examined in the context of the other five groups. The reliquary histories, for example, ascribe to Buddhism, its institutions, and its personnel a special, central role in the life of the community. What happens to Buddhism, and to religion, in the other texts? Or, to cite another example, each of the texts defines the community of the *müang* of Nan with a somewhat different shape and substance. What is a *müang*? To the Buddhist monks? To the king's administrators? Furthermore, all our texts, in one way or another, deal with the nature of power in the society of Nan—both the human, secular power that controls people's bodies and the suprahuman (or subhuman) power that controls their minds and their souls.

Two particularly tantalizing questions arise out of the combination of texts we have here. First, notice the small assortment of almost-anecdotal additions that *Sænluang* Ratchasomphan apparently made to the sources. Two come particularly to mind, though there are others: the "stand-off" between Cao Sumana and Cao Atthawalapanño, when Sumana thrice attempted to shoot his nephew and the gun repeatedly failed to fire (§6.34); and the story of the "ghosts" haunting the city of Nan (§7.21). Why might Ratchasomphan have chosen to insert these and other such tales?[46] Similarly, why did Ratchasomphan choose to omit certain references to Nan in the Chiang Mai chronicles (which surely were available to him)?

Second, consider when the Nan Chronicle was written: 1894. Just a year earlier, Nan had suffered the loss of much of its territory and wealth to the French, in the aftermath of the Paknam Crisis. Why is there not the slightest, even elliptical, mention of this calamity in the Nan Chronicle? Is it possible that, perhaps, the Nan Chronicle *does* refer to the Paknam Crisis, even on every page? Might the emphasis on Nan's powerlessness throughout history be telling us something? Does the recurrent image of the orphan—the frequent depiction of Nan as an "orphan" state, abandoned by its patrons who should have taken care of it—suggest something important in the political or intellectual realm? We shall see.

---

[46] I already have dealt with the second of these: "Assault by Ghosts: Politics and Religion in Nan in the 18th Century," *Crossroads* 4, 2 (1989): 63-70.

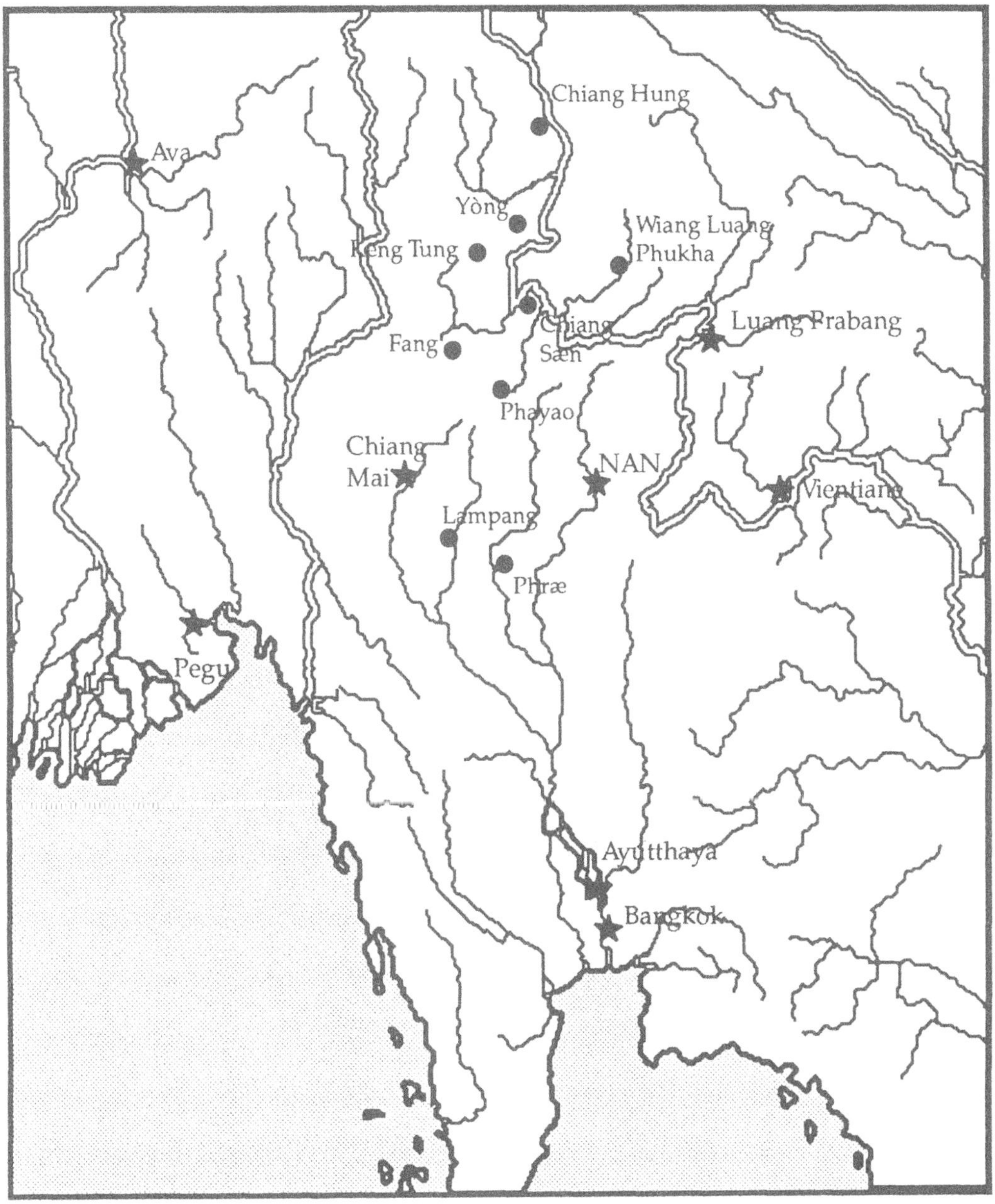

Map of Nan and its Neighbors

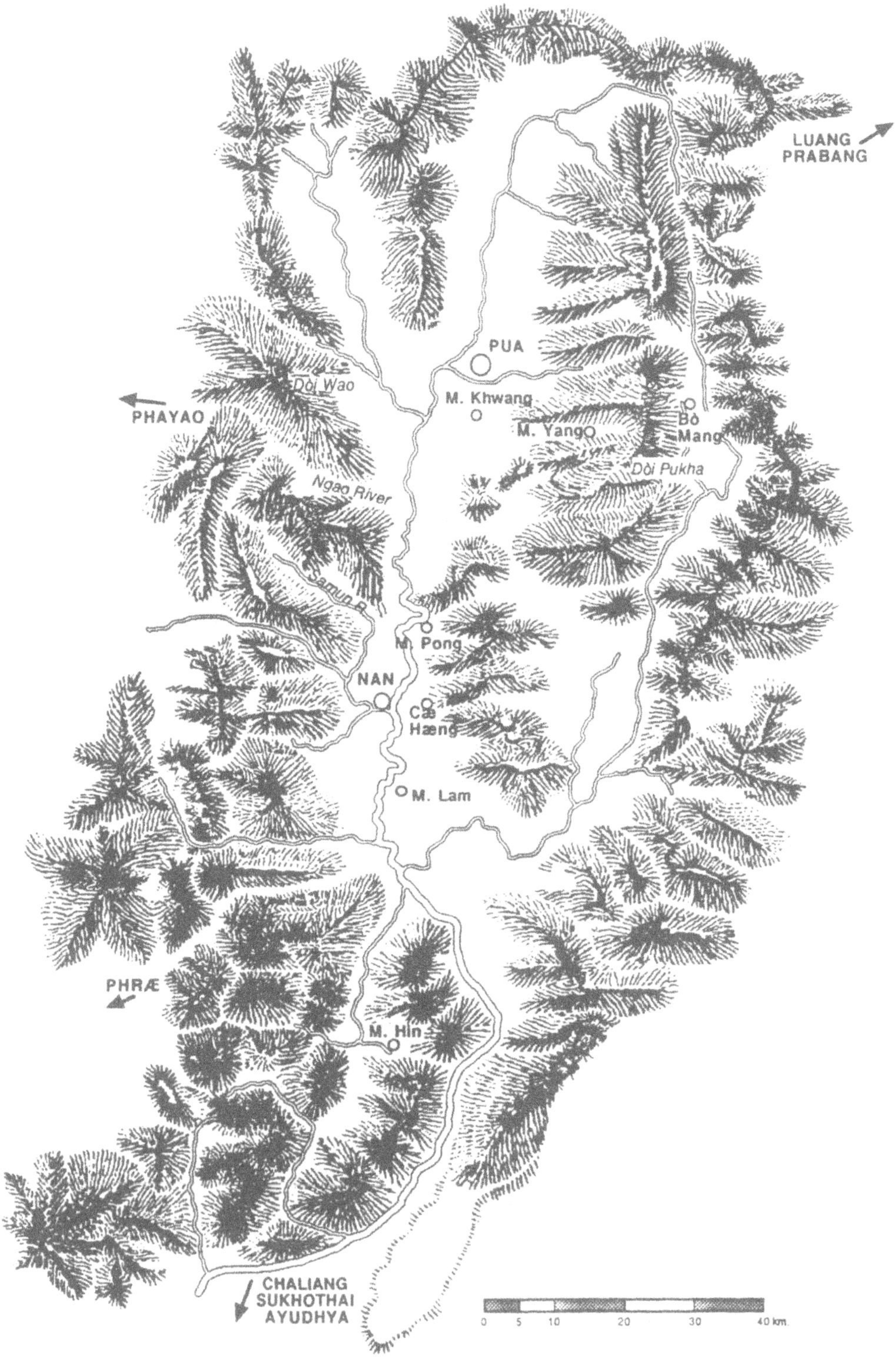

Map of the modern province of Nan, constituting the core of the ancient kingdom of Nan. Based upon provincial map in the Akkharanukrom phumisat prathet Thai [Gazetteer of Thailand] *of the Royal Academy, 1964.*

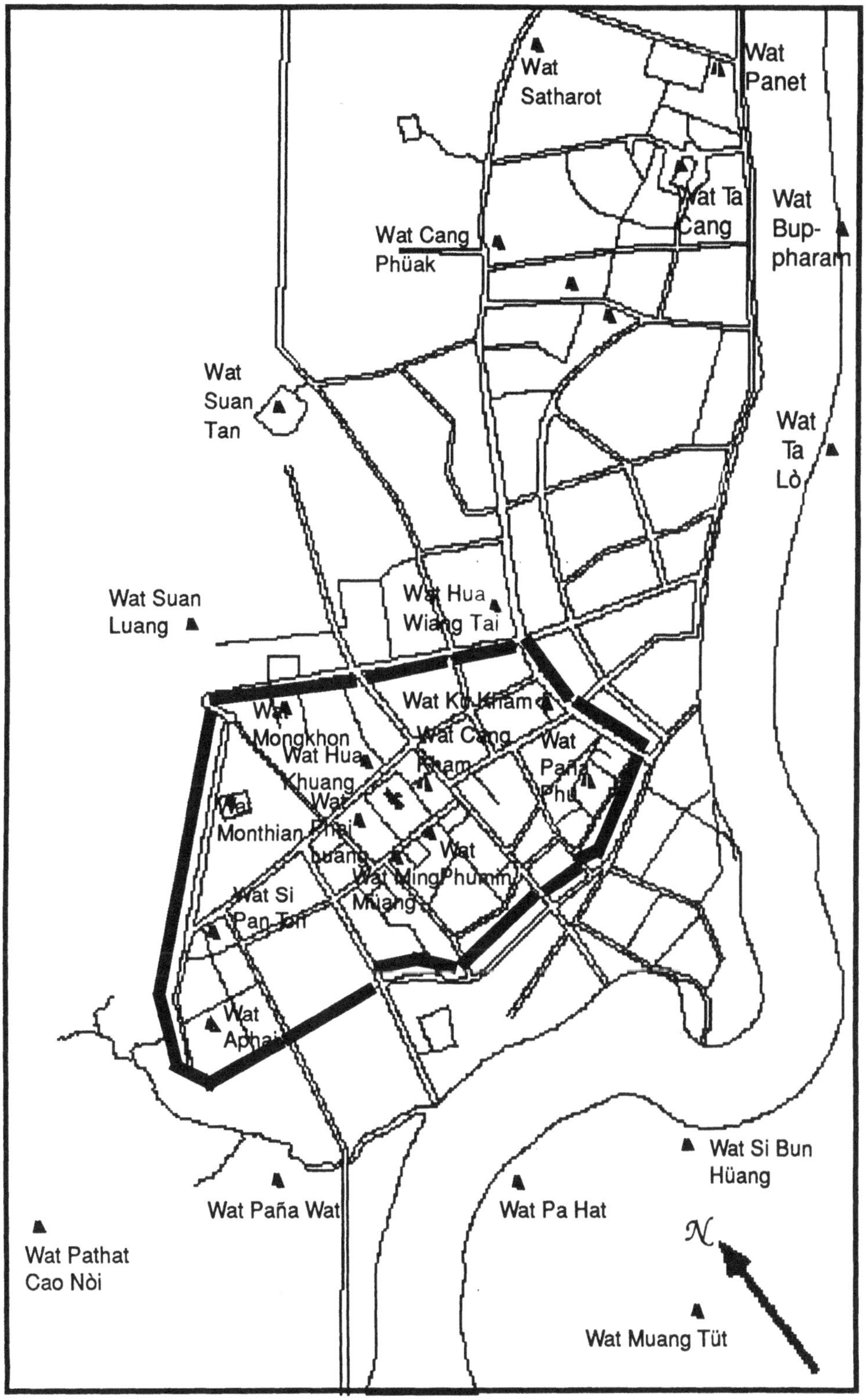

Map of the city of Nan. The heavy lines mark a hypothetical reconstruction of the nineteenth-century city walls. City layout based upon a 1953 city planning map; Buddhist monasteries supplied from a 1992 city planning map.

Cao Suliyaphong Phalittidet (d. 1918), the penultimate King of Nan, who sponsored the compilation of the Nan Chronicle by Sænluang *Ratchasomphan.*

ÂRAMBHAKATHÂ[1]

"Suraṇamahiniyaṃ buddhaseṭṭhaṃ namitvā sugatabhavadhammaṃ saṅghaṇca namitvā ahaṃrājā dāyādaraṭṭhādhipatiṃ vakkhāmi sabbadukkhā bayādhirogā vināsasantu."

Ahaṃ. *I who am lord, Cao Suriyaphongphrittadet Kunlachetsathamahanta Chaiyananthaburamahâratchawongsâthibòdî, becoming ruler on November 1,* RS *113, a Thursday, Thai day* müang met, *4th waxing of the second month,* CS *1265, a* kâp sangâ *year, a* mamia *year, first of the decade, in the 20th lunar mansion, called Pubbâsâdha, in the 3rd great lunar mansion, in the tæ watch,*[2] *have carefully reflected on the history of the line of kings and rulers who have been lords and reigned since santânusantati, that is, since our Bodhisatva took birth as Phraya Samantarat, and have continued in regular succession down through the generations to the present age. They are totally gone, and we know little of them and can find out even less. I who am lord have thus commissioned Saenluang Ratchasomphan to investigate this past and to write as a secure basis for the future, that our sons and grandsons and great-grandsons and great-great-grandsons may know.*

INVOCATION

Sādhavo! Look here, all just men! The learned one who recounts the tales, practices, and succession of the princely families, all those lords who have been rulers enjoying sovereignty in Müang Varanagara, i.e. Müang Pua and Müang Nandapuri here, in succession down to the prince of today, here reverences the Triple Gems with the verse beginning; "Saraṇamahiniyaṃ buddhaseṭṭhaṃ"—like this—ahaṃ, that is, I; namāmi, prostrate myself; Buddhaseṭṭhaṃ, to the Lord Buddha who is the most excellent in all the three worlds, namely the world of desire, the world of forms, and the world of formlessness, in the present age. Ahaṃ, that is, I; namāmi, prostrate myself; Dhammaṃ, to the Lord of Dhamma; sugatabhavadhammaṃ, he who cannot be revealed to the world of creatures, that all creatures may attain to paradise, that is, Nibbāna; namitvā, that is; vandāmi, I

[1]This passage occurs in the Kaona edition of the *Prachum phongsawadan*, vol. IV, pp. 333-34.

[2]Thursday, November 1, 1894. Most, but not all, of the elements in the date check out correctly: However, the CS year is transposed as 1265 instead of 1256, and the year was the fifth of the decade, not the first. The date as given places the sun in the 20th lunar mansion (*rœk*), called Pubbâsâdha, while that day began (at 6 a.m.) with the sun entering the last third of the 19th lunar mansion; so the event recorded in the date given here must have occurred late in the day.

reverence; Saṃghaṃ ca, i.e., the two groups of the Saṅgha, that is; the Ariyasaṅgha and the Sammatisaṅgha; dakkhiṇeyyaṃ, which should receive the alms of all people; ahaṃ, that is, I; vakkhāmi, will now declare; rājadāyādaraṭṭhādhipatiṃ, to the princely families of all those who have been rulers descending down to the present age; sabbadukkhā sabbabhaya sabbarogā sabbaantarāyāpi vināsantu, which is to say that all suffering and dangers and cares and accidents; vināsantu, may they all disappear, and not befall me.[1]

---

[1]This entire passage is given in Pali at the beginning of Part I of the text: Suraṇamahiniyaṃ buddhaseṭṭhaṃ namitvā sugatabhavadhammaṃ saṃghañca namitvā ahaṃ rājādāyādaraṭṭhādhipatiṃ vakkhāmi sabbadukkhā bayādhi rogā vināsasantu.

CHAPTER ONE

ORIGINS OF THE *MÜANG*

1.1 *Tatrâyamânupubbikathâ.*[1] We shall now relate [the story] from the beginning, as told by an ancient sage learned in the affairs of the royal lines, as follows. /

1.2. In the beginning, Paña[2] Pukha ruled in Müang Yang.[3] There was a hunter in Yang who regularly traversed the forests and mountains seeking game. One day, having found none, / he [went as far as] the foot of Mount Pukha,[4] and there discovered the tracks of game. He followed the tracks for some distance, but could not find the animal which had made them, and so lay down to rest under / a very large and lovely tree. While resting there, he discovered two large eggs the size of coconuts, which he took and presented to Paña Pukha.[5]

1.3. When Paña Pukha saw the eggs he was delighted and amazed. He took good care of them, placing one in a basket of kapok and the other in a basket filled with cotton. He constantly watched over them, and before long, the egg embedded in kapok /85/ hatched, and from it came a handsome baby boy whom the lord loved as his own son. Not very long afterwards the egg in the basket of cotton also hatched, and from it came a second handsome baby boy as beautiful as the first. Paña Pukha raised both boys, / and loved them as if they were his own flesh and blood. When they had grown, he named the elder brother, the one hatched in the basket of kapok, Cao Khun Nun, and the younger brother / he named Cao Khun Fòng.[6]

---

[1]Pali. This might roughly be translated as, "Here is the story from the beginning." The text begins on f° 84 of the manuscript. The diagonal slashes scattered through the text mark folio (/*number*/) and / line breaks. There are usually five lines per folio. Page numbers were added to the manuscript when it was microfilmed by the Social Research Institute.

[2]Romanized according to pronunciation. Written *phraya*.

[3]There is an old M. Yang in Nan, north of modern Nan city, at 19° 06′ 38″N, 100° 59′ 31″ E. (McCarthy triangulation map.) This would place it south of Pua. It does not appear on modern maps; but should be associated with a small valley 8-10 miles south-southwest of Dòi Pukha; 25 km. or 15 miles northeast of Nan. For a brief discussion of the locale of this story, see Richard B. Davis, *Muang Metaphysics* (Bangkok: Pandora, 1984), p. 28, n. 4.

[4]Dòi Pukha is the high mountain (1980 m.) that dominates the upper valley of the Nan River. It is located 16 km./10 miles southeast of Pua.

[5]This story, continuing down to §1.6, also appears in PTMN, ff° 22/2-25/4, and TMN, ff° 1-3. There, the language is similar, but not identical, to this version.

[6]The names of the two princes comes from *nun*, "kapok," and *fòng*, "eggs." An interesting parallel to this myth of human birth from eggs is to be found in the chronicle *Sasanavamsa*, written by the monk Paññasami in Burma in 1861. It has been translated by B. C. Law as *The History of the Buddha's Religion* (London, 1952); cf. esp. pp. 40–41. In this version, the eggs were

1.4. When Cao Khun Nun was eighteen years of age and his brother sixteen years, they said to each other, "Let us go and pay respects to our father, and ask him to make us rulers of our own domains." The two brothers / then paid reverence to Paña Pukha, their father, saying, "O father, our lord, we wish to be lords [of domains]. May our honored father be pleased to grant our request." Their father then replied to the two brothers, "If you two / really wish [to have domains of your own] to rule, go together and seek out Paña Thera Tæng, who may have mercy upon you." The brothers saluted their father and asked where they might find Paña Thera Tæng, and were told that he lived between Dòi Tiu and Dòi Wao.[1] /86/ The two brothers went in search of Paña Thera Tæng.

1.5. [Upon seeing them], Paña Thera Tæng asked the two brothers what their purpose was in coming to see him. They respectfully answered, "Because we wish to be rulers, our father told us to come / and see you and ask for your kindness in establishing domains for us to rule." "Very well," Paña Thera Tæng replied, "if you are really desirous of being rulers, I will consider the matter." / After careful deliberation, he took the princes[2] to the east of the Khong River.[3] When they came to a certain place east of the river suitable for a domain, Paña Thera Tæng indicated that one prince should found his domain there. On the ground, he scratched with his walking stick / the outline of a city, and named it Candapuri.[4] He appointed Cao Khun Nun, the elder brother, as lord of the new city, and made the people living in that area his subjects.

1.6. The younger brother then appealed to Paña Thera Tæng, "Since / you have so graciously made my elder brother ruler of a domain, will you not kindly grant me the same favor?" Paña Thera Tæng then led the younger brother, Cao Khun Fòng, back to the west. When they were about 5,000 fathoms[5] east of the Nan River /87/ at a place suitable for establishing a domain, the Paña Thera stopped and scratched on the ground the outline of a new city and named it Varanagara. Later it would be called Müang Pua.[6] Paña Thera Tæng handed over that domain to the younger brother, Khun Fòng, as ruler there, and made all the Kwao[7] there his subjects. / Then Cao Thera Tæng delimited the border

---

brought forth by a female serpent who had been intimate with a "knower of charms" and who abandoned them out of shame. Each of the two boys born from the eggs was given a country to rule, one at Thaton in the Burma Delta.

[1]Doi Tæo and Doi Wao in PTMN, f° 23/4. Doi Wao (elev. 1674 meters) is 12 miles (19.5 km.) west-northwest of the administrative center of Tha Wang Pha district, on the present border between Nan and Phayao provinces. Doi Tiu/Tæo cannot be located, but we might expect to find it an equal distance east of the river. See Davis, *Muang Metaphysics*, p. 28, n. 4.

[2]The text suddenly switches to calling them *kumara*, "princes."

[3]I.e., the Mekong.

[4]Candanapuri is the classical name of Vientiane, capital of Laos.

[5]*wa*, about 10 km. PTMN, f° 25/1, says 4,000 *wa*. 4 and 5 are easily confused in some Northern Thai writing systems. A *wa* is equivalent to about 2 meters, or 2 yards; a fathom.

[6]Varanagara is, literally, the "venerable city." Pua is 5 miles (9 km.) east of the Nan River. The old city must have been where the modern district center is today. Somchet Vimolkasem (*Khrongkan samruat læ cat tham khòmun sing wætlòm sinlapakam*, Nan, 1990, p. 15) argues that the old city was centered around Wat Phrathat Beng Sakat, and he illustrates remains of the old city walls.

[7]Also Kao/Klao, below; the traditional name for the Tai people of the Nan River valley; a name which occurs in the 1292 inscription of Ramkhamhæng (face IV, line 2). See the Index for other occurrences of this ethnonym.

between the realms of the two brothers, extending it from Ta Nun in the north to Sala Müang Lang[1] in the south. As for the line between the Kao and the Lao, that has already been mentioned.[2] Paña Thera Tæng was chief of the ascetics.[3] /

1.7. Having been made ruler, Cao Khun Fòng was king of Varanagara. He had one son whom he named Cao Kao Küan. When Cao Khun Fòng / died, not so long afterward, all his councillors consecrated Cao Kao Küan to rule in his father's place.

1.8. Not much later, his grandfather, Paña Pukha, came to learn that his grandson was ruling [Varanagara] to the great satisfaction of his councillors and subjects. / Paña Pukha thereupon sent two ladies to invite Cao Kao Küan[4] to become the ruler of a domain in Müang Pukha, namely Müang Yang. Cao Kao Küan, however, declined the invitation, but the two ladies would not hear of it and insisted that he accept. Cao Kao Küan finally submitted to the ladies' entreaties and accepted his grandfather's invitation to rule Yang.[5]

1.9 The two court ladies returned and reported to the king his grandson's acceptance /88/ of the invitation. So informed, Paña Pukha sent a delegation of councillors and elders and musicians of Yang to conduct Paña Kao Küan to / Yang in state.[6] When the delegation arrived, Cao Kao Küan told his wife and councillors, "Now, Paña Pukha, my grandfather, has / invited me to rule Yang. I must thus go to live in Yang with him. As for Varanagara, I entrust it to my lady and all my councillors to rule. My lady is now with child. If, when she comes to term, she gives birth to a son who grows to be a brave man, I will enlarge and improve this place [Varanagara] in a manner befitting such a son." Speaking thus, Paña Kao Küan / handed over the domain to his queen[7] and councillors and set out for Yang with his councillors.

---

[1]There is a Ban Müang Rang (=Lang) at 15°04′ N., 102°31′ E., the location of which is about right. Tha Nun cannot be located.

[2]Where has this already been mentioned? In the earlier (untranslated) portion of the chronicle?

[3]The TPMCM, p. 7, interestingly says that the legendary King Cüang was succeeded by his first son, by his queen, and that his second and third sons, by another mother, were sent to rule Lan Chang and Nanthaburi, i.e., Nan, respectively. This supposedly happened in AD 1134/35. The interesting point, of course, is the fraternity of the rulers of Laos and Nan.

In an unpublished chronicle of Luang Phrabang, the *Tamnan müang Lan Sang*, Phraya Thera Tæng is not a hermit (*rishi*) but a *devata*, a heavenly spirit whose special function it is on earth to build and construct, much in the same way that Vishvakarman is employed in other Siamese legends. Sanguan Chotisukkharat, *Tamnan müang nüa* (Chiang Mai, 1955-56), vol. I (2nd ed.) p. 44, footnote.

[4]Variously Kao Küan, Klao Küan, 9 Küan; here the last.

[5]The same story is given in PTMN, ff° 25/4-26/4. In that version, however, Cao Kao Küan made both ladies pregnant. TMN, f° 3, has a version closer to MS.1, but without any lady emissaries.

This is a rare case where the text from which I am working is less complete than the text given in the Prachum Phongsawadan edition. It is quite clear that a haplography ("*müa* . . . *müa*") has taken place. The Thai text has been amended to follow the published version [*Prachum Phongsawadan*, pt. 10; Kaona edition vol. IV (Bangkok, 1964), p. 409].

[6]Note that this section consistently writes Müang Yang where the printed edition says Müang Pukha.

[7]PTMN, f° 27/1, indicates that he left Pua in the hands of two women, Mæ Tao Kham Ua Sim and Mæ Tao Kham Pin, together with his son by the former, Am Pom.

1.10. When he reached Yang, his grandfather, Paña Pukha, and his officials inaugurated him as ruler. Paña /89/ Pukha had ruled for a long time in Yang, and had invited many to succeed him. Not long afterwards, he died and left this world for the next. Paña Kao Küan ruled the domain justly.

1.11. Not much later, there was a certain ruler / named Ngam Müang ruling Phayao[1] who, learning that Varanagara—that is, Pua—was ruler-less, governed only by a queen, invaded and attacked Pua.[2] The invasion was so sudden and unexpected that the queen, Mæ Tao Kham / Pin, could not contact her husband, Paña Kao Küan, to ask for help, nor did she or her councillors have sufficient time to defend / the city. She could only gather her valuables, her gold ornaments and jewelry, and make an escape with her maid. She hid in the jungle for many days. Later she came to a hut / and decided to rest there. That same night she gave birth to a baby boy.

1.12. Near that hut there was a stream, but it was dry, and there was no water for drinking or for bathing. The queen lamented, saying to her [absent] husband, "On the day you left me, you said that if I gave birth to /90/ a boy you would build a magnificent city for him when he grew up. Look at us now! I cannot even find a drop of water for drinking or bathing." Then suddenly there was a heavy rainstorm and flood. / When the storm was over, the queen took the baby to the stream and bathed it. It was a night of the full moon, an *ubosatha sila* day.[3]

1.13. The queen took the child down to the stream and bathed it, and then returned to the field shelter. / The next morning the village headman, a farmer,[4] came around inspecting his fields. He heard an infant crying in the hut, so he went to the hut and recognized the queen, and asked her what had brought her to the hut. The queen then related to him that her city had been suddenly invaded and that she had just managed to escape the invaders. The owner of the hut, / who happened to be the ruler's former cook, indicated she should not remain there, and invited the queen to come and stay in his house. The queen accepted his invitation, and he accompanied the queen and her infant girl[5] back to his home. / The householder cared for the queen and her child, and fed them well. When the child was old enough to travel, the former cook, concerned for their safety, helped the queen and her daughter to flee to another village, Ban

---

[1] I have chosen to render toponyms like Phræ and Phayao in modern Central Thai usage in order to minimize confusion.

[2] This story is in PTMN, ff° 27/1-31/4, including all up to the accession of Cao Sai Yok/Yot.

[3] On the *uposatha sila*, see Kenneth E. Wells, *Thai Buddhism: Its Rites and Activities* (Bangkok, 1960), pp. 51-55. These are days when devout laypersons choose to follow several of the austere precepts of Buddhism.

[4] *chao rai*, the tiller of a dry-rice field, as opposed to *chao na*, the tiller of a wet-rice field.

[5] Here the child is a daughter (*dek ying*), while elsewhere it is a son, a *kumara* (prince). PTMN, ff° 28/3 and 29/1 is similarly confused. TMN f° 4 clears up the problem: the girl is her maidservant, who accompanied her into the forest: near the bottom of the folio it states that "The Queen had her [servant] girl carry the prince in search of water, and [then] the Queen herself bathed the prince seated atop a large rock." Later, the TMN explicitly states that the farmer invited the queen, the prince, and the maid into his home (f° 5).

Saban.[1] This village happened to lie in the territory of[2] /91/ Paña Ngam Müang [of Phayao].

1.14. The two headmen[—the former cook, and the headman of Ban Saban—] raised the young prince[3] to the age of sixteen years, when they presented the young prince before Paña Ngam Müang of Phayao. The ruler was much impressed with the prince, who served him well, and gave him the name of Cao Khun / Sai, making the headman [of Ban Saban] his foster-father.

1.15. Later, Paña Ngam Müang realized that the business of ruling was becoming too much for one man. He therefore appointed Cao Khun Sai to do a large share of his work for him, delegating to him much power. The ruler was very pleased, and had a house built for the young prince, and gave gold and silver presents and jewelry to the young man's mother, [Mæ Cao Kham Pin of Pua].

1.16. Not very long afterwards, [Cao Khun Sai] was appointed Mün Cæ Tang,[4] and [later] he was sent to rule Müang Pat, / when the ruler titled him Cao Sai Yok.[5] At that time, Paña Ngam Müang bestowed the rule of Pua upon one of his wives, Ua Sim, and her son, Am Pòm. Annually, at the turn of the new year and new month, the ruler of Pua presented tribute / to Paña Ngam Müang, paying respect to the ruler by presenting him tribute.

1.17. On one occasion, while visiting Paña Ngam Müang with her son, the queen of Pua made a buffalo-meat curry for the king. After having eaten the curry, the king said to the queen, in a jesting manner, "Your buffalo curry /92/ was delicious and sweet, but it was a little watery." The queen of Pua was highly offended, but kept it to herself. The next day, she returned to Pua with Cao Am Pòm, her son. Cao [Am Pòm] also was offended, and was determined to take the lands in the valley of the Yom for himself and his mother.[6]

1.18. Upon returning to Pua, the mother immediately wrote to the lord of Pat, asking him to come quickly. Cao Sai Yok responded by hurrying to Pua with a large number of elephants, horses,[7] and men. When the lord of Pat arrived at Pua, the queen rushed to welcome him, and on that day the queen and the lord of Müang Pat agreed to become husband and wife.

1.19. Soon, when Paña Ngam Müang learned that Ua Sim [the queen of Pua] had married the lord of Pat / he became highly incensed, and came with a large force to attack Pua. He established his base at Ban Nòng Liang,[8] and declared his intention of capturing Pua. Cao Sai Yok's force was led by Cao Am Pòm. After brief fighting, Paña Ngam Müang recognized his son, Am Pòm, at

---

[1]Spelled Ban Sraban; also in PTMN, f° 29/2. Not in standard gazetteers.

[2]TMN, f° 5, states that the village of Saban paid labor service (*pen khom bân khom wiak*) to Ngam Müang of Phayao. This particular archaic phrase does not occur in the other accounts.

[3]Here, clearly a male child. TMN, ff° 5-6 gives the full history of this young man.

[4]PTMN, f° 30/1, adds that he was in that position for two years. TMN f° 5 says six years.

[5]The printed edition consistently has Cao Sai Yot, while all the manuscript versions I have seen consistently have Cao Sai Yok; e.g. PTMN, f° 30/2, and TMN, f° 5.

[6]The "watery curry" story is also in TMN, ff° 5-6.

[7]Here and elsewhere in this MS., "horses" is spelt *mla*. Other Chiang Mai and Nan manuscripts also spell it this way, which is linguistically curious.

[8]PTMN, f° 31/2, has "Liang." The gazeteers locate a Ban Nòng Liang at 17°13′ N., 99°47′ E.

the head of the opposing army, and Ngam Müang took his armies and retreated back to Phayao.[1]

---

[1]TPMCM, pp. 14-16, relates the famous story of how King Mangrai of Chiang Mai mediated a quarrel between King Ngam Müang of Phayao and Phra Ruang, i.e., Ramkhamhæng, of Sukhothai, which centered on Ngam Müang's queen. The story is *very* close to the story of Ua Sim and Ngam Müang. The Chiang Mai version calls her Lady Ua Chiang Sæn, and gives an expanded version of the "watery curry" story. See also Prasert na Nagara, "Samphanthaphap rawang ratchawong Phra Ruang kap ratchawong Nan [Relations between the dynasties of Phra Ruang and Nan]," in his *Ngan carük læ prawattisat* (Bangkok, 1991), 156-58.

CHAPTER TWO

THE THAI KAO RULERS, CA. 1300-1448

2.1. The councillors of Müang Pua, /93/ headed by Cao Am Pòm, installed the former ruler of Müang Pat, Cao Sai Yok, as the ruler of Pua. He was given the name Cao Pha Nòng because before he was born there was no water for drinking or bathing, and as soon as he had been born there was a rainstorm and a flood that was powerful enough to carry big rocks down the stream; so he was given / the name of Cao Pha Nòng ["Rock-Deluge"].[1]

2.2. At that time, Paña Kao Küan, who had ruled Pukha-Yang for a long time, died in his domain. Cao Pha Nòng therefore [went to Yang and] arranged for the funeral of his father. Pha Nòng then returned to rule as lord of Pua. He was a just and upright ruler. The city was prosperous and the people contented. Cao Khun Fòng, his grandfather, had died. He was the first king of the dynasty. Next came Cao Kao Küan, father of Pha Nòng, second of the dynasty, who also had died. Cao Pha Nòng was made ruler of Pua in the *kot san* year, Culasakkarat 684.[2] He ruled Pua for thirty years. He had six sons. The eldest was Cao Kan Müang, [followed by] Cao Lao, Cao Lün, Cao Ba Cai, Cao Khwai Tom, and Cao Sai.[3]

---

[1]Also in TMN, f° 6. PTMN, ff° 38/4-39/4, tells a curious story of this period. It says that a *yiba*, apparently an ascetic of some sort, who lived in a cave, came to Cao Sai Yok at Pua and told him of a good place to found a town. Sai Yok had Cao Am Pom take people there, and it was named Müang Khwang. Am Pom ruled it, with the title of Paña Kao Kœn. (Does *paña* indicate a degree of independence? Consider that Am Pom might have resented his stepfather, Cao Sai Yok/Pha Nòng.) Am Pòm soon fled to join his father, Ngam Müang, in Phayao. He died there, but returned to Khwang as a tutelary or guardian spirit (*arak*). Khwang is listed among the larger towns of Nan in the PNMN, f° 2/4 (printed edition page 2); and later in that text is listed as having been 3,000 *wa* (6 km.) south of Pua (f° 39/4; printed page 21). It has been placed on the map accordingly.

[2]Culasakkalat (CS) 684 was a *tao set* year, not a *kot san* year. The nearest *kot san* year was CS 682 (AD 1320/21). PTMN, f° 32/1, and TMN, f° 6, says he began his rule in a *ka kai* year, which would be CS 685 (AD 1323/24), and ruled for thirty years. I follow PTMN in dating his reign 685-714. On these chronological problems, see David K. Wyatt, "The Chronology of Nan History, AD 1320-1598," *Journal of the Siam Society* 64, 2 (July 1976): 202-6. Such dates can readily be checked using the table in Thawi Swangpanyangkun, *Sakkarat thiap hon Thai* (Chiang Mai, 1988), p. 8 and back cover.

[3]PTMN, f° 32/1: he had five sons, Tao Lao, Tao Lœn, Ba Cai, Khwai Tom, and Tao Sai. TMN, f° 6 says 7 sons, but it lists only the six given by MS.1. It also adds that Cao Am Pòm returned to Ngam Müang in Phayao.

I find it curious that the Nan chronicle makes no mention of the major episode in which Nan figures in the early portion of the Chiang Mai chronicle—when Nan participated in a military

2.3. When Cao Pha Nòng died, the councillors anointed[1] his youngest son, Cao Sai, to rule the domain in his father's place, in the *kat pao* year.[2] As he was considered the brightest of the lot, the councillors chose him to rule.[3] Cao Sai ruled [only] three years, and died in the *luang mao* year, CS 715.[4] The councillors, acting in concert, anointed Cao Kan Müang, the eldest of Pha Nòng's sons, as ruler of the domain in that *luang mao* year. Cao Pha Nòng, his late father, was third of the line. As for Cao Sai, he was the fourth king of the [Pukha] Dynasty.

2.4. Soon after he became king, / Cao Kan Müang was invited by the ruler of Sukhothai, Paña Sopattagandhi,[5] to go to Sukhothai to help him design and build Wat Luang Aphai, / so Paña Kan Müang went down to assist Paña Sopattagandhi.[6] When the temple was finished, the king of Sukhothai was highly pleased with Paña Kan Müang. To show his appreciation, the king of Sukhothai presented him with seven holy relics and twenty gold and twenty silver votive tablets. / The relics were of different types: two were the size of mustard seed and looked like crystal, three looked like pearl, and two were the size of sesame seed and looked like black ivory. Paña Kan Müang was delighted to have these good and marvellous things.

2.5. Taking the relics and tablets, Paña Kan Müang [returned to Pua] and showed /95/ the treasures to Mahâthera Dhammapâla[7] of Pua, and asked his

---

expedition against Phayao in CS 700-702; see T15RW fascicle 2, Notton (III, 81), and Sanguan, p. 39.

[1]Here, *abhiseka*, while other kings sometimes undergo *ussarâjâbhiseka*. What is the distinction? The Pali compound implies anointing.

[2]The nearest *kat pao* year would be 711 (AD 1349/50). PTMN, f° 32/2: *tao si*, CS 714 (AD 1352/53); TMN, f° 7: *tao si*, CS 713, which is wrong. I follow PTMN.

[3]Note in the accession of the youngest son, Cao Sai, a possible example of a succession pattern noted by Kachorn Sukhabanij, "The Thai Beach-Head States in the 11th-12th Centuries," *Sinlapakon* I, 3-4 (Sept.-Nov. 1957). Such a pattern is common in the chronicles of this earliest period.

[4]715 was a *ka sai* year; the nearest *luang mao* was 713. TMN, f° 7, and PTMN, f° 32/3: he ruled five years, and died in *kap sanga*, which would be 716 (AD 1354/55), though TMN says 718! I follow PTMN.

[5]The TCH (1931), p. 9, dates this episode in [CS] 718, a *lwai san* year. It states that there were seven relics, not six. The date checks out, = AD 1356/57. PTMN ff° 123/2-125/4 gives a similar story, stating that in the *lwai san* year "There was a lord named Kan Müang, son of Paña Sai of Müang Pua, and a ruler named Sopatthakhanthirat ruling Sukhothai in the Southern Country, who invited Paña Kan Müang to assist him in building Wat Phra Luang Aphai, in return for which he gave him seven relics and twenty silver votive tablets." In the TCH, ff° 3/5-4/3, the ruler of Sukhothai is named Paña Srisogandhipattidhammarâjâ. (Note the final element, *-dhammarâja*, of this name.) TCH/PP, pp. 9-10, gives the same names, but has Wat Luang Phaipheyya. The king of Sukhothai at this time (AD 1351) was the well-known Lü Thai (Mahâdhammarâjâ I), whose piety and religious good works have been admirably described by A. B. Griswold and Prasert na Nagara, "The Epigraphy of Mahâdharmarâjâ I of Sukhodaya (Epigraphic and Historical Studies, No. 11)," *JSS* 60, pt. 1 (Jan. 1973): 71-82, and 60, pt. 2 (July 1973): 91-128; or *Epigraphic and Historical Studies* (Bangkok, 1992), pp. 425-570. TMN omits this story, curiously.

[6]Wat Phra Phai Luang is among the oldest temples in Sukhothai. See A. B. Griswold, *Towards a History of Sukhodaya Art* (Bangkok, 1967), pp. 4, 64; and *Raingan khwamkaona kandamnœn ngan süksa wicai anurak læ phatthana Wat Phra Phai Luang* (Bangkok, 1986).

[7]Name spelled identically in TCH/SF, f° 4/2. Dhammapâlathera in TCH (1931), p. 10; and PTMN f° 123/4.

advice as to the best place to enshrine these holy objects. After careful deliberation, the Mahâthera decided that the ruler should enshrine them at Dòi Pu Piang Cæ Hæng, between the Tian and Ling rivers.[1]

2.6. Paña Kan Müang was filled with delight at the advice of the Mahâthera, and proclaimed to his ministers and people his intention of building a shrine for the relics. / In concert with the Mahâthera, he organized a procession with five groups of musicians, and took the relics from Pua to Dòi Pu Piang Cæ Hæng. They stayed at the site for the shrine and the construction work was begun / the next day. Kan Müang had a bronze urn cast, in which he and the Mahâthera and his ministers placed the relics and the gold and silver votive tablets. The cover of the urn was affixed / and sealed with plaster.

2.7. The king and the Mahâthera inspected the work, and then all the *devaputra* and *devata* and powerful forces[2] accompanied the Mahâthera and the ruler in conveying the urn to the site, where a pit one fathom deep was dug. /96/ The urn was placed respectfully in the pit and sealed with bricks and plaster, and over it a cetiya one fathom high was built. Many monks then chanted. The ruler performed rites of worship by his own regular fashion. Then, when he had finished, he accompanied his forces back to Pua.

2.8. Not long afterwards, the ruler longed to be near the relics so that he could regularly pay divine honors to them. He announced to his councillors and forces that he would go down to build a city near the relics / [at Dòi Pu Piang Cæ Hæng]. He first had the city moats dug and earthen walls and beautiful gates constructed.

2.9. In the *muang lao* year CS 721,[3] all the Kwao Tai people were called in to build Paña Kan Müang's palace.

2.10. Paña Kan Müang ruled / Pua for six years, and stayed at Cæ Hæng for five years. In the *luang pao* year CS 725,[4] Khun Inta of the South Country[5]

---

[1]TMN, f° 7, omits any reference to Sukhothai as the source of the relics, which it says were dug up on the spot at Cæ Hæng. TCH/SF, f° 4/2; TCH (1931); TCH/PP, p. 10, and PTMN f° 124/1, also have the Ling and Tian rivers. These streams are not on the best maps (1:250,000) available to me. They show the Mæ Tuan to the north and the Mæ Hæt to the south, both emptying into the Nan River from the east, above and below the Cæ Hæng Reliquary. TCH/PP, p. 11; TCH (1931), p. 10, and PTMN f° 125/2 also note that Cæ Hæng gets its name from a temporary drought.

[2]*tewabut læ tewada læ mahesak tang muan*.

[3]721 was a *kat kai* year; the nearest *muang lao* year was 719 (AD 1357/58). According to TCH/SF, f° 4/3, the decision to move the city was made in the *kat kai* year 181, which has to be 721 (AD 1359). TCH (1931), p. 10, says 721, a *kat kai* year. PTMN f°125/2 states that the relics were enshrined in the *kat kai* year 727, which has to be 721. The sources appear to agree on the *kat kai* year = CS 721.

[4]TCH/SF, f° 4/5; TCH/PP, p. 11; TCH (1931), p. 10; and PTMN, f° 32/4, date these events in the *ka mao* year. TCH (1931) states that this was 725, while PTMN states that it was CS 715. 725 was a *ka mao* year (AD 1363). Thus, in this case our text has the numerals right but the cyclical years wrong, which is unusual. A later version of the same story in PTMN f° 125/3 also says that he stayed there five years before Inta came from the South, dating these events, again, in the *ka mao* year, = 725 (AD 1363/64).

[5]The king of Ayudhya at this time (AD 1361) was Ramathibodi I. Ayudhya activity so far north as Nan at this date may seem early; but cf. A. B. Griswold and Prasert na Nagara, "The Pact Between Sukhodaya and Nân (Epigraphic and Historical Studies, No. 3)," *JSS* 57, pt. 1 (Jan. 1969): 57-108. Might Khun Inta be Indraraja of Ayudhya, who reigned from 1409/10 to

came to pay his respects to Paña Kan Müang and brought him as a present a valuable piece of cloth. The cloth had been treated with a mantra so that one could not tell that it had been poisoned. / Paña Kan Müang, not knowing that the cloth was poisoned, stroked the cloth. As soon as he touched the cloth he collapsed and immediately died, in the *luang pao* year, CS 725, in Wiang Pu Piang Cæ Hæng. He was the fifth king of the Pukha Dynasty.

2.11. The ministers in concert /97/ anointed his son, Cao Pha Kòng, to succeed him as ruler in the *luang pao* year, CS 725. After Cao Pha Kòng had ruled in Wiang Pu Piang Cæ Hæng for six years / there was a drought.[1] There was no water for bathing or for elephants and horses. Cao Pha Kòng then proclaimed to his ministers and people that the city had to be moved, and he selected Ban Huai Kai as the site for his new city, which is the present-day city of Nan.

2.12. Cao Pha Kòng built the city *(wiang)* of Nan here in the *lwai sanga* year / CS 730, on Tuesday, the sixth day of the waxing moon of the twelfth month, in the evening watch.[2] He had ruled in Wiang Pu Piang for six years, and had ruled at Wiang Nan for twenty-one years when he died in the *lwai yi* year, CS 750.[3] He was the / sixth of the line. The councillors anointed Cao Khamtan,[4] his son, to rule the domain in that *lwai yi* year.

1424/25—perhaps before he became king? According to vV, p. 62, he was the son of Phangua of Suphanburi. The geographical designation *"müang tai"* (Southern Country) used here in conjunction with the name of the official, Khun Inta, seems very vague, but it is used throughout to refer to Ayudhya and Bangkok.

[1]TCH (1931), p. 10: the drought occurred after he had ruled 3 years. Tao Pha Kòng is explicitly named in the Luang Prasœt Chronicle of Ayudhya, *sub anno* CS 738, which correlates with the dates given here.

[2]728 is the nearest *lwai sanga* year; 730 was a *pœk san* year. Much better and fuller information on this very important date—the first building of the city of Nan—is given in the PTMN, which provides the information in two places. First, at the head of the manuscript, on the first folio, there is a *duang*, an astrological diagram placing all the heavenly bodies at the moment the city was founded in the *pœk san* year, CS 730. Then, at f° 33/2, the date is given as Tuesday, the third day of the twelfth month. Our manuscript here says Tuesday the 6th. TCH/PP, p. 11, and TCH (1931), p. 10, say 730, a *pœk san* year, on Tuesday the 6th waxing of the 12th month. The TCH/SF, f° 5/2, says *pœk san* 690(!), but gives the day as Tuesday, the full-moon day of the twelfth month. TMN, f° 7, has the 3rd day of the 12th month in the *pœk san* year 730. The nearest Tuesday to our chronicle's date is the 2nd day of the twelfth month, which was 15 August 1368, while the Cæ Hæng Reliquary Chronicle's date best works out to Tuesday, the 1st day of the waning moon of the twelfth month, 29 August 1368. In neither case do the actual planetary positions match the *duang*. There is little question as to the year, as the position of Saturn changes so slowly as to narrow the choices very considerably.

On the various hours ("watches") of the day, see Appendix 2.

[3]748 is the nearest *lwai yi* year; 750 was a *pœk si* year. TMN, f° 7; TCH (1931), p. 11; TCH/SF (f° 5/4); and the PTMN (f° 33/4) all give the *lwai yi* year, CS 748 or AD 1386/87. The TCH/SF (f° 5/5) adds a curious story about people then coming from Sajjanâlai to try to loot the Cæ Hæng Reliquary, which was protected by its guardian spirits, making the intruders ill and driving them away. TCH/PP, p. 11; TCH (1931), p. 11, and PTMN f° 126/2 state that he ruled nineteen years and died aged 80 years in the *lwai yi* year.

[4]TCH/SF, f° 6/1, says Cao Khampan. TCH (1931), p. 11, and PTMN f° 126/2 state that he had three sons: Khamtan, Sican, and Tao Hung (TCH (1931)) or Lahung (PTMN). TMN, f° 7, says he also had a daughter, Mæ Tao Ia.

2.13. [Cao Khamtan] had ruled for eleven years, when a ruler of the South named Khun Luang[1] came up / to Nan to perform the ceremony of consecration for Cao Khamtan. Everyone had joined in building a pavilion for the ceremony at Ta Li[2]. During the ceremony the ruler of the South and all the people poured consecrated water over the head of Cao Khamtan. After the pouring of holy water, Cao Khamtan developed a severe headache, and on returning to his palace he died the same night. He died in the *lwai cai* year /98/ CS 760.[3] Khun Luang of the South fled. [Khamtan] was the seventh of the dynasty. The councillors and ministers together consecrated his son[4] Cao Si Canta to succeed him as ruler in that *lwai cai* year.

2.14. When Cao / Si Canta had ruled Nan for a year, the two brother rulers of Phræ, the elder Paña Thera, and his younger brother, Paña Un Müang, invested and captured Nan and Cao Si Canta was put to death in / the *müang pao* year CS 761.[5] He was the eighth king of the dynasty.[6] Cao Hung, the younger brother of Cao Si Canta, escaped to the South country, and took refuge with Paña Chaliang.[7]

---

[1]TMN, f° 7, says "The ruler of the South had a person named Khun Luang" come to Nan, 11 years after Khamtan ascended the throne. TCH (1931), p. 11, just says "Khun Luang, a person of the Southern Country." TCH/PP, p. 11, and PTMN f° 126/3 have "Khun Luang Si (Sri) of the Southern Country." It is interesting to note the suddenly increased role of the South (Siam) in Nan. Again, any identification with the known name of any specific Ayudhya king is impossible. The name used here, "Khun Luang," is no more than a vague title (although it occurred in the name of at least one king of Ayudhya, Khun Luang Ha Wat, in the eighteenth century, and is one way of referring to the third king of Ayudhya, Borommaracha I [1370-88]—"*khun luang phangua*"). Cœdès, in his translation of the *Jinakalamali* ("Documents ...," *BEFEO* 25, p. 100) makes an intriguing identification of the Vattitejo of that text, who was sent by King Ramathibodi to rule Chainat, with "Khun Luang Phongua," the governor of Suphanburi who succeeded his brother-in-law Ramathibodi on the throne of Ayudhya in 1370 as Borommaracha I. Throughout the chronicle, references to Ayudhya and Bangkok kings are very vague. Ayudhya is frequently mentioned even after the capital was moved to Thonburi and later to Bangkok.

[2]This place is not locatable. It is probably one of the boat landings on the west bank of the Nan River somewhere near the city; perhaps where the bridge is today, where there is low, flat ground?

[3]758 is the nearest *lwai cai* year; 760 was a *pœk yi* year. 758 = AD 1396/97. TCH (1931), p. 11, says 758, a *lwai cai* year. TCH/PP, p. 11; TCH/SF, f° 6/1, and the PTMN (f° 34/2, also f° 126/4) agree on the *lwai cai* year.

[4]PTMN f° 126/2 says that Si Canta was his younger brother. TCH/PP, p. 11, states that Pha Nong had three sons—Khamtan, Sri Canta, and Hung. TMN, f° 8, says Canta was Khamtan's son, and concurs with the date.

[5]759 is the nearest *müang pao* year; 761 was a *kat mao* year. TMN (f° 8), TCH/SF (f° 6/1) and PTMN (f° 34/2) agree on *müang pao*, which would be CS 759 (AD 1397). TCH (1931), p. 11, gives no date.

[6]This sentence occurs at the end of the paragraph in the text, but it makes better sense to place it here.

[7]This is to be identified as the old city of Satchanalai. See A. B. Griswold and Prasert na Nagara, "A Fifteenth-Century Siamese Historical Poem," in *Southeast Asian History and Historiography: Essays Presented to D.G.E. Hall* (Ithaca, 1975), p. 128 and the maps on pages 124-25.

2.15. Paña Thera[1] ruled Nan for six months / and ten days[2] and developed a kind of sickness in which blood oozed from the pores of his body and he died in that *müang pao* year. He was the ninth king of Nan, but of a different lineage.

2.16. Cao Un Müang,[3] his younger brother, became / ruler in the *müang pao* year CS 761.[4] After he had been ruling for a year, Cao Hung came up to Nan with an army from Chaliang and invaded and captured Nan. Cao Un Müang was captured and sent to the ruler of the South, where he remained for ten years and died. Cao Un Müang /99/ left the domain in the *pœk yi* year, CS 762.[5] He was [the tenth ruler of Nan,] from a different lineage.

2.17. Cao Paña Hung then became ruler in the *pœk yi* year, CS 762. He ruled for eight years,[6] and died in the *dap lao* year / CS 769[7] from an abscess. He was the eleventh in the line.

2.18. Cao Pu Kheng,[8] the son of Cao Hung, succeeded his father as ruler in the *dap lao* year, CS 769.[9] Cao Pu Kheng ruled for eleven years before dying / of diarrhea in the *dap met* year, CS 779.[10] He was the twelfth of the line.

2.19. Cao Pan, his son, succeeded him in the *dap met* year. He ruled for ten years and died in the *kap yi* year / CS 788.[11] He was the thirteenth of the line.

2.20. Cao Pan was succeeded in the *kap si* year by his son, Cao Ngua Pha Sum, who ruled for eight years and died / in the *luang kai* year CS 795.[12] Cao

---

[1]TCH/SF, f° 6/1, has Paña Cæn.

[2]TMN (f° 8) alone agrees exactly with this interval. TCH/SF, f° 6/1, has 2 mos., 2 days; PTMN, f° 34/3, has 2 mos. 10 days; f° 127/2 has 1 mo. 20 days; TCH (1931), p. 11, has 1 month and 20 days.

[3]TCH/SF (f° 6/2), and TMN (f° 8) have Paña Ờn Mông.

[4]759 is the nearest *muang pao* year; 761 was *kat mao*. TCH (1931), p. 11, says in the *lwai cai* year, which would be 758.

[5]760 is the nearest *pœk yi* year; 762 was *kot si*. None of the other manuscripts mentions a year.

[6]TCH/PP, p. 12; TCH (1931), p. 11, and PTMN f° 127/3 say 9 years.

[7]TCH (1931), p. 12, says he also was the nephew/grandson of Pha Kòng, and he succeeded in the *lwai set* year, 768. 767 is the nearest *dap lao* year; 769 was a *müang kai* year. TMN (f° 8), TCH/SF (f° 6/2), and PTMN (f° 34/4) all have *lwai set*, which was CS 768 (AD 1406).

[8]TCH/SF, f° 6/3, has Paña Pu Piang; TMN, f° 8, TCH/PP, p. 12, and PTMN f° 127/4 have Paña Pu Kheng, nephew/grandson of Cao Pha Kòng.

[9]TMN, f° 8, TCH/PP, p. 12, and PTMN f° 127/4 say it was the *lwai set* year, 768.

[10]777 was *dap met*; 779 was *müang lao*. TCH/PP, p. 12; TCH/SF (f° 6/2), TMN (f° 8), and PTMN (f° 35/1, f° 128/1) all have *lwai san*, which was CS 778 (AD 1416). TCH/PP, p. 12, and PTMN f° 127/4 say that he built Wat Luang Paña Phu in the *tao si* year 774. TCH (1931), p. 12, states that he built Wat Luang Paña Phu Kheng, finished the vihara in the *tao si* year 774, and died in the *lwai san* year 778, having ruled 11 years. This has to be Wat Paña Phu, within the old city walls nearest the river on the east side. See the city map.

[11]This has to be *kap si*, not *kap yi*. The nearest *kap si* was 786; 788 was *lwai sanga*. But TCH/PP, p. 12; TCH/SF (f° 6/3) and PTMN (f° 35/1) all say *dap sai*, which was CS 787 (AD 1425). PTMN f° 128/1 says this was Tao Phan, who ruled 10 rainy seasons (*vassa*). TCH (1931), p. 12, says that Tao Pan ruled 10 years, and in the *dap sai* year 787 was succeeded by Tao Pa/Pha Sum, who obtained a white elephant. He built the city walls of Nan.

[12]Pha Sum is mentioned in three inscriptions dated CS 788 from Nan, in which he is styled Somdet Cao Paña San Pha Sum. MNBPS, pp. 247-55. CS 793 was *luang kai*; 795 was *ka pao*. TCH/PP, p. 12; TCH (1931), p. 12; TCH/SF (f° 6/3); and PTMN (f° 35/2) all say the *tao cai* year, which was CS 794 (AD 1432). The TMN (f° 8) and PTMN add the information that Pha Sum sent his predecessor to the South (i.e., Ayudhya). TMN (f° 8) says Pha Sum became ruler in the *dap sai*

Ngua Pha Sum had three sons, Cao Intakæn, Cao Pæng, and Cao Hò Pom.[1] The councillors consecrated Cao /100/ Intakæn, the eldest son, as ruler.[2] Cao Ngua Pha Sum was fourteenth in the line.

2.21. Cao Intakæn succeeded his father in that *luang kai* year. When he had ruled for a year and three months,[3] his two younger brothers, Cao / Pæng and Cao Hò Pom, seized power and put Intakæn in a cage,[4] where he was left to die. While imprisoned, Intakæn practiced a ruse [to deceive his captors]. He smeared his bedding / and clothing with buffalo blood, then told his keepers that he had a bad case of diarrhea and was sure to die. The keepers informed Cao Pæng, who came to look at Intakæn through the cage door. / He then said to the keepers, "He is going to die anyway, so we might as well let him die outside." Intakæn was released. That night he escaped to Ban Tao Hai.[5] From there he went to Müang Lam,[6] where he was given food by a white-robed ascetic.[7] / The ascetic wrapped him in a cloth and took him to the South Country, where he took refuge with the ruler of Chaliang.[8]

2.22. Cao Pæng then ruled in place of his eldest brother in the *tao cai* year, CS 796.[9] He had ruled for one year when, in the *ka pao* year, CS 797,[10] /101/ Cao Intakæn obtained troops from the ruler of Chaliang and led them [towards Nan], setting up his base at the mouth of the Samun [river], north of Cæ Pang.[11]

---

year, = 787, AD 1425; and that he died in the *tao cai* year (794/AD 1432). PTMN f° 128/1 says his son Tao Pha Sum Cao Cang Phüak—"Lord of the White Elephant"—succeeded him in 795. He is said to have built the fortified town *(wiang)* and died in the *tao cai* year.

1TCH (1931), p. 12, says his three sons were Intakæn, Tao Pæng, and Tao Lok. TCH/PP, p. 12, puts the names in a curious form: Phananta Kæn Tao, Tao Pæng, and Tao Tho.

2TMN (f° 8) and TCH/SF (f° 6/5) consistently call him Kæn Tao, as do the Chiang Mai chronicles.

3TMN (f° 8) says 6 years and 4 months. TCH/SF (f° 6/4); TCH (1931), p. 12; and PTMN f° 128/2: 6 months; PTMN (f° 35/2): 4 months.

4The word used is comparable to the modern word for "prison;" but it seems better to use "cage." This story is not included in TMN.

5TCH (1931), p. 12, just has Ban Tao: though *hai* follows, it is needed grammatically as a verb, and should not be part of the village's name. TCH/PP, p. 12, however, has Ban Tao Hai Cæliang! There are three villages by that name, at 16°51′ N, 100°15′ E; 17°14′ N., 101°19′ E.; and 17°24′ N., 100° 07′ E.

6TCH (1931), p. 12, and PTMN f° 128/4 have Müang Lam Ban Hua Lin. TCH/PP, p. 13, has Müang Lam Ban Hua Lin. Müang Lam clearly is located in the domain of Nan: it is listed in the 17th-century(?) PNMN, f° 3/3 (printed p. 2).

7TCH/PP, p. 13 names the ascetic: Sanghapâla.

8TMN (f° 8) alone names him: Phraya Sai Si Yot, ruler of Chaliang.

9var. Tao Pæng (TCH/SF, f° 6/4), Paña Pæng (PTMN, f° 35/2). 794 was the nearest *tao cai* year; 796 was *kap yi*. TCH/SF and PTMN both have *tao cai*, which is CS 794 (AD 1432).

10795 was the nearest *ka pao* year; 797 was a *dap mao* year. TMN (f° 8) and PTMN (f° 35/3) give the *kap yi* year, which would be CS 796 (AD 1434). TCH/SF gives no date, and says that Pæng ruled for one year and four months. TCH (1931), p. 13, says 1 year 3 months. TMN does not give the details of this battle, but briefly refers to a contest on elephant-back.

11The Samun River flows from the northwest, emptying into the Nan River immediately below Nan. Cæ Pang poses a puzzle. That village is located to the *east* of the river, some distance from the mouth of the Samun, southwest of Cæ Hæng and *west* of what looks on the map as though it could be an old course of the river. One strong possibility, then, is that the course of the Nan River changed, placing Cæ Pang on the west bank of the Nan River. (Owing to official

Cao Pæng brought down an army to engage the invaders, mounted on his war elephant, Prap Cakravala, and crossed the river north of the mouth of the Samun. Intakæn, mounted on his war elephant, / Khwan Phek Paña Mara, charged the elephant Prap Cakravala. Khwan Phek engaged [his adversary], and was struck right at the end of his tusk(s). Khwan Phek was wounded by the tusk of Prap Cakravala.[1]

2.23. Prap Cakravala then withdrew back across the Nan River [and got set in a position] using the Nan and Samun rivers as moats, [along which] the army assembled. Cao Pæng decided to fight [Intakæn] there. Cao Intakæn, mounted on Khwan Phek Paña Mara, crossed the Nan River [in pursuit]. Tao Pæng, heedless of his elephant's royally decorated tusks, engaged Tao Intakæn's elephant Khwan Phek, and the tips of [Prap Cakravala's] tusks stabbed into the mouth of his opponent, and the latter lost all taste for battle. Then Intakæn slashed with his lance, and Cao Pæng, bleeding profusely, fell from his elephant and died.

2.24. Intakæn's troops then made short work / of their opponents, killing them and driving them into the Samun to drown. The place where the two princes dueled on the Samun north of Cæ Pang,[2] where Cao Pæng was killed, is popularly known as the Na Khacat ["Massacre Field"];[3] and the place where their armies battled is called / Ban Khwai Mæng Ngang ["Village of the Rout"].[4] Cao Pæng died in the *ka pao* year, CS 797.[5] He was the fifteenth in the line.

2.25. Cao Intakæn ruled a second time, from the *ka pao* year, for sixteen years.[6] He had / one son.[7]

2.26. At that time he sent a servant to take salt from Bò Mang[8] to present to Paña Tilok of Chiang Mai.[9] Soon afterwards, Paña Tilok decided to make Nan

---

Thai and US resistance to allowing scholarly access to the 1:50,000 maps, I have to work with a poor xerox, which is not clear.)

According to PTMN f° 129/2, the army was led by Khun S(r)i. TCH/PP, pp. 13-14, and TCH (1931), p. 13, give a fuller version of this episode. The troops were led by Khun S(r)i, came to the east of the city, along the river, and sent a letter announcing their presence to Intakæn's brother. The ministers counselled against fighting, but Cao Peng ignored them. The rest of the account is very much as given here, though the language in places seems more archaic.

[1]Essentially the same story is given in PTMN f° 129/3. Translation very uncertain. Prap Cakravala might translate as the "Conqueror of the Mountains that Ring the Universe" or "Conqueror of Multitudes," while Khwan Phek Paña Mara translates as "Prince of Darkness, Thunderbolt Battleaxe." On the elephant names, compare the names in Sanguan Chotisukkharat, *Tamnan müang nüa* (Chiang Mai, 1955), vol. 2, p. 18.

[2]TCH (1931), p. 13, has Cæ Pang. Somchet Vimolkasem tells me that Cæ Pang is located on the east side of the Nan River between Nan and Wiang Sa; but the context requires a location on the Samun River, which is on the west side of the Nan River. Cæ Pang therefore has to be either south or west of Nan.

[3]TCH (1931), p. 13 has Ban Dòn Khacat.

[4]TCH (1931), p. 13, has Ban Mæng M(l)ang. (Note the ML cluster again.)

[5]See previous note on this date.

[6]TCH/SF (f° 6/5) and PTMN (f° 130/4) agree on 16 years. TCH (1931), p. 14, explicitly says 796, a *kap yi* year, and agrees on 16 years.

[7]The printed version says one son and two daughters. TMN (f° 8) says one son and one daughter, and agrees on 16 years.

[8]On the salt wells, located in the valley east of Pua adjacent to the modern Lao border, see *Müang Nan* (Bangkok, 1987), p. 16, which includes a photograph. PTMN (ff° 42/3-44/3) includes

a tributary of Müang Ping Chiang Mai. He mobilized / a fourfold army and led it out of Chiang Mai to Müang Lò, putting Lò people in the vanguard. The army then went by way of[1] the base of Mount Wao to Nan. The army was based at the Sugar-Palm Orchard.[2] / They set up cannon and bombarded[3] the city gate, and then took the city. When Paña Intakæn realized that he could not resist the superior forces of the enemy, he took his wives and children and fled to the South Country, taking refuge with his friend, the ruler of Chaliang. Intakæn fled / from Nan in the *pœk si* year, CS 812.[4] He was the sixteenth in the ruling line.

---

a story accounting for the names of four salt wells in this region, citing an otherwise unknown *Tamnan Nâng Klüa*. They were called Bò Wa, Bò Næ, Bò Mang, and Bò Pak. The third surely was in the headwaters of the Mang River, where a salt well remains to the present day. The Wa and Mang rivers flow south from the valley behind Pua, while the headwaters of the Nan River flow north.

[9]The great King Tilok of Chiang Mai ruled from CS 804 to 849 (AD 1442-1487). Cf. Camille Notton, tr., "Chronique de Xieng Mai," *Annales du Siam*, III (Paris, 1932), pp. 104-44. His expedition against Nan, according to Notton (pp. 110-11), took place in CS 805-6 (AD 1443/44). The Jkm., written by a monk of Chiang Mai in 1516, gives the date as CS 810 (AD 1448), which agrees with this chronicle. Cf. Cœdès, "Documents ...," p. 109. The confusion continues in other sources. The TPMCM, pp. 52-53, depicts a long war ending in the *kat sai* year, 811. The TPMCM, p. 66, varies. T15RW, f° 4/14/2, says the war began in the *ka kai* year (805) on the 13th day of the second month (Tuesday, 5 November 1443), and the city fell to Chiang Mai in the *pœk si* year 810 (f° 4/19/4). The preponderance of the evidence indicates CS 810 (AD 1448/49).

[1]The printed edition adds that they went by way of Müang Pong and Müang Khwan (Khwang?). TCH (1931), p. 14, says they went by way of Müang Pong and Dòi Tiu and Dòi Tua Cao.

[2]Probably the vicinity of Wat Suan Tan on the north side of the city of Nan.

[3]The words used in the text with reference to this bombardment indicate that cannon were used: the words used are *amòk sinat*. The same words are used in TCH/PP, p. 14, and PTMN f° 131/1; while TCH (1931), p. 14, simply says they set up their cannon (*amòk*) to shoot in through the Utthayan Gate. The glossary to the printed edition defines *amòk* as artillery. This is not impossible: cf. W. A. R. Wood, *A History of Siam* (Bangkok, 1959), p. 77, n. 1, for early references to the use of firearms.

[4]See lengthy note above concerning the date, which has to be 810. PTMN (f° 6/5) adds that, from the foundation of Nan in the *pœk san* year (730) to the fall of the city to Chiang Mai in the *kat sai* year, 811, was 82 years (current, not elapsed), which confirms 730 as the date of the foundation of the city. Another version of this invasion reads as follows: In AD 1476, King Tilok of Chiang Mai was engaged in expanding his territory. He entered the territory of Nan and encamped at Suan Tan Luang, where he set up his artillery and commenced firing into the city. Cao Intakæn, convinced that he could not hold the city, fled to Chaliang. When Tilok entered the city the next morning, he decided that since he had taken it without bloodshed, as if aided by the angels (*deva*), he would commemorate the victory with a golden image of the Lord Buddha. Having asked publicly for donations of gold, and collecting 12 *tü* of gold within seven days, he gathered craftsmen—local men, Burmese, Shan, Lao Kao, and men of Chiang Sæn—and commenced the casting of the image. After three months and seven days, the image was finished, and named "Phracao Thong Thip." Not long afterwards, King Tilok returned to Chiang Mai. Sanguan Chotisukkharat, *Tamnan müang nüa*, vol. I, pp. 253-55. Early Buddha images from Nan are depicted in *Muang Nan* (Bangkok, 1987), esp. pp. 32-33, and MNBPS, esp. pp. 177 ff.

TMN (f° 8) agrees on the year, but seems to say that Kæn Tao (or Intakæn) fled to Phayao, not Chaliang or the South; and it offers no explanation of Tilok's motivation.

2.27. When Paña Tilok captured Nan, he appointed Cao Pha Sæng, son of Cao Pæng, to rule the city in the *pœk si* year /103/ CS 812.[1] Pha Sæng ruled for twelve years, and died in the *kat mao* year, CS 823.[2] He was the seventeenth in the ruling line. As for the ruling line of Kao Tai of Nan, that is, from Cao Khun Fòng all the way down to Cao Pha Sæng, / it ends with this Pha Sæng. After him, all [the rulers] were appointed from outside the domain.[3]

---

[1]PTMN (f° 131/2) says *kat sai*, which has to be *pœk si* 810. TCH (1931), p. 14, says he was appointed in the *kat met* year 801 (AD 1439/40), which has to be wrong (cf. Jkm.). TCH/PP, p. 14 says that Phâ Sæng began ruling Nan in the *kot sai* year, which would be CS 822 (AD 1460/61).

[2]TCH/PP, p. 14; TCH/SF (f° 7/1), TMN (f° 9), and PTMN (f° 36/1, also f° 131/3) all have the *kot si* year, CS 822 (AD 1460/61), which has to be correct. TCH (1931), p. 14, states that he ruled 12 years and died in the *kat sanga* year 812.

[3]This seems to be the last reference in this text to the distinctive ethnic identity of the Kao/Kwao of the Nan valley. TCH (1931), p. 14, also uses the word, with inserted L—*müang Klao Thai*. TCH/PP, p. 14, also puts this in ethnic terms: the line of Kwao Tai rulers ended here. TMN makes no such statement.

CHAPTER THREE

NAN UNDER CHIANG MAI RULE, AD 1448-1558

3.1. [After the death of Cao Pha Sæng,] King Tilok then appointed Mün Sòi of Chiang Khong to rule in the *kot si* year, CS 824.[1] He ruled for four years and was transferred to rule Fang.[2] He was the eighteenth to rule Nan.

3.2. The king then appointed Mün Nòi Nai to come and rule in the *kap san* year, 828.[3] He ruled for three years, then committed an infraction and was killed, dying in the *lwai / set* year, 830.[4] He was the nineteenth ruler.

3.3. The king next appointed Mün Khwa Tao Ba Lai in the *muang kai* year 831.[5] He ruled for four years, and died in the *kot yi* year.[6] He was the twentieth ruler.

---

[1]The chronology of this and the next chapter is exceedingly difficult. 824 was a *tao sanga* year; the nearest *kot si* year was 822. PTMN (f° 36/1), agreeing with the TCH that Cao Pha Sæng died in the *kot si* year (= CS 822 = AD 1460/61), says that Mün Cæ Lo then came to rule for 3 months. TCH/SF f° 7/1 and PTMN f° 36/2 then have Mün Sòi of Chiang Khong coming to rule in the *lüang sai* year, = CS 823 (AD 1461/62). TCH/PP, p. 14, TMN (f° 9), and PTMN (f° 131/3) say that a temporary ruler Mün Cæ Mò came for 3 months, followed by Mün Sòi of Chiang Khong. TCH (1931), p. 14, says that, after the death of Pha Sæng in *kat sanga* 812, Mün Cæ Mò came as acting ruler for 3 months; and then Mün Sòi of Chiang Khong came, in *luang met* 813. He ruled for 5 years, and then went to Chiang Sæn. I conclude that Mün Cæ Lo/Mò came for 3 months in CS 822 *kot si*, followed the same year by Mün Sòi of Chiang Khong.

[2]TMN (f° 9) says he was sent to Chiang Sæn, and adds that, after him, there were no more rulers titled Phraya Nan—an assertion which it later contradicts!

[3]The nearest *kap san* year was 826 (= AD 1464/65). TCH (1931), p. 14, says that Mün Noi Nai came in *dap kai* 817, ruled 3 years, and was killed in *pœk yi* 820. TMN (f° 9); TCH/PP, p. 14; TCH/SF f° 7/1 and PTMN f° 36/2 and also f° 131/4 bring Mün Chiang Nòi to Nan in the *dap rao* year, = CS 827 (AD 1465/66), which would appear to be the correct date.

[4]The nearest *lwai set* year was CS 828 (= AD 1466/67). TCH and PTMN do not mention the ruler's death, but they have the next ruler come in *pœk cai* 830, which seems correct. TMN (f° 9), and TCH/PP, p. 14, have him killed in the *pœk cai* year.

[5]The nearest *müang kai* year was CS 829 (=AD 1467/68). TCH/SF f° 7/1 and PTMN ff° 36/2 and 131/4 have Mün Khwa Tao Ba Lai appointed in the *pœk cai* year, = CS 830 (AD 1468/69), which would appear to be the correct date.

[6]TCH (1931), p. 14 says Mün Khwa ruled 3 years and died in *luang sai* 823. PTMN f° 131/4 says that he ruled 3 years. The nearest *kot yi* year was CS 832 (AD 1470/71). TMN (f° 9), TCH/SF (f° 7/1), and PTMN (f° 36/2) place this event in the *luang mao* year, = CS 838 (AD 1471/72).

3.4. The king then appointed Mün Kham[1] to rule in the *luang mao* year, 835.[2] He ruled for three years, and in the *ka sai* year[3] was transferred to rule Fang. He was the twenty-first ruler.

3.5. The king then appointed Tao Kha Kan, /104/ son of the ruler of Fang, to come and rule in the *kap sanga* year, CS 838.[4] Tao Kha Kan sent Mün Nai Kham to see Paña Tilok in Chiang Mai. There he met Mahâthera Vajirabodhi, who gave him the history of the famous shrine [Wat Cæ Hæng] to take to Tao Kha Kan. When the ruler was apprised of the account of Wat Cæ Hæng, he / decided to restore it.[5]

3.6. Tao Kha Kan[6] then convened all the monkhood and the population to rebuild the Pu Piang Cæ Hæng reliquary. At this time, Wat Cæ Hæng was in ruins and almost completely obliterated, overgrown with bamboo and / vines. The place where the relics were enshrined was only an ant-hill. Tao Kha Kan had the place cleared of undergrowth and bamboo, and performed an act of worship. He then built a pavilion for the ceremony. /

3.7. That night there was an emanation of brilliant light from the ant-hill, indicating the location of the relics. Tao Kha Kan dug down in the ant-hill to a depth of one fathom, and found a large, round, smooth rock. He then had the rock broken open, and found inside a large golden urn with its cover still intact.

3.8. He asked the white-robed ascetic Chiang Khom, who lived in Wat Tai nearby, to open the urn. Inside the urn were seven relics, and the twenty golden and twenty silver votive tablets which Paña Kan Müang had brought from the ruler of Sukhothai in the South Country and enshrined, and which King Asoka had enshrined, /105/ ten fathoms below the surface, just as the chronicle had

---

[1]TCH/PP, p. 14, and TMN (f° 9) call him Mün Khâo Kham, but otherwise confirm the information given here. TMN adds that he was the son of the previous ruler.

[2]The nearest *luang mao* year was CS 833 (AD 1471/72), which I take to be the correct year. TCH/SF f° 7/1-2 and PTMN ff° 36/2 and 131/4 give this person's name as Mün Khwa Kham, and bring him to Nan in the *luang mao* year. TCH/PP, p. 14, calls him Mün Khâo Tao Bâ Lâi, and has him rule for 3 years before dying in the *luang mao* year.

[3]The nearest *ka sai* year was CS 835 (AD 1473/74). TCH (1931), p. 14 says Mün Kham, the previous ruler's son, ruled 3 years and went to rule Fang. TCH/SF f° 7/2 says that he ruled 3 years and fled in the *kap sanga* year (= CS 836), which I take as the correct year. PTMN f° 36/3 adds that he died in that year.

[4]838 was a *lwai san* year: the nearest *kap sanga* year was CS 836 (AD 1474/75), which I take as the correct year; a year which is given correctly in TCH/PP, p. 14. TCH (1931), p. 14, says Tao Kha Kan, "son of Müang Fang" (presumably the previous ruler), came to rule in *kap san* 826. TCH/SF f° 7/2 simply says that Mün Khwa Kham ruled 3 years and fled in the *kap sanga* year (= CS 836), when the king appointed Tao Kha Kan. PTMN ff° 36/3 and 132/1 says that Mün Khwa Kham went to rule Fang in the *kap sanga* year. However, PTMN then diverges from the other texts: "He [then] went to rule Chiang Sæn in the *kat kai* year [CS 841], for 4 years, and died in the *ka mao* year [CS 845]. His son then succeeded him in the *ka mao* year, ruling for 4 years and leaving in the *müang met* year [CS 849." There appears to be a haplography here, omitting the name of the ruler of Nan who went to Chiang Sæn in CS 841.

[5]TCH/PP, pp. 15-17; and TCH (1931), pp. 15-17, give an extended version of this story. The first section of PTMN omits this story of the renovation of the reliquary, but it appears in the later section at ff° 132/2-4. TCH/SF ff° 7/3-8/3 has it, though it is told somewhat differently. TMN omits this story.

[6]Note that, as soon as rulers begin to be appointed from Chiang Mai, their titles change—usually to *tao* or *cao*.

stated. He kept the relics and votive tablets in the city for a month, and then reported his find to Paña Tilok in Chiang Mai. Paña Tilok told Tao Kha Kan to enshrine the relics at the original site, at Mount Pu Piang. Informed of King Tilok's advice, Tao Kha Kan returned the relics and built a cetiya six fathoms high over them.[1]

3.9. In the *pœk set* year, CS 842, a Kæo[2] army invaded Nan.[3] Paña Tilok ordered Tao Kha Kan to meet them with a force of / forty thousand. He defeated the Kæo, and killed a large number of the enemy and sent their heads to Paña Tilok. He also captured a large number of prisoners and their families, as well as elephants and horses, which he presented to King Tilok. Paña Tilok was not pleased with what Tao Kha Kan had done, and said to him, "You should have allowed the enemy to escape / instead of following them and killing them to capture their families. The wrath of enemies and tigers is awful. The Kæo [prisoners] should not be allowed to settle in Müang Nan." Tilok then transferred Tao Kha Kan to Chiang Rai.[4] He was the twenty-second ruler.

3.10. The king then appointed Tao / Ai Yuam to rule in the *kat kai* year, 843.[5] He ruled for four years, and died in the *tao yi* year, 847.[6] Tao Ai Yuam together with the monkhood and laity of the domain further restored the [Cæ Hæng] reliquary by building a larger and higher cetiya over the one built by Tao

---

[1]According to PTMN f° 136/3, apparently in the *lwai san* year, CS 838 (AD 1476/77), which I take to be the correct year.

[2]Kæo is the conventional term for Vietnam/Vietnamese, though in some contexts it can mean otherwise. That it here indicates Vietnam is supported by Lao sources.

[3]842 was a *kot cai* year. The nearest *pœk set* year was CS 840 (AD 1478/79). TCH does not mention this Kæo invasion, nor is it in the first section of PTMN. It does, however, occur in the later section of PTMN, ff° 104/4-108/3, dated in the *luang pao* year 823, which has to be 843 (AD 1481/82). It also figures in the TPMCM, p. 65 (see also Notton, III, pp. 136-38), with a date in the 8th month (May) of the *kat kai* year, CS 841 (AD 1479/80). See also T15RW, II, 52 (*phuk* 5, f° 16); Phraya Prachakitkòracak, *Phongsawadan Yonok* (Bangkok, 1973), p. 345; and Sanguan Chotisukkharat, *Nangsü phün müang Chiang Mai* (Chiang Mai, 1972), pp. 80-81. All these Chiang Mai sources agree on a Kæo war in CS 841, and I have accepted 841 (AD 1479/80).

Paul le Boulanger, *Histoire du Laos français* (Paris, 1931), pp. 64-67 writes of the Vietnamese invasion in 1478/79, as does Maha Sila Viravong, *History of Laos* (New York, 1964), pp. 44-46. Cao Khamman Vongkotrattana, *Phongsavadan sat Lao* (Vientiane, 1973), p. 33, dates it one year earlier.

[4]TCH/PP, p. 17, TCH (1931), p. 17, and PTMN f° 136/4 say that Kha Kan renovated a cetiya, ruled 3 more years, and went to rule Chiang Sæn in the *kat kai* year 841. TMN (f°9) does not mention the religious work, and states that Khao Kham (Kha Kan) was transferred to Fang, not Chiang Rai. I have accepted 841 (AD 1479/80), not least because he ruled 3 years from 838, when he built a cetiya.

[5]843 was a *luang pao* year: the nearest *kat kai* year was 841 (AD 1479/80), which is given for this event in TPMCM, p. 65; TCH/SF f° 8/3; and PTMN f° 136/4. I have accepted 841. TCH/PP, p. 17, and TCH (1931), p. 18, say that Ai Yuam came in *tao yi* 844, ruled for 4 years, built a 17-fathom high cetiya, and died in *ka mao* 845. TPMCM, p. 65: Tao Kha Kan was succeeded by Mün Kha Tap.

[6]847 was a *dap sai* year: the nearest *tao yi* year was CS 844 (AD 1482/83), which I take to be the correct year. TCH/SF f° 8/3-4 and PTMN f° 137/1 say that Ai Yuam ruled for 4 years and built a 7-fathom-high cetiya atop what Tao Kha Kan had built. TMN (f° 9) baldly gives only the chronology, as here.

Kha Kan. /106/ This cetiya was ten fathoms wide and seventeen fathoms high. The work took four years to finish. Tao Ai Yuam was the twenty-third ruler.[1]

3.11. The king next appointed Tao Müang, son of Tao Ai Yuam, to rule in the *tao yi* year, 847.[2] He ruled for five years and died in the *lwai sanga* year, CS 851.[3] He was the twenty-fourth ruler.

3.12. The king then appointed Mün Mong of Chiang Lüa[4] in the *lwai sanga* year.[5] He ruled only / six months before dying. He was the twenty-fifth ruler.[6]

3.13. The king appointed Tao Bun Fæng in the *lwai sanga* year, CS 851.[7] He ruled for eight years and was transferred to rule Chiang Sæn in the *ka pao* year, CS 858.[8] He was the twenty-sixth ruler.

3.14. The king then appointed Mün Tin Chiang to rule in that *ka pao* year, CS 858. He ruled for ten months,[9] and was transferred to rule Chiang Sæn in the *kap yi* year, CS 859.[10] He was the twenty-seventh ruler.

---

[1]I have omitted a sentence here which simply repeats another sentence above.

[2]TCH/SF f° 8/5 has Mün Phlon succeed in the *ka mao* year (CS 845 = AD 1483/84). PTMN f° 36/3 seems to agree. I have taken 845 to be the correct year. TCH/PP, p. 18, has his son Cao Müang Nanta rule for 4 years, dying in the *müang met* year. TMN (f° 9) says he was the son of Ai Yuam, but does not name him. It also says that he "lost favor," not that he died, in the *müang met* year (=845/AD 1483).

[3]851 was a *kat lao* year: the nearest *lwai sanga* year was CS 848 (AD 1486/87). TCH (1931), p. 18, says the previous ruler's son (unnamed) ruled 4 years, and was succeeded in *müang met* 849 by Mün Mongkhon Chiang Hüa. I follow TCH in taking 849 as the correct year (AD 1487/88).

[4]Where is Chiang Lüa? Somchet Vimolkasem suggests that it might be in the Sayaboury province of Laos, to the east of Nan. TCH/PP, p. 18, has Mün Mongkhon Chiang Lüa come to rule for 6 months. TMN (f° 9) says Mün Mongkhon of Chiang Lœt, who ruled for just 6 months and lost favor, not that he died.

[5]TPMCM, p. 68: in the *lwai sanga* year 848, the South attacked Müang Kip and Müang Hin, which were dependent on (*luk phannâ* of) Nan, killing their rulers. (M. Hin is in the extreme south of Nan province, in Na Nòi district. McCMap.) King Tilok started for Nan, but had only reached the mountains south of Lamphun when word arrived that the enemy had withdrawn, and Tilok returned to Chiang Mai.

[6]TCH/SF f° 8/5: Mün Mongkhon came to rule in the *müang met* year (CS 849 = AD 1487/88). TCH (1931), p. 18, and PTMN f° 36/3-4 are fuller: Cao Mün Mongkhon of Chiang Lüa/Hüa came in that year to rule for 6 months before dying. The correct year is 849.

[7]TCH/SF f° 8/5 has Tao Pun Pæng; TMN (f° 9) and PTMN (f° 36/4) have "the ruler of Lampang" (*cao müang Nakhòn)* Tao Bun Fæng, while f° 137/2 has Cao Mün Nakòn Tao Bun Fæng in the *dap mao* year. 851 was a *kat lao* year: the nearest *lwai sanga* year was 848 (AD 1486/87). TMN says he came in the *müang met* year and left after 7 years in the *kap yi* year. The chronology of Bun Fæng is very messy, partly because he came to rule in Nan several times, and because it seems that PTMN and TCH have confused several of his periods of rule. Let us assume 849 (AD 1487/88) for the beginning of his rule.

[8]TCH (1931), p. 18, says the Governor of Lampang (not the king in Chiang Mai) appointed Tao Bun to rule in that same *müang met* year: he ruled for 7 months, and went to Chiang Sæn. PTMN f° 36/4 says 7 years; TCH/SF f° 9/1 says 8 years; PTMN f° 137/2 says 15 years, dying in the *muang mao* year. 858 was a *lwai si* year: the nearest *ka pao* year was CS 855 (AD 1493/94). TCH/SF f°9/1 says a *dap mao* year (CS 857); PTMN f° 36/4 says a *kap yi* year (CS 856). I conclude that Bun Fæng's first rule lasted from 849 to 856—8 years current.

[9]PTMN f° 36/4 agrees on 10 months. TCH/SF f° 9/1 says he was the ruler of Müang Ngua, and ruled for 7 months and 20 days.

[10]859 was a *müang sai* year: the nearest *kap yi* year was CS 856 (AD 1494/95). TCH/SF f° 9/1 and PTMN f° 37/1 say *dap mao* (CS 857). TMN (f° 9) and TCH (1931), p. 18, say Mün Tin Chiang came in *kap yi* 856, ruled for 10 months, and went to Chiang Sæn.

3.15. The king then had the ruler of Lakòn [Lampang], Tao Bun Fæng, son of the Chiang Sæn [ruler], come to rule in the *kap yi* year, CS 859. He ruled for twelve years, and died in the *dap pao* year, CS 869.[1] He was the twenty-eighth ruler. /107/

3.16. The king then appointed Mün Sam Lan to rule in that *dap pao* year, CS 869. He ruled for three years, and then went to rule Fang in the *müang mao* year, CS 871.[2] He was the twenty-ninth ruler.

3.17. The king then appointed Sòi, the ruler of Phræ,[3] to rule in the *pœk si* year, 872.[4] He ruled for three years, and went to rule Lakòn [Lampang] in the *kot sanga* year, CS 875.[5] He was the thirtieth ruler.

3.18. The king then appointed Mün Tao Bun Khwang[6] to rule in the *kot sanga* year, CS / 875. He ruled for three years, and went to rule Thœng in the *tao san* year, 877.[7] He was the thirty-first ruler.

---

[1]869 was a *müang mao* year: the nearest *dap pao* year was CS 867 (AD 1505/06). TCH/SF f° 9 and PTMN f° 37/1 agree that he ruled for 12 years and died in a *müang mao* year (CS 869 = AD 1507/08). TCH/PP, p. 18, has Mün Tin Chiang come in the *yi* [sic] year to rule for 10 months, after which he went to Chiang Sæn; *then* Tao Bun Fæng came to rule in the *dap mao* year for 12 years, dying in the *müang mao* year. TCH (1931), p. 18 just says that Cao Müang Tao Bun Fæng came "again" in *dap mao* 857, ruled 12 years, and died in the *mao* year. Yet another variant comes from the TMN (f° 9), which says that Bun Fæng came again in the *dap mao* year, ruled for 16 years, and died in the *müang mao* year. I conclude that Bun Fæng's second rule lasted from 857 to 869.

[2]869 was the nearest *müang mao* year; 871 was a *kat sai* year. TCH/SF f° 9/1 says that Dam Pa Cin ruled 3 years from the *müang mao* year to the *kat sai* year (CS 869-871). (Aroonrut Wichienkhieo tells me that Dam Pa is an old Northern title.) TMN (f° 9), TCH/PP, p. 18, and PTMN f° 37/1 and f° 132/2-3 say that Mün Sam Lan ruled for 3 years from *müang mao* to *kot sanga* (CS 869-872). TCH (1931), p. 18, says Cao Mün Sam Lan ruled 3 years, and went to Fang in *kot sanga* 872. I conclude that this governorship lasted from 869 to 872 (AD 1507/08-1510/11).

[3]Is this possibly a repetition of §3.1?

[4]870 was the nearest *pœk si* year; 872 was *kot sanga*, which is the correct year (AD 1510/11).

[5]872 was the nearest *kot sanga* year; 875 was a *ka rao* year. TCH/SF f° 9/2 has Cao Müang Phræ Sòi for 4 years from the *kat sai* year to the *tao san* year. TMN (f° 9), TCH/PP, p. 18, and PTMN ff° 37/1-2 and 137/3 have the ruler of Phræ, Sòi, for 3 years, from *kot sanga* to *ka rao*. TCH (1931), p. 18, has Cao Müang Sòi, who ruled for 3 years and went to Lampang in *ka sao* [sic] 875. I conclude 872-875 (AD 1510/11-1513/14), which is 4 years (current). TPMCM, p. 69, reports an Ayudhya invasion of Phræ in 872 *kot sanga*.

[6]The printed edition writes "Fang;" but the MS. unmistakeably has "Khwang." TCH (1931), p. 18, has Cao Bun Khwang, son of Tao Bun Fæng, come to rule for 3 years, transferred to Müang Sœng (sic) in *dap kai* 877. TCH/PP, p. 18, seems to say that Tao Bun Fæng himself came to rule for 3 years, and went to Thœng in the *dap kai* year. TMN (f° 9) curiously refers to Cao Phræ Kham Yòt Fa coming in the *ka cai* year, without further details or comment. It then brings in Cao Mün Tao Bun Khang in the *ka lao* year for 2 years, after which he was transferred to Khrœng (Sœng/Thœng) in the *dap kai* year.

[7]874 was the nearest *tao san* year; 877 was a *dap kai* year. TChC f° 9/2-3 says that Mün Khwa ... Phò Thai Bun Khwang, the son of the ruler of Kæn Tao named Kham Khan, came in the *tao san* year and ruled for 4 years and 4 months, leaving in the *dap kai* year. PTMN f° 37/2 has Cao Mün Khwa Tao Bun Khwang coming in the *ka rao* year for 2 years, going to Müang Chrœng (Thœng) in the *dap kai* year. PTMN f° 137/3-4 has Cao Mün Khwa Tao Bun Fæng, for 3 years. I conclude 875-877 (AD 1513/14-1515/16), which is 3 years (current).

3.19. The king then appointed the ruler of Fang to rule in that *tao san* year. He ruled for / ten months, and then went to rule Phayao in the *ka rao* year, 878.[1] He was the thirty-second ruler.[2]

3.20. The king then appointed the ruler of Phræ, Kham Yòt Fa, to rule in the *ka lao* year, CS 878. He ruled / for three months and went to rule Phayao in that *ka lao* year.[3] He was the thirty-third ruler.

3.21. The king of Chiang Mai then appointed Cao Paña Nò Chiang Sæn to rule in the *kap set* year 879.[4] He ruled for three years, and went to rule Phayao in the *lwai cai* year /108/ 881.[5] He was the thirty-fourth ruler.

3.22. The king appointed Paña Kham Yòt Fa to rule for a second time in the *lwai cai* year, CS 881.[6] He had ruled for four years when, in the *kat mao* year, CS 884,[7] he, with the monks headed by the *kuba*[8] of Wat Cæ Hæng and the lead-

---

[1] 875 was the nearest *ka rao* year; 878 was a *lwai cai* year. TCH (1931), p. 18, and TMN (f° 9) have Cao Müang Fang rule for 10 months and go to Phayao in *lwai cai* 878. TCH/SF f° 9/3 has Cao Mahinda coming in the *dap sai* year for 10 months. Under the date *kat mao* 881, the TPMCM, p. 70, mentions a Cao Müang Mahinda, ruler of Chiang Sæn, who died on a military expedition in the Shan states. Another Mün Mahinda went to govern Chiang Sæn in CS 900 (p. 72). PTMN ff° 37/2-3 and 137/4 have him coming to Nan in the *dap kai* year for 10 months, leaving for Phayao in the *lwai cai* year. The latter passage specifies a year, 878. CS 878 was indeed a *lwai cai* year (AD 1516/17). I conclude 877-878 (AD 1514/15-1515/16).

[2] TCH/PP, p. 18, states that the ruler of Fang came to rule for 10 months, and went to rule Phayao in the *lwai cai* year 878. TCH/SF f° 3/4 adds: "From the *ka mao* year when the cetiya was built to the *tao sanga* year, 40 years, there were 7 rulers—Mün Mongkhon, Tao Bun Fæng, Cao Müang Ngua, Dam Pa Cin, Cao Müang Sòi, Tao Bun Khwang, and Mahinda, altogether 7, none of whom renovated the [Cæ Hæng] cetiya."

[3] The nearest *ka rao* year was CS 875 (AD 1513/14). TCH/PP, p. 18, and TCH (1931), p. 18, have Müang Phræ Kham Yòt Fa come to rule 3 months and go to Phayao in *müang pao* 879. TCH/SF f° 9/4-5 says that Kham Yòt Fa succeeded Cao Mahinda in the *lwai cai* year and ruled for 8 months and 50 (?) days. PTMN ff° 37/3 and 137/4 has Cao Müang Phræ Kham Yòt Fa coming in the *lwai cai* year for 3 months, leaving for Phayao in the *müang pao* year. And TMN (f° 10) says Cao Phræ Kham Yòt Fa came in the *ka lao* year for 2 years and was transferred to Müang Khring (Thœng?) in the *dap kai* year. I conclude 878-879, probably in the first half of AD 1517.

[4] The nearest *kap set* year was 876: 879 was a *müang pao* year. TMN (f° 10) inserts another ruler here: the ruler of Fang came in the *lwai cai* year for 3 months and was transferred to Phayao. Or is this a reference to the ruler in the previous paragraph? TMN then specifies a date for the arrival of Nò Chiang Sæn, the 7th waning of the fourth month in the *müang pao* year, for a rule of 4 years.

[5] 878 was the nearest *lwai cai* year; 881 was a *kat mao* year. TCH (1931), p. 18, says Cao Paña Nò Chiang Sæn came to rule 3 years and went to Phayao in *kat mao* 881. TCH/SF f° 9/5 says that first Paña Chiang Khong came in the *müang pao* year, and then Cao Müang Kham Yòt Fa came again in the *kat mao* year. PTMN ff° 37/3-4 and 138/1 are nearly identical: Paña Nò Kham Chiang Sæn came on the 7th waning of the 9th month for 4 years, or 5 years, and left for Phayao in the *kat mao* year. TCH/PP, p. 18, has a defective date here: he came to rule in the 9th month on the [blank] day of the waning moon, ruled 4 years, and went to Phayao in the *kat mao* year. Probable date: Wednesday 27 May 1517.

[6] 878 was the nearest *lwai cai* year: 881 was a *kat mao* year, which is the correct year (AD 1519/20). TCH (1931), p. 18, says the ruler of Phayao, Kham Yòt Fa, came in *tao sanga* 884. TCH/SF f° 9/5 has Kham Yòt Fa come again in the *kat mao* year. TCH/PP, p. 18, and PTMN ff° 37/4 and 138/1 say that the ruler of Phayao, Kham Yòt Fa, came in the 2nd month (November 1519) of the *kat mao* year.

[7] 881 was the nearest *kat mao* year; 884 was a *tao sanga* year. TCH/PP, pp. 18-19, and PTMN f° 138/1-3 most clearly approximate this passage, stating that after Kham Yòt Fa had ruled for 4 years, in the *tao sanga* year (CS 884 = AD 1522/23) a group of ecclesiastical dignitaries joined the

ing officials, cast a [Buddha] image, Pa Cao Lan Tòng, and built walls around the cetiya of Wat Cæ Hæng. He ruled for twenty-three years, and was called Paña Müang Nan.[1] In the *pœk set* year,[2] the king / recalled him to Chiang Mai. He was the thirty-fifth ruler.

3.23. The king of Chiang Mai then had Cao Sæn Songkham come to rule in that *kot set* year, on the sixth day of the waxing moon of the twelfth month, CS 888.[3] He ruled for one month and eleven days, and was sent to rule Müang Lakòn [Lampang] as before. He was the thirty-sixth ruler.

3.24. The king of Chiang Mai then raised Cao Paña Kham Yòt Fa to the title of Cao Paña Sæn Songkham and had him come to rule Nan for the third time in the *pœk set* year, 888.[4] After ruling for one year, he went on a campaign

---

ruler in casting the Lan Thòng image and renovating the cetiya. The dignitaries are named: the abbot of Wat Cæ Hæng, named Dhammasena, the *thera pa* Surasila, the Sangharaja Surasila Si Bun Hüang, and the Mün Sai Dhammapaya. There is a similar, but less clear, passage in TCH/SF ff° 9/5-10/2. TCH (1931), p. 18, has a clearer list of these dignitaries: the abbot of Cæ Hæng named Dhammasena, the *thera pa* Surasila, the Mahasangharaja Surasira S(r)i Bun Hüang, and the Sangharaja Sipañña. 884 was the correct year.

[8]*khruba*, a learned Buddhist monk.

[1]PTMN ff° 37/4 and 138/3: after he had ruled 20 years, he was given the title Paña Nan in the *pœk set* year (CS 900 = AD 1538). TCH/PP, p. 19 and TCH (1931), p. 19: Kham Yòt Fa ruled 20 years, and in *pœk set* 900 was ordered recalled to Chiang Mai as Cao Sænsongkham. TMN (f° 10) gives him a rule of 40 years (perhaps including all the various intervals?) and confirms that he was called Paña Müang Nan, from the *pœk set* year.

[2]TCH/SF f° 10/2-3 states that Kham Yòt Fa went to become Sæn Mongkhan (sic) to Paña Ket in Chiang Mai in the *kat kai* year CS 888. PTMN (f° 138/3-4) is clearer: Yòt Fa went to Lampang as Cao Sæn Songkham Cao Paña Nakhon in the *pœk set* year. The nearest *pœk set* year is CS 900. This date causes problems, however: see below. Note that the next ... *set* year, in the next paragraph, is *kot set* in 888. I have had to settle on 900 (AD 1538/39) as the end of his period of rule, however.

[3]888 was a *lwai set* year. *Kot set* years fell in 852 and 912. TCH/SF f° 10/3 has Tao Chiang Khòng come to rule in the *kat kai* year for 3 years. PTMN f° 38/1 states that Cao Sæn Songkham of Lampang came on the 2nd day of the 12th month in the *pœk set* year (Monday 26 August 1538) and ruled for 1 month, 11 days before going back to Lampang. F° 138/3-4 , and TCH/PP, p. 19, say the 2nd day of the 6th month (Wednesday 19 February 1539) for 11 days. TMN (f° 10) says he came on the 6th of the 12th month in the *pœk set* year and ruled for 1 month and 11 days before returning to Lampang. TCH (1931), p. 19, says the ruler of Lampang came to rule on the 2nd of the 6th month for 11 (units not specified) and then returned to Lampang as before.

[4]900 was the nearest *pœk set* year; 888 was a *lwai set* year. The date has to be CS 900 (AD 1539/39), presumably in the early months of 1539. TCH/PP, p. 19, and TCH (1931), p. 19, say Cao Kham Yòt Fa returned to rule, "this his third time," in *kat kai* 901 for just a month, before going to Chiang Mai, where he died on the 11th day of the 6th month. TCH/SF f°10/3-11/1 goes into some detail for this confusing period: Paña Ket, the ruler of Chiang Mai, went to Müang Pæng and Tao Chiang became ruler of Chiang Mai. Tao Chiang Khòng went to rule Lampang, and Kham Yòt Fa came to rule Nan in the *kat kai* year. After 5 months, he went to Chiang Ten, and died. Tao Chiang then ruled instead. Chiang Mai then had Cao Müang 3 [Sam] Kæo rule instead, in the *kat kai* year. After 3 years, Paña Ket returned to rule Chiang Mai, and had Cao Müang 3 Kæo go to Chiang Sæn and Cao Müang Sano come to rule Nan. He ruled for 10 months, and then went to rule Müang Lò; whereupon Cao Müang Sang Yi Mongkhon come to rule Nan from the *kap si* year to the *dap sai* year.

PTMN f°38/1-2 states that Cao Sæn Kham Yòt Fa came to rule for the 3rd time in the *pœk set* year in the *kat kai* year [sic]. One month after he arrived, the ruler of Chiang Mai died, on the 8th day of the 6th month in the *kat kai* year. On the 11th day of the 6th month (Tuesday 17 February 1540), Cao Müang Nakhòn 3 [Sam] came to rule Nan. TMN (f° 10) is similar: Yòt Fa came for the

and returned. A month later he went on a military campaign to Chiang Mai and fought there. He died in Chiang Mai from an abscess in the *kat kai* year, 889.[1] He was the thirty-seventh ruler.

3.25. The king of Chiang Mai then appointed Cao Paña Palatep Lü Cai to rule Nan, /109/ in the *kat kai* year, CS 889, on the 11th day of the waxing moon of the sixth month.[2] After he had ruled for ten years, in the *pœk san* year, CS 898,[3] he built Wat Luang in the center of Nan.[4] He had ruled for thirty-two years when, in the *pœk sanga* year CS 920, the king of Hongsa (i.e., Pegu) / captured Chiang Mai.[5] Paña Palathep Lü Cai escaped to Müang Lan Cang [Luang Prabang]. He was the thirty-eighth ruler.[6]

3rd time in the *pœk set* year, and went to Chiang Mai when the king died on the 1st of the 6th month.

Yet a third version appears at f° 138/4-5 of the same text: Cao Sæn Songkham came to rule for a third time in the *kat kai* year, attacked Chiang Mai, and died on the 11th day of the 6th month in the *kat kai* year.

[1]There is a dated Nan inscription from CS 889, a *müang kai* year. MNPBS, pp. 258-59. CS 901 was the nearest *kat kai* year; 889 was a *muang kai* year. I have taken 901 (AD 1539/40) to be correct.

[2]TCH (1931), p. 19, says that on the 11th waxing of the 6th month, the ruler of Lampang came to rule Nan. The date has to be Tuesday 17 February 1540. The next sentence names him, Paña Teplücai. TCH/SF f° 11/1-4 says that in 894, on the full moon of the month of Visakha, Sæn Kao, the client of Paña Ket, ruler of Chiang Mai, died. The people and queen invited the ruler of Lan Cang (Luang Prabang) named Phothisalat to rule Chiang Mai. The ruler of Nan, named Yi Mongkhon, paid homage to the ruler of Lan Cang at Chiang Sæn. The ruler of Lan Cang gave the insignia of rule to Palatep Lü Cai to rule Nan in the *lwai sanga* year. After he had ruled for one year, the prince of Pegu (Cao Fa Hongsa) named Mangtharatu *(min-taya Tu)* took Chiang Mai. Palatep fled from Nan to Lan Chang on Saturday, the 14th day of the 6th month, a Thai *luang lao* day (Thursday 26 January 1559).

PTMN again has two versions. In the first (f° 38/3), on the 11th day of the 6th month in the *kat kai* year, Cao Müang Nakhòn 3 came to rule Nan; and here the listing of rulers abruptly ends. In the second (f° 139/1), the ruler of Lampang came as Paña Palatep Lü Cai, and had ruled for ten years when, in 910, a *pœk san* year, he built Wat Luang in the center of the city of Nan (Wat Luang Kang Wiang Nan). After he had ruled (another?) twenty years, the Burmese took Chiang Mai in the *pœk sanga* year. Lü Cai fled to Lan Cang in the same year, on Saturday the 12th day of the 6th month, a *muang lao* day.

TPMCM, p. 74, mentions that the governor of Nan, Yi Mangkhala, defeated Ayudhya forces during their siege of Chiang Mai in CS 907.

TMN (f° 10) simply states that the ruler of Lampang returned in the 6th month of the *kat kai* year, and then states that the story of the history of Nan ends here, which suggests something about its early date of composition.

[3]This has to be in *pœk san* 910, AD 1548/49, following PTMN f° 139/1.

[4]TCH/PP, p. 19, says he built this temple in the *pœk san* year, 910 (AD 1548/49). It possibly can be identified as Wat Cang Kham, directly opposite the National Museum in the center of Nan.

[5]TPMCM, p. 78, gives the exact date: Saturday 15th waxing of 7th month, a *tao set* day. Saturday, 14th waxing, 2 April 1558, was a *tao set* day.

[6]TCH (1931), p. 19, says that Lü Cai had ruled 10 years when he built Wat Luang, and after another twenty years the king of Pegu invaded, in *pœk sanga* 920, when Lü Cai fled to Laos on Saturday, 12th waxing of the 7th month, a Thai *müang lao* day. There was no Saturday *müang lao* day that year: the closest was Friday, 10th waning of the 6th month (Northern, 4th month Southern), 3 March 1559. This source and PTMN f° 139/2-3 agree that there were 30 rulers from Kan Müang to Lü Cai.

3.26. After the king of Pegu captured Chiang Mai, he appointed Paña Nò Kham Sathian Cai Songkham as ruler / of Nan.[1]

3.27. The king of Pegu stayed in Chiang Mai for a month and twelve days, and then returned to Pegu.

---

[1]TCH/PP, p. 19: he came to rule in the *kot san* year 922 (AD 1560).

CHAPTER FOUR

NAN UNDER BURMESE RULE, AD 1560-1727

4.1. In the *kot san* year, CS 922, Cao Paña / Nò Kham Sathian Cai Songkham became governor of Nan [then under Burmese rule].[1]

4.2. The large cetiya [of Wat Cæ Hæng] that Tao Ai Yuam had built [in 847], seventeen fathoms high and ten fathoms wide, was by this time in a bad state of disrepair, / especially the northern platform.[2] On becoming ruler, Paña Nò Kham Sathian Cai Songkham decided to restore it. He appointed Mahâsâmi Kalyâno[3] of Wat Si Bun Hüang supervisor of the work of restoration and repair.[4] Working together, all the people of the domain restored the northern platform and, on the approaches to the cetiya, built walls 1300 fathoms long and six fathoms apart.[5] They also built a sala for monks, the small *vihara*, and the ubosot hall.[6]

---

[1]922 was a *kot san* year; AD 1560/61. TCH (1931), p. 19, and PTMN f° 139/3 say the Pegu king appointed Cao Paña Nò Kham Sathian Cai Songkham as ruler of Nan in the *kot san* year 922. TCH/SF f° 11/4-12/1 reads very differently. It seems to say—and the text is difficult—that, after Lü Cai had fled, five days later the Burmese entered the city, on a Wednesday, a *luang pao* day (28 August 1560). On Sunday, the 5th day of the waxing moon, a *tao sanga* day (cannot be converted), Sæn Luang Ping Cai came to rule Nan. Then, in the month of Citra (15 March-12 April 1561), the king of Pegu had *mün* Phi ....(?) The king of Pegu, Mangthara, had a *paña* named Sin Paña and Paña Sæn Hua Khian named Cai Kham. (?) The ruler of Lampang named Nò Kham Sathian Cheyyaraja Songkham to come to rule Nan. *Mangthara* is obviously a Northern Thai rendering of the Burmese *min-taya[-gyi]*, "king."

[2]The present cetiya is much larger, but it has been renovated—and even completely rebuilt—so many times that present-day dimensions are irrelevant. TCH/SF f° 12/1-3 says the new ruler brought a royal order commanding the building of a sala and renovations at Wat Utthayan Noi, and enlisting elders in Nan and a number of named individuals—Pan Nangsü Panño, Pan Nangsü Nòi, Phra Maha Sangharaja Dhammabodhi ... Maha Swami Bhu Müang ... Thera Cao Uddhayana named Sanghasena, and the Phra Maha Sangharaja Wat Sri Bun Hüang named Kalyanabuddhamkura. The new ruler apparently solemnly promised not to oppress the people (cf. f° 13/2-4) in the *kot san* year 921, 10th waning of the month of Visakha, a Thai *kat met* day, at noon. TCH (1931), p. 19, says these renovations did not occur until the ruler had ruled for 14 years, and took from the *ka lao* year until the *lwai cai* year, 937. Date cannot be converted.

[3]TCH (1931), p. 19, has Cao Sami Kalyâno Si Bun Hüang. The title *sami* used with the names of monks was conferred by the king of Sri Lanka on foreign monks receiving ordination there. Cf. Cœdès, "Documents," p. 95, n. 5.

[4]Ban Si Bun Hüang is pretty much due west of Cæ Hæng, on the banks of the Nan River directly opposite the old city walls, and symbolically between Cæ Hæng and the old palace.

[5]The modern pathway leading up to the reliquary, which was rebuilt much later, is 50 fathoms long and 20 fathoms wide.

[6]PTMN f° 139/3-140/2 states that it was 14 years from the *kot san* year to the *ka lao* year, when Tao Ai Yuam built the cetiya; and 92 years from the *tao yi* year to the *ka lao* year, when the

4.3. On the second day of the waning moon of the sixth month in the *pœk yi* year, 942,[1] the king of Chiang Mai, the Tharrawaddy Prince, stopped at / Cæ Hæng on his way to Lan Cang. When he heard the full story of the Cæ Hæng Reliquary, he became piously enthusiastic. He commanded Paña Nò Kham Sathian Cai Songkham, the governor, to do more restoration so as to make it more beautiful and appropriate to the reliquary's illustrious history.[2] /

4.4. The governor delegated the work of restoration and building to the monks of Wat Si Bun Hüang. The members of the congregation of the temple were required to furnish 66 timbers and seventeen workmen. The people of Cæ Hæng village furnished nine workmen.[3] In the *tao sanga* year[4] they dug a well, and built a bathing shed, a latrine, and a *kuti* for the Somdet Sangharâja Cao of Müang Pò,[5] who had come [to reside] there in charge of all the carpenters and

---

cetiya was destroyed. Kham Sathian built it anew as before in the 3 years from the *ka lao* year to the *lwai cai* year (CS 938). The building of the sala, *vihara*, and ubosot hall is put in the *pœk yi* year (= CS 940, AD 1538/39). TCH (1931), pp. 19-20 agrees with the dates and details given in PTMN, but gives numerals to the years: 14 years, from *ka lao* 935 to *lwai cai* 947.

TCH/SF ff°13/4-19/1 has a very different run of events, all pointing to the year, 942 (AD 1580/81) when the history of the reliquary was related to the Burmese ruler (see below). Briefly, after [Kham Sathian] had ruled for 4 years, in the *ka kai* year (CS 925) Paña Mæku Cao [of Chiang Mai] "had Paña Lò come to rule the Left and Right, named Paña Sò Müang. In the *tao san* year 933, 9th waning of the month of Assayujja, a Tuesday, a Thai *müang pao* day, at the 8th lunar mansion, he got a white elephant." (Date does not convert.) He then built a vihara, covered the Dibbacetiya, built the *vihara* of Wat Chang Klòng ..., built the Mahabodhi Nòi vihara, built the Brahma *vihara*, built kuti at Wat Hò Pa Kæo and Wat Paña Wat and Wat Phu Müang Uddhayana Noi, and the cetiya of Wat Khua Müang. In the *ka lao* year [935 = AD 1573/74] the Cæ Hæng cetiya collapsed on its northern side, and the ruler had Mahaswami Cao Sri Bun Hüang fix it, together with Mahaswami Cao Kalyano. In the *lwai cai* year [938 = AD 1576/77] the ruler had Maha Sangharaja Cao Sri Bun Hüang organize laymen, presumably for renovations at Wat Cæ Hæng, for which purpose a ceremony was conducted on the 1st waning of the 7th month (f° 16/2). From the *müang pao* year [939 = AD 1577/78], various donations of money and slaves were made to Wat Cæ Hæng. Then, in the *pœk yi* year [940 = AD 1578/79] there were more donations and building there, including donations of land.

Is it really walls that were built? Or a balustrade leading up to the cetiya?

[1]940 was the nearest *pœk yi* year; 942 was a *kot si* year. Sunday 19 February 1581. PTMN f° 140/2-3 has the date as 142 [sic], a *kot si* year, on the 2nd waning of the 3rd month. This has to be 942 (= AD 1580/81), which was a *kot si* year. This text has the Burmese prince invite the Maha Sangharaja Cao Sri Bun Hüang to come to Wat Cæ Hæng and tell him the story. Might this be the occasion when the story was written down and disseminated? The text goes on to say that the work was completed in the *ruang sai* year (= 943 = AD 1581/82). TCH (1931), p. 19, says that in *kot si* 942, on the 2nd waning of the 6th month (Sunday 19 February 1581), the Tharrawaddy Prince, ruler of Chiang Mai, en route to Lan Cang, made the Mahasangharaja Sri Bun Hüang go to dwell at the Cæ Hæng *vihara*. On his way back from Laos he ordered the restorations listed here.

[2]I find it curious and interesting that there are at least two implicit references in the chronicle to the importance of the book of the history of the great reliquary.

[3]TCH (1931), p. 20, dates this work in *luang sai* 943. TCH/PP, p. 20, is even more specific: the 2nd waning of the 6th month: Saturday 10 March 1582.

[4]CS 944 = AD 1582/83. PTMN f° 141/1 concurs. TCH (1931), p. 20, *tao sanga* 944. From this point, our text is very close to the PTMN.

[5]PTMN f° 141/2 has Cao Wat Luang Müang Bò. TCH/PP, p. 20, has Somdet Sangharaja Wat Luang Müang Phò. TCH (1931), p. 20, says Cao Wat Luang Müang Pua. There is much confusion about this toponym, but here it has to be associated with Pua.

craftsmen. Nantapu It was the chief carpenter.[1] / In the *ka met* year,[2] the villagers of Ban Bun Hüang and Ban Cæ Hæng brought in 86 timbers. On the twelfth day of the waning moon of the sixth month in the *kap san* year,[3] the main *vihara* was whitewashed. On the *kat pao* day, a Wednesday, the fourth day of the waning moon of the sixth month in the *dap lao* year 949,[4] at three *bat* past noon, they inaugurated the main *vihara*, /111/ and in the *pœk cai*[5] year it was completed. On the fifth day of the waxing moon of the eighth month in the *kat pao* year, CS 953, in the *kòng leng* watch, Paña Nò Kham Sathian Cai Songkham died.[6] He ruled for thirty years, and was the thirty-ninth ruler. The king then appointed the ruler's son[7] to succeed him.

4.5. Paña Nò Kham Sathian had four sons: Cao Cetabut Pommin,[8] Cao Nam Bò, Cao Si Sòng Müang, and Cao / Un Müang. When Cao Si Sòng Müang was born, Paña Nò Kham Sathian had the boy's horoscope read by an astrologer. The astrologer prophesied that the boy would grow up to be a great man and would / surpass his own father. Upon hearing what the astrologer said, Paña Nò Kham decided to do away with the child. [The boy's elder brother,] Cao Nam Bò, intervened, said he had no child of his own, and said that if his father would spare the life of the boy, he would adopt him. The father relented, and gave Cao Si Sòng Müang to Cao Nam Bò to raise as his own.[9]

---

[1] TCH/PP, p. 20, writes his name as Antaphu It. PTMN f° 141/2 states that there were 8 *dam khwan*—carpenters, according to Aroonrut Wichienkeeo—and Nantapu It headed the carpenters. TCH (1931), p. 20, in *tao sanga* 944: he built a well and a bathing shed; and there were eight chief carpenters, headed by Nanthaphu It.

[2] CS 945 = AD 1583/84. PTMN f° 141/2 concurs. TCH (1931), p. 20, in *ka met* 945, the Bun Hüang and Cæ Hæng people brought 86 timbers for building; and more in *kap san* 946.

[3] CS 946 = AD 1584/85. Wednesday 28 March 1585. TCH/PP, p. 20, and PTMN f° 141/3 concur. All AD dates after October 1582 are expressed in the Gregorian calendar.

[4] CS 947 was the nearest *dap lao* year; 949 was a *müang kai* year. TCH/PP, p. 20, has the same day and hour, but CS 947, not 949. TCH/SF f° 19/3 ends here with a bad date: 945, a *dap lao* year. The rest of the date is as given here. Tuesday 11 February 1586. It adds that the main *vihara* was 7 fathoms 3 elbows wide, and 20 fathoms long. This is much the size of the larger of the two *vihara* within the reliquary compound today. The fact that this chronicle ends here seems to suggest that it might have been written down for the Burmese Tharrawaddy Prince who had expressed so much interest in it in 942 (see above).

[5] CS 950 = AD 1588/89. PTMN f° 141/3-4 here is somewhat confused: It miswrites 957 instead of 947 for the beginning of construction, and states that it was completed in 950, which is correct. TCH (1931), p. 20, in *kap san*, 5th waning of 7th month, a Thursday, Thai *kat pao* day, at 3 *bat* past noon, inaugurated Cæ Hæng *vihara*, construction taking 5 years, from *kap san* until *pœk cai* 950, when it was completed. There was a Wednesday *kat pao* day on the 3rd waning of the 7th month (17 April 1585) and a Thursday *kat pao* day on the 5th waning of the 11th month (15 August 1585).

[6] 951 was the nearest *kat pao* year; 953 was a *luang mao* year. Wednesday 19 April 1589. TCH/PP, p. 20, and PTMN f° 141/4 have the same date, in the *kat pao* year, = AD 1591/92. TCH (1931), p. 20, in *kat pao* 951, 4th waning of the 8th month, in *kong læng* watch, Nò Kham Sathian Cai Songkham died, after a reign of 30 years.

[7] PTMN f° 141/4 names the son, Cao Cettabut (Jesthaputra).

[8] var. Phummin, Phumin.

[9] The same story is given in the 18th-century(?) PNMN, p. 8 (ff° 13-14). Dates given are at some variance with those given here: Si Sòng Müang is said to have become ruler of Nan in 1621? (Text very unclear.)

4.6. When Paña Nò Kham Sathian Cai Songkham died, Cao Cetabut, his eldest son, succeeded him[1] in the *kat pao* year, CS 953.[2] Cao Cetabut had ruled for six years when, in the *kap sanga* year, CS 958, /112/ on the third day of the waning moon of the eighth month,[3] he went to live in Müang Pò.[4] He built Wat Dòn Tæn, and then consecrated Sâmi Cao Khwam Khwæn as Sangharâja. Around that time, the officials in Müang Pò had a large quantity of gems gathered from the Sa River, and presented them [to the ruler, who] ordered them used in the making of an ornamental girdle four fathoms long and five *plong* wide, decorated with the shapes of white lotuses, and another girdle three *sòk* long and three *plong* wide,[5] each of which required more than a thousand stones. At the full moon of the ninth month[6] he installed the abbot of Cæ Hæng as the Sangharâja; and the next day the girdles were affixed to the great cetiya which Tao Ai Yuam had constructed.

4.7. In the *dap met* year, CS 959, on the ninth day of the waning moon of the second month,[7] Cao / Cetabut Phumin,[8] ruler of Nan, fought the Tharrawaddy Prince [the Burmese viceroy of Chiang Mai] at the mouth of the Ngao River.[9] Cao Cetabut's army was defeated, and he fled to Lan Cang. The Tharrawaddy Prince then appointed all the officials, led by Paña Khæk,[10] to take care of Nan.

---

[1]PNMN, p. 8 (ff° 13-14) consistently refers to this ruler as Paña Phumin. It notes that, during his reign, a red elephant was found which the ruler presented to Mahathammacao, i.e. the king of Burma, in return for which the towns of Chiang Ròn and Chiang Lom were bestowed upon Nan, only to be taken back from Nan in 1622 after the end of his rule.

[2]951 is the nearest *kat pao* year; 953 was a *luang mao* year. CS 951 = AD 1589/90. TCH (1931), p. 21, Cao Cettabut, son [of Nò Kham Sathian Cai Songkham] ruled in his father's stead. In *kap sanga* 956, on the 3rd waning of the 3rd month (Wednesday 30 November 1594), he went to live in Müang Phò—i.e., Wiang Sa—and built Wat Dòn Tæn. He consecrated Sami Kham Khwæn as Sangharaja.

[3]956 was the nearest *kap sanga* year; 958 was a *lwai san* year. Date confirmed in TCH/PP, p. 21; but here given for building Wat Dòn Tæn. Saturday 7 May 1594.

[4]This might be read as meaning he went to live in his father's *müang (müang phò)*; but here it has to be Wiang Sa, the main district town in what is now the southern part of the province of Nan, because of the additional information provided three lines below. Cf. PTMN f° 141/4-142/1. Note other references to Müang Pò, Wiang Pò, and Ban Pò.

[5]*sòk*, "elbow," is approximately 18 inches; and *plong* is the distance between two joints of a bamboo, not further specified.

[6] Friday 3 June 1594. TCH (1931), p. 21, concurs on both dates.

[7]The nearest *dap met* year was 957; 959 was a *müang lao* year. Saturday 25 November 1595. TCH/PP, p. 21, has the same date. PTMN f° 142/3 concurs with the *dap met* year, which would be 957 (AD 1595/96), and adds that this was a Friday, in the *kòng læng* watch. TCH (1931), p. 21, however, says this battle took place on the 4th waning of the second month. The Chiang Mai Chronicle (*sub anno* CS 957) suggests why the attack occurred: "In 957, a *dap met* year, the king of Lan Chang came to [try to] make the governor of Nan the king of Lan Na, but unsuccessfully; and he returned to Lan Chang."

[8]Earlier (§4.5), Cao Pommin.

[9]The Ngao empties into the Nan River 12 miles (19 km.) due north of Nan, and flows from the northwest.

[10]TCH/PP, p. 21, has Paña Khæng.

4.8. Three years later, that is, in the *pœk set* year, CS 962,[1] Cao Cetabut managed to gather a force of Lao soldiers at Lan Cang. He and his Lao army /113/ went to Chiang Mai to invade the city.[2] His Lao army, however, only took his money and did not fight. Paña Khæk, acting governor of Nan, upon hearing of Cetabut's invasion of Chiang Mai, rushed his troops to Chiang Mai [to help the ruler of Chiang Mai.] [Meanwhile, when he failed to take Chiang Mai,] Cao Cetabut returned to Nan and made himself governor. In the *kat kai* year,[3] Paña Dòi Nòi took Nan people, / so on the fourth day of the waning half of the month of Asadha,[4] the Lao fled Chiang Mai.

4.9. In the *luang pao* year,[5] Paña Sæn Ma made an unsuccessful attempt to take Nan, and fled. In the *tao yi* year,[6] Cao Cetabut, ruler of Nan, again tried to take Chiang Mai, but failed in the attempt and fled back [to Nan].

4.10. In the *ka mao* year, CS 965,[7] the / king of Chiang Mai, the Tharrawaddy Prince, attacked Nan. Cao Cetabut and Cao Nam Bò appointed their younger brother, Cao Si Sòng Müang, to guard the Hing Nòi Gate.[8] Instead / of guarding it, he opened the gate to the forces of the Maha Dhamma, who captured Cao Cetabut Phumin and Cao Nam Bò, his foster father and elder brother. They tortured Cao Nam Bò by squeezing his chest with timbers, and he died seven days later. They / disposed of his body by throwing it down a well west of Wat Phumin, which is why he is called "Prince Water Well" (Cao Nam Bò).[9]

4.11. As for Cao Cetabut Phumin, the ruler of Nan, the group of Maha Dhamma—i.e., the Tharrawaddy Prince—captured him and took him to Chiang Mai. When he reached Chiang Mai, he was killed on the ninth day of the waning moon of the ninth month.[10] /114/ On the day he was killed, there was an earthquake.[11] Cao Cetabut Phumin had ruled Nan for seven years, then had taken refuge in Müang Lan Cang for three years, and then returned to Nan and

---

[1]960 was the nearest *pœk set* year; 962 was *kot cai*. AD 1598/99. PTMN f° 142/4 has the *pœk set* year. TCH (1931), p. 21, says *pœk set* 960.

[2]TCH (1931), p. 21, says they invested the city in the fourth month (January 1599).

[3]CS 961 = AD 1599/1600. PTMN f° 143/1 concurs. TCH (1931), p. 21, says *kat kai* 961.

[4]Sunday 11 July 1599. PTMN f° 143/1 also has just the 4th waning of Asadha; and TCH/PP, p. 21, and TCH (1931), p. 21, say 4th waning of Asalha. This is the Northern 10th month, Southern 8th month.

[5]CS 963 = AD 1601/02. TCH/PP, p. 22, and PTMN f° 143/1 agree. TCH (1931), p. 21, says the governor of Chiang Sæn tried to take Nan in *luang pao* 963. There is a laconic reference to this campaign in TPMCH, p. 80, *sub anno* 963.

[6]The nearest *tao yi* year was CS 964 = AD 1602/03. PTMN f° 143/1 agrees. TCH (1931), p. 22, says that Nan failed to take Paña Sæn in *tao yi* 964.

[7]Date is correct. AD 1603/04. PTMN f° 143/2 gives a fuller date: the *ka mao* year 965, the 9th waning of the 9th month (Tuesday 3 June 1603); while TCH (1931), p. 22, has just *ka mao* 965.

[8]The glossary to the published edition notes that this was a small gate which contained a hall for an image of the municipal guardian spirit (*sala teparak*) and opened into monks' cells. The context of the reference suggests a gate in the walls on the west or south side; probably the south.

[9]Wat Phumin is best known for its extraordinary mural paintings. See the bilingual *Wat Phumin and Wat Nong Bua* (Bangkok, 1986).

[10]See note above. Tuesday 3 June 1603. TCH/PP, p. 22, and TCH (1931), p. 22, agree on the 9th waning of the 9th month.

[11]TCH/PP, p. 22, gives a different date for the earthquake: Friday, 7th waxing of the 9th month: Friday 16 May 1603.

ruled a / second time for four years. He died in the *ka mao* year, CS 965.[1] He was the fortieth ruler.

4.12. After having captured / Cao Cetabut, the Tharrawaddy Prince appointed Cao Si Sòng Müang to rule, in the *ka mao* year, CS 965, on the sixth day of the waxing moon of the ninth month, in the *kòng ngai* watch.[2] He was given the name of Cao Paña Palasük Sai Cai Songkham. After he had ruled for eight years,[3] in the *kot set* year,[4] the cetiya that had been restored by Tao Ai Yuam was in a bad state of repair. The ruler therefore, / with his councillors and all the Sangha of Nan, headed by the Râjaguru of Wat Cæ Hæng and the Râjaguru of Wat Bun Hüang, started the restoration of the great cetiya, on the eighth day of the waning moon of the sixth month, in the *tut sai* watch.[5] They dismantled the top of the cetiya /115/ as far down as the part restored by Tao Kha Kan, of which a small part remained.

4.13. In the *luang kai* year, CS 973, on the thirteenth day of the waning moon of the second ninth month, at noon,[6] the work of construction began on the 23 fathom-high cetiya. In the *ka pao* year,[7] Lan Cang attacked.[8] On the seventh day of the waxing moon of the third month,[9] Cao / Paña Palasük Sai led out a force which defeated the Lao, killing 270 men. On the fifth day of the

[1] AD 1603/04.

[2] PTMN f° 143/2-3 gives the same date. Friday 16 May 1603. TCH (1931), p. 22, says this was Friday, 7th waxing of the tenth month. It notes that Ponsük Sai ruled in place of his elder brother.

[3] TCH (1931), p. 22: three years. TCH/PP, p. 22, says 80 years!

[4] CS 972 = AD 1610/11. PTMN f° 143/3 concurs. It adds the information that the cetiya built by Ai Yuam was 17 fathoms high. TCH (1931), p. 22, says *kot set* 972.

[5] Sunday 6 March 1611. PTMN f° 143/4 , and TCH (1931), p. 22, agree on date and hour.

[6] Saturday 6 August 1611. PTMN f° 143/4-144/1 gives the full date, including the numerals, as here. CS 973 was an *adhikamasa* year (thirteen months). But it places this in the second *tenth* month, not the second *ninth* month. TCH/PP, p. 22, says Friday, 13th waxing of the second *tenth* month. TCH (1931), p. 22, has something even stranger: Friday the 13th of the third first month (*düan 1 tatiya*).

[7] CS 975 = AD 1613/14. Cf. PTMN f° 144/1. TCH/PP, p. 22, says Sunday, 7th waxing of the 3rd month: Sunday 17 November 1613.

[8] This war, at least under this particular date, is mentioned neither in the various annals of Laos nor in the Chiang Mai Chronicle. However, Maha Sila Viravong mentions a Lao military expedition to Phayao, Thœng, Chiang Sæn, and Chiang Rai sometime between 1598 and 1603 (*Phongsavadan Lao*, 1957, pp. 148-49; English ed. [New York, 1965], pp. 72-73). Cao Khamman Vongkotrattana (*Phongsavadan sat Lao*, Vientiane, 1971, p. 52 states only that "In the *kot cai* year, CS 962 [AD 1600/01] the king raised an army and attacked and took Chiang Sæn, and the governor, Phraya Ram Decho, fled." This corroborates the evidence of the Chiang Mai Chronicle (C. Notton, *Annales du Siam, III: Chronique de Xieng Mai*, Paris, 1932, p. 172), which states that "In the *ruang pao* year, 963, Phraya Ramadecho was named to the government of Chiang Sæn. The Lao of Lan Chang took Lan Na, with the exception of Phayao, Fang, and Chiang Mai. Phraya Ramdecho fled from Chiang Sæn in that year." Notton has a long footnote that gives additional information.

[9] Tuesday 19 November 1613. PTMN f° 144/1 adds that it was in the *tut sai* watch. TCH (1931), p. 22, has Sunday, 7th of third month in the *tut sai* watch.

waning moon of the fourth month,[1] the Lao withdrew. In the *kap yi* year,[2] the prince of Ava attacked Lakòn [Lampang] and took it, though with difficulty. Many Lampang and Chiang Mai people died.[3] The prince / of Ava rounded up many Chiang Mai people to send to Pegu.

4.14. In the *dap mao* year, CS 977, in the fifth month,[4] the councillors and elders of Chiang Mai together invited Cao Si Sòng Müang Palasük / Sai Songkham, ruler of Nan, to become king of Chiang Mai.[5] He accepted their invitation and appointed his younger brother, Cao Un Müang, to rule Nan in his stead.[6] In the tenth month, Cao Un Müang / took many Nan people to Chiang Mai.[7] Inasmuch as he had further restored the Cæ Hæng Reliquary, from Saturday the second day of the waning moon of the ninth month,[8] his expenses were enormous, including the maintenance of the Sangha and /116/ construction costs. When it was completed, he installed a golden finial and gilded it from top to bottom.

4.15. Cao Si Sòng Müang ["Glory of Two Cities"], i.e., Cao Palasük Sai Cai Songkham, the ruler of Nan, after having ruled / Nan for thirteen years, became king of Chiang Mai and lord over all of Lan Na Tai.

4.16. He had been king of Chiang Mai for seventeen years when, in the *luang / met* year, CS 993,[9] Cao Fa Phawa Mangthara Suttho Thammarat [of Burma][10] successfully invaded Chiang Mai.[11] The king of Chiang Mai, Cao Si Sòng Müang, was captured and taken to Pegu. Prince Suttho / appointed Paña Tippanet of Chiang Sæn as ruler of Chiang Mai. This marks the end of the Chiang Mai kings. Cao [Si Sòng Müang] Palasük Sai Cai Songkham had ruled Nan and then became king of Chiang Mai. He was the forty-first ruler [of Nan].[12]

---

[1]Monday 16 December 1613. TCH (1931), p. 22, and TCH/PP, p. 22, say this was a Sunday, in which case the proper date is 15 December 1613.

[2]CS 976 = AD 1614/15. PTMN f° 144/1-2 says this was a Sunday; and that this was the day when the king of Ava came, not the day the Lao withdrew. TCH/PP, p. 22, and TCH (1931), p. 22, agree on *kap yi* 976.

[3]PTMN f° 144/2 adds that the ruler of Chiang Mai died. Cf. TPMCM, p. 80.

[4]PTMN f° 144/2, and TCH (1931), p. 22, agree on the date. 19 January-16 February 1616.

[5]TPMCM, p. 80, where the date given is identical.

[6]PTMN f° 144/4 says that in the *dap mao* year (CS 977), on the 5th waning of the 8th month, (Sunday 17 May 1615) at noon, Paña Sòng began rule in place of his elder brother. TCH/PP, p. 23, says his rule began on Saturday, 4th waning of the 8th month: Saturday 16 May 1615.

[7]PTMN f° 144/3 says that people of Nan were taken to Chiang Mai, on Saturday, 2nd waning of the 10th month (Sunday 26 June 1611), in the *luang kai* year, which was CS 973, a retrospective reference. Or did the compiler mistake the year for a *luang kai* day? TCH (1931), p. 22, does not give a year.

[8]Saturday 28 May.

[9]I find this date, in its context, to be very confusing, but the manuscript and the printed editions agree.

[10]This king is usually referred to as Thalun (r. 1629-48); but Phayre (*History of Burma*, 1883) refers to him as Thado Dhammâ Râjâ (p. 134), which corresponds neatly to this reference.

[11]TPMCM, p. 81.

[12]TPMCM, p. 80, seems to say that Lan Cang, i.e. Luang Prabang, unsuccessfully invaded Nan in 957 *dap met*.

4.17. Cao Un Müang, the younger brother, ruled Nan in place of his elder brother from the *dap mao* year, CS 977.[1] He had ruled for nine years when, in the *ka kai* year, CS 985, in the twelfth month, /117/ on Friday the full-moon day,[2] he rebelled against the Burmese and fled to the South Country in the waning half of the twelfth month of the *ka kai* year, abducting with him the soldiers of Pegu.[3]

4.18. Early on Tuesday, the fifth day of the waxing moon of the tenth month in the *kap cai* year, 986, the Burmese surrounded Nan to capture Cao Un Müang, / but he escaped to Phræ.[4] On Tuesday, the eighth day of the waxing moon of the twelfth month,[5] he returned with an army from Lan Cang and encamped at Wat Uttayan Nòi.[6] On Thursday, the tenth day of the waxing moon of the third month,[7] in the watch before noon, he regained the city.

4.19. At the full moon of the second month,[8] Prince Suttho again surrounded Nan. Cao Un Müang, seeing that he could not defend the city, fled to Lan Cang, and most of the inhabitants of Nan also fled. The Râjaguru / of Wat Bun Hüang also fled with all his pupils and laymen by way of Bò Wa.[9] The Burmese army took a large number of prisoners to Pegu. The people of Nan suffered greatly. Cao Un Müang, who had fled, was the forty-second ruler, and had ruled for nine years.

4.20. In the *dap pao* year, CS 987, on the Thursday, the fifth day of the waxing moon of the fourth month, at the twenty-second *lunar mansion,* called Phumabala,[10] the ruler of Müang Nakòn [Lampang], besieged Nan and entered

---

[1]AD 1516/17. TCH (1931), p. 23, says he began his rule on Saturday, 5th waning of the eighth month, at noon. Sunday 17 May 1615. TPMCM, p. 80, has a date in the same year that is not as full.

[2]Saturday 9 September 1623. PTMN f° 144/4 agrees that Paña Sòng (= Cao Un Müang) ruled in place of his elder brother from the 5th waning of the 8th month of the *dap mao* year (CS 977 = Sunday 17 May AD 1615/16), and that he had ruled for 9 years when, on the date given in the text, he rebelled against the Burmese and went south. TCH/PP, p. 23, and TCH (1931), p. 23, agree on date. TPMCM, p. 81, dates the rebellion in the *dap pao* year 987.

[3]September 1623. But see TCH (1931), p. 23: "The Southerners swept up the Pegu army." The Chiang Mai Chronicle (*sub anno* 987) says simply that "In 987, a *dap mao* year, Nan rebelled, and King Suttho went and took Nan."

[4]Thursday 21 June 1624; or two days earlier? PTMN f° 145/1, and TCH (1931), p. 23, concur. Under this date, the TPMCM, p. 80, mentions only Chiang Mai's suppression of a revolt in Chiang Khong. A revolt in Nan is mentioned in *dap pao* 987 (p. 81), when Suttho "again" takes Nan.

[5]Wednesday 22 August 1624, or one day earlier? TCH (1931), p. 23 concurs.

[6]MS. has different reading. TCH (1931), p. 23, simply says at Utthayan Noi. Staff at the municipal public works office in Nan tell me that this is on the small hill just southwest of the city.

[7]Wednesday 21 November 1624; or one day earlier? PTMN f° 145/2. TCH (1931), p. 23, says the twelfth month. Date confirmed in TCH/PP, p. 23.

[8]Saturday 27 October 1624. TCH (1931), p. 23, says a Tuesday, in the *tut chao* watch.

[9]PTMN f° 145/2-3 gives a date, Tuesday, the full-moon day of the 2nd month (has to be a Keng Tung-style month; Monday 26 November 1624), when the people of Nan, Un Müang, and "both the *rajaguru*—of Cæ Hæng and Sri Bun Hüang—fled with their pupils and laymen to Lan Cang, by way of Bò Wa," one of the salt-well villages northeast of Nan, on the way to Luang Prabang, in the headwaters of the Wa River. TCH/PP, p. 23, and TCH (1931), p. 23, agree.

[10]Friday 2 January 1626; or one day earlier? TCH/PP, p. 23, PTMN f° 145/4 , and TCH (1931), p. 23, concur, including the CS number. This has to be Wednesday 31 December 1625, which has the correct lunar mansion.

the city through the Elephant Landing Gate,[1] /118/ and took possession of the city.[2] Having become ruler, he viewed the dilapidated condition of the Great Reliquary of Cæ Hæng. He announced to his councillors and to his people and household that he would have them, led by Somdet Cao Tipangkara[3] at the head of the monkhood, / restore and renovate it and place a golden [copper?] casing upon the base and second stages right down to the ground, and he provided 1,500 weights [ca. 1.82 kg.] of gold for the gilding on all four sides. Furthermore, since the galleries / of the holy reliquary, which had been built by Paña Kham Yòt Fa, southwards from the Small Vihara, which had eleven rooms, were in ruins, the ruler of Nan invited the monkhood, headed by Somdet Cao Tipangkara, / and the public to rebuild them.[4] This construction began in the *kat sai* year, CS 991.[5] The work of applying the adhesive lacquer and affixing the gold leaf was entrusted to the monks of Wat Ku Kham,[6] and they accomplished it with great faith / from the second tier down to the ground, which was a great service to the Holy Reliquary, beyond measure. ...[7] /119/ The work of reconstruction lasted for fourteen years, from the *dap mao* year to the *pœk yi* year, and was carried on without interruption until completed.[8]

4.21. This ruler of Nan, Cao Paña Müang Lakòn [Lampang], died on the *luang mao* day, the second day of the waxing moon of the first ninth month, in the *kòng ngai* watch, in the *pœk yi* year, CS 1000.[9] / His funeral ceremonies were begun on the sixth day of the waxing moon of the third month,[10] and he was cremated on the seventh day of the waxing moon. In / that same year[11] by the Lao reckoning his cremation was concluded at the full moon of the second month. He was the forty-third ruler.

4.22. Cao Paña Chiang Rai then came to rule Nan in the *pœk yi* year 1000. He ruled for eleven years and died on Tuesday, the twelfth day of the waxing moon of the second month, in the morning watch, in the *pœk cai* year, 1010.[12] He was the forty-fourth ruler.

---

[1]This gate probably should be associated with Wat Ta Cang, now at the north end of the city. It would then reinforce the idea of an earlier, more northern site for the city. Older city walls are faintly suggested in this area. See the city map.

[2]TPMCM, p. 81, *sub anno* 987. The full date is not given in the Chiang Mai Chronicle.

[3]TCH (1931), p. 23, has Somdet Cao Pâladipankara (Palathipangkon).

[4]PTMN f° 145/4-146/2 has this information also.

[5]AD 1629/30. TCH/PP, p. 24, and PTMN f° 146/2 concur.

[6]The easternmost temple within the old city walls, due east of the palace. See the city map.

[7]One sentence not translated. See MS., f° 118, line 5.

[8]Confirmed in TCH/PP, p. 24, and PTMN f° 147/1. TCH (1931), pp. 23-24, gives a similar account, and says that the work continued to *pœk yi* 1000. *Dap mao* has to be a mistake for *dap pao:* see first line of previous paragraph.

[9]The MS. as it stands is not correct: the only *luang mao* day near this date was the 15th waning of the first 8th month, Saturday 10 July 1638. CS 1000 (AD 1638/39) was a *pœk yi* year. However, PTMN f° 147/1 gives CS 109 (clearly 1009, = AD 1647/48), a Thai *luang mao* day, in the *kòng ngai* watch. TCH (1931), p. 24, agrees: the ruler died in *müang khai* 1009, on Monday, 2nd waxing of the first tenth month, (A)sadha, a *luang mao* day. TCH/PP, p. 24, has only the year CS 1009 and the first *tenth* month.

[10]Saturday 11 December 1638.

[11]PTMN f° 147/1-2 also gives these dates. TCH (1931), p. 24. 6th waxing of the third month.

[12]Wednesday 29 October 1648, or the previous day. TCH/PP, p. 24, PTMN f° 147/2, and TCH (1931), p. 24, all concur on the date.

4.23. Next, Maha Dhamma appointed the three brothers who ruled Chiang Khong. The eldest was Cao Paña Læ / Mum, and his younger brothers were Cao Paña Yòt Cai and Cao Paña Pa Müang Laca.[1] Cao Paña Læ Mum came to rule Nan in the *kat pao* year, CS 1011. On Sunday, the full-moon day of the eighth month, a *ka lao* day, in the watch near noon, in the fifteenth lunar mansion, he /120/ took his place in the audience hall.[2] He ruled for fourteen years and seven months.

4.24. In the *tao yi* year, CS 1024, on the third day of the waning moon of the third month,[3] the king of the South attacked Nan. He captured Paña Læ Mum and sent him to the South, where he died. He was called Paña Khong.[4] He was the forty-fifth ruler.

4.25. In the *dap sai* year, CS 1027,[5] Maha Dhamma had Paña Yòt Cai, a younger brother of Paña Læ Mum, come to rule Nan. The new governor first stayed at Pua, and moved to Nan in the *lwai / sanga* year.[6] He ruled for twenty-three years.[7] He died in the *müang mao* year, 1049, on Sunday, the seventh day of the waning moon of the second month, in the *kòng leng* watch.[8] He was the forty-sixth ruler.[9]

4.26. In the *kat sai* year, CS / 1051, Maha Dhamma appointed Cao Paña Pa Müang Lacha, another brother of Paña Læ Mum, to rule Nan.[10] He ruled for fifteen years. In the *ka met* year, CS 1065, on Saturday, the first day of the waxing moon of the twelfth month, near dawn,[11] / Lao Con Sæn Kæo brought word that the Burmese were coming. The ruler lent his ear to Lao Con Sæn Kæo [who urged him] to stand up against the Burmese. All the members of the Sangha, upon learning of this, kindly [tried to] dissuade him, but he did not listen.[12]

---

[1]PTMN f° 147/2-3 gives different relationships, both here and below. It says that there were two brothers, plus the son of one; and the elder brother was Paña Læ Mum.

[2]Monday 26 April 1649; or the previous day, Sunday 25 April 1649. TCH/PP, p. 24, PTMN f° 147/3, and TCH (1931), p. 24, concur. This day had the correct lunar mansion.

[3]Tuesday 28 November 1662. PTMN f° 147/3 gives the year as 124 TCH/PP, p. 24, and TCH (1931), p. 24, concur, and have 1024. They goes on, however, to say that the South's attack *failed*, and many died. TPMCM, p. 81, says the South attacked Chiang Mai unsuccessfully in 1022 *kat cai*.

[4]So called because he is said to have come from Chiang Khong.

[5]PTMN f° 148/1-2 has CS 127 (=1027), a *dap sai* year (AD 1665/66), and states that the younger Paña Khòng, named Yòt Cai, became ruler. TCH (1931), p. 25, has the full numeral, 1027.

[6]PTMN f° 148/2 has CS 128 (=1028), *lwai sanga* (AD 1666/67). TCH (1931), p. 25, has 1028.

[7]TCH/PP, p. 25, says 13 years.

[8]Tuesday 28 October 1687. TCH/PP, p. 25, PTMN f° 148/2, and TCH (1931), p. 25, concur.

[9]The MS. actually says "forty-fifth."

[10]PTMN f° 148/2 agrees: CS 1051 *kat sai* (= AD 1689/90). But it says that Pa Müang Laca was the son of the previous ruler, not his brother. TCH (1931), p. 25, also calls him a son, and concurs on date.

[11]PTMN f° 148/3, and TCH (1931), p. 25 concur. Tuesday 11 September 1703. If the month is expressed in Burmese style, then Thursday 11 October. The chronology seems to be off especially in cases when the year was supposed to be a leap year (13 months), suggesting that Nan chronographers might have intercalated months irregularly.

[12]Thanks to Harald Hundius for suggesting a reading of this final sentence. The Chiang Mai Chronicle (*sub anno* 1065) is not very helpful: "In 1065, a *ka met* year, Lawâ fell upon Lan Na, setting themselves up at Chiang Khòng, and then fled to Nan in that Year."

4.27. On Friday, the tenth day of the waxing moon of the seventh month, at midday,[1] as the Burmese were approaching the city, Cao Paña Pa Müang Laca, seeing that he could not resist the Burmese, /121/ gathered up his retainers and family and fled to Lan Cang, together with Con Lao Sæn Kæo[2] and Tao La. All the Sangha fled, and the people were defeated and fled to the wilderness.[3] On the fourteenth,[4] the Burmese / entered the city.

4.28. After having been in Lan Cang a short time, Paña Müang Lacha fled to the South.[5] He was the forty-seventh ruler.

4.29. When the Burmese army entered the city, they destroyed it. They tore down the city walls, burnt down houses, and looted the west-facing image of the Buddha / at Wat Phumin.[6] They also tore off the finial of the cetiya of Wat Cæ Hæng, and did the same to the cetiya of Wat Luang in the center of the city and the Dibbacetiya, which they leveled to the ground.[7] All that was left of Nan was the earth itself. Many people / died. All this occurred because they did not heed the commands of the king,[8] and because no work of [religious] building or restoration was done.[9]

4.30. On Tuesday, the second day of the waxing moon of the fifth month in the *müang kai* year, CS 1069,[10] the king of Ava appointed Nòi In, of the Fai Kæo villages,[11] as Pa Na Sai to act as governor of Nan.[12] /122/ When the

---

[1]TCH/PP, p. 25, PTMN f° 148/3, and TCH (1931), p. 25, concur. Saturday 15 March 1704; Burmese-style month. Cf. TPMCM, p. 82, *sub anno* 1065.

[2]Two paragraphs above this name is rendered Lao Con Sæn Kæo.

[3]The text says, literally, to "the forests, streams, caves, and mountains." "Wilderness" seems an appropriate translation.

[4]TCH/PP, p. 25, and PTMN f° 148/4 agree. Wednesday 20 March 1704; Burmese-style month.

[5]PTMN f° 148/4 actually states that he fled to "Ayotthiya." TPMCM, p. 82, *sub anno* 1065, states only that the Lao invaded Lan Na, took Chiang Khong, and went on to Nan. It does not explicitly mention a Lan Na counterattack.

[6]Indicating that the quadruple Buddha image at Wat Phumin is of some antiquity. Illustrated in *Wat Phumin and Wat Nong Bua*, p. 10.

[7]PTMN f° 148/4-149/1 agrees, and gives the date as CS 166 (= 1066), a *kap san* year (AD 1704/05). It adds that the Dibbacetiya and Wat Phumin also were pillaged. TCH (1931), p. 25, varies: three cetiya were razed—Cæ Hæng, Luang Klang Wiang, and Tip. The year given is *kap san* 1066. Wat Luang Klang Wiang is probably Wat Cang Kham.

[8]TCH (1931), p. 25, also gives this account, including the admonitory phrase. The reliquary chronicle ends here, save for two colophons by copyists; one in *kot cai* 1242 (AD 1880), 4th waxing of the second month (Saturday 6 November 1880); and the other *tao yi* 1262 (AD 1900), Wednesday, 3rd waning of the fifth month (7 February 1901). The manuscript is stated as having been presented to Cao Paññа of Wat Pa Singhalam in Chiang Rai.

[9]TCH/PP, p. 25, ends with the crumbling of various cetiya, arguing that "many died because they did not heed the word of the king." The final date given in this manuscript is in the *kap san* year 1066. TCH/MT concludes similarly, and TCH/TC includes an identical passage shortly before concluding.

[10]PTMN f° 149/3 has the same date. 24 January 1708.

TPMCM, p. 82, speaks of something like this only later, in connection with the year 1077 (see below). In 1069 *müang kai*, it states, Cao Nò Müang was sent to be governor (*wun*, a Burmese term) of Nan.

[11]Ban Fai Kæo is less determinate than it appears. There is a village by that name just to the northwest of the Cæ Hæng reliquary. However, Aroonrut Wichienkeeo explains that *kæo*, in addition to referring to gems, also is used to denote the callouses on the palms of the hands of

Burmese were surrounding Nan, it had been Nòi In who cooperated by burning homes and temples, thus scaring away the people, who evacuated the city and went into the forests and upland valleys. When the Burmese retreated, he persuaded the people / to return. A year later the Kæo and Lao armies yet again captured Nan and took people away to Müang Lao as prisoners. Many then fled to the wilderness. / After the enemy retreated, Nòi In—who was a very clever man, always able to save himself—again persuaded the people who had fled to return to the empty land as before.[1]

4.31. The king of Ava heard about his cleverness and especially his ability to persuade people to return and rebuild the city. The Burmese king therefore appointed him Pa Na Sai, in charge of gathering / people and putting them into villages and towns. In the same year, the king of Ava sent a prince, Cao Fa Wiang Khòng, to administer Nan with Nòi In.[2] In that year, Prince Wiang Khòng came to Müang Lim.[3] On the sixth day of the waxing moon of the sixth month in the *pœk cai* year,[4] /123/ the prince visited Pa Na Sai at Ban Cang Pha,[5] and commanded Pa Na Sai to issue a proclamation to the people compelling them to rebuild the country and resume their farming and rebuild dams and irrigation ditches. If any able-bodied dry- or wet-rice farmer refused to comply, / his land would be worked by others, and the owner would have no right to reclaim his land. The people complied.

4.32. In the *kap sanga* year, CS 1076,[6] the ruler died / in Nan. Cao Wiang Khòng had ruled Nan for seven years, and was the forty-eighth ruler. In that same *sanga* year, the king of Ava appointed a *myosa* prince to come as ruler of Nan.[7] / On becoming ruler of Nan, the *myosa* prince, together with the Pa Na Sai

---

those who have to work especially hard, as in maintaining irrigation works. Thus the *fai kæo* villages might well be those, separately administered, which have irrigated fields. I am all the more encouraged to think this way because of the title that *nai* Nòi In is given, Pa Na Sai, which means something like Officer in Charge of the Left-hand [Irrigated or Wet] Rice Fields. Might it be that the Pa Na Sai traditionally was an officer in charge of the irrigated fields (and their populations) on the left (east) bank of the Nan River, and the Pa Na Khwa had similar responsibilities on the right (west) bank?

[12]The Chiang Mai Chronicle (*sub anno* 1069) says that "In 1069 ... on the 6th waning of the eighth month [the Burmese commander at Chiang Mai] appointed the man who ruled Müang Rai to come to rule Chiang Rai and Cao Nò Müang to go as governor of Nan."

[1]PTMN lacks this passage about Nòi In. Curiously, TCH/TC, in the final passage summarizing the reigns from CS 1066 to CS 1197, says only that "in the *kat pao* year 1071, Paña Ti came to rule Nan, [and ruled] for 45 years, to the *ka lao* year, 1115, when he died." This would seem to be a reference to Cao Luang Tin.

[2]PTMN f° 149/3-150/1 has the same date, but speaks only of Paña Na Sai (= Nòi In) and Cao Mayòng Khòng, son(s?) of (the ruler of?) Chiang Sæn. "Mayòng Khòng" is repeated, at 150/2, so this is not a singular misreading.

[3]The best I can tell from the meagre maps available is that Müang Rim/Lim/Lem seems to be more or less identical with present-day Tha Wang Pha.

[4]Thursday 15 February 1709.

[5]Village located on the east bank of the Nan River, directly opposite the northern part of the modern city of Nan. There is a temple there called Wat Chang Pha (Cang Pha). The name suggests an economic specialization in weaving cloth.

[6]AD 1714/15.

[7]The Chiang Mai Chronicle (TPMCM, p. 82) concurs: The Burmese governor of Chiang Sæn consulted the king of Ava and "brought back a royal order stating that, since Cao In Müang who had been appointed to rule Nan had died, Chiang Mai and Chiang Sæn concurred in sending

and all the Sangha renovated the Holy Reliquary; that is, they extended the cetiya by erecting a seven-tiered finial, in the *lwai san* year, at the full moon of the eighth month, a Tuesday and Tai *kap set* day.[1] / The *myosa* prince ruled Nan for three years, and died in that *lwai san* year, CS 1078.[2] He was the forty-ninth ruler.

4.33. On the death of the *myosa* prince, the king [of Ava] appointed Pa Na Sai (Nòi In) as /124/ governor, and his rank was raised to Pa Na Khwa. Pa Na Khwa became governor in the *lwai san* year, CS 1078. Together with all the officials, he built the *vihara* of Wat Pu Kòng,[3] / and had his own portrait painted on the wall of the *vihara* for future generations to see.

4.34. Later, in the *lwai sanga* year, 1088,[4] Pa Na Khwa considered the fact / that Nan had no ruling prince. He and all the officials decided to invite a prince of Chiang Mai to come and rule Nan. The governors of Chiang Mai and Chiang Sæn together went to Ava and asked permission of the king. / He granted their request, and sent the governor of Chiang Sæn to Chiang Mai to accompany Cao Paña Tin to Nan to begin his rule. Pa Na Khwa, the former Nòi In of the *fai kæo* villages, / had ruled for eleven years. He was the fiftieth ruler. He handed the domain over to Cao Paña Tin.

Phraya Tin to go and rule Nan." But it adds that "The king of Ava [also] issued a royal order that, of the two brothers ruling the principality, [the elder,] Khattiyawong, should be the new Nâ Khwâ and Phutthawongsa, the younger brother, should be the Nâ Sâi" and that the various northeastern principalities should form military units under Chiang Sæn. A *myosa* prince is given territories or domains (*myo*) to eat (*sa*); i.e., they provide him with sustenance.

[1]PTMN f° 150/2 adds that it was CS 1078. The 8th waning of the 6th (Northern) month, Tuesday 12 March 1715, was a *kap set* day.

[2]PTMN f° 150/4 agrees that he died after ruling 3 years, but does not give a date.

[3]Not identified.

[4]Sunday 2 March 1727, or the following day. PTMN f° 150/4 has CS 168 (= 1068), *lwai sanga*, which has to be 1088, the nearest *lwai sanga* year. It also adds that Paña Tin Mahawongsa came to rule Nan on Monday, the 11th day of the 6th month, a *müang mao* day.

CHAPTER FIVE

THE DESCENDANTS OF CAO LUANG TIN

5.1 Cao Paña Luang Tin Mahawong of Chiang Mai became ruling prince of Nan in the *lwai sanga* year, CS 1088, on Monday, the eleventh day of the waxing moon of the sixth month, /125/ a *müang mao* day.[1] Soon after, Pa Na Khwa regretted that he had brought Cao Paña Luang Tin to rule Nan and was thinking of overthrowing him, but before he even said anything, Cao Paña Luang Tin knew of his intention. He therefore sent for Pa Na Khwa and asked / him about it. Pa Na Khwa did not know what to reply, for he had already done wrong [by even considering such an act].

5.2. Cao Paña Luang Tin then said to him, "You have rehabilitated the people of Nan and rebuilt the city and ruled over them. Then you / realized that Nan had no ruling prince, and you invited me to become ruler. Now you are turning against me and are intending to overthrow me. Do not do it, for it would mean senseless killing and sacrifice of lives. I am willing to / return to my country, and you can become ruler once more. I will not interfere with you or invade your city. I am here now because you invited me. That was your own idea." Pa Na Khwa became frightened, for the power of a ruling prince was great. He no longer wanted to live, so he went to Tung Ciang Læng and shot himself in the mouth.[2]

5.3. When Cao Luang Tin came from Chiang Mai /126/ to rule in Nan, he left all his family behind, and came only with a few servants. Later he took Nang Yòt of Ban Na[3] as his wife. By his wife in Chiang Mai he had / three sons and one daughter. His first son was named Cao Aliyawong Wantòk, his second son Cao Malæ, his third son Cao Nalin, and his daughter was named Cao Nang Tep. All his children later joined him in Nan.[4]

---

[1]2 March 1727.

[2]This story is given in TCRM, ff° 1-3/4. The printed edition inexplicably writes Thung Fiang Læng.

These two paragraphs logically go at the end of the previous chapter. I have left them here because they form the initial folios of the TCRM manuscript.

[3]TCRM, f° 3/5 has Ban Na Pang.

[4]TCRM, f° 4/3-4, for these children by his Chiang Mai wife; here, Cao Manglæ, not Malæ.

5.4. By his Nan wife, Nang Yòt, / Cao Luang Tin had three daughters: Cao Nang Malimala,[1] Cao Nang Yòt Manola,[2] and Cao Nang Kham Kha.[3]

5.5. Cao Aliyawong Wantòk (son of Cao Luang Tin) brought his wife with him from Chiang Mai. He had six sons. They were named / Cao Nan[4] Cantapacot Cao Mongkhonwalayot who joined his father later; Cao Witun, also called Cao Na Khwa; Cao Tepin; Cao Nòi Tayu; Cao Nan Som;[5] and Cao Nan Mahawong.[6] All later joined their father. Cao / Aliyawong Wantòk later joined his father [in Nan]. He took a lady of Müang Lam as wife, and they had three sons: Cao Khwa, Cao Sai, and Cao Samana.[7]

5.6. Cao Malæ, [a son of Cao Luang Tin,] took a wife /127/ and had one son and one daughter. The daughter was named Nang Si Mahamaya, and the son was named Cao Nan Mahawong.[8]

5.7. Cao Nalin, [third son of Cao Luang Tin,] married Cao Nang Pimpa, daughter of Cao Nang Tep. They had one daughter and one son. The daughter was named Cao Nang Sukanta and the son was Cao Tu Nai Nakkasena.[9]

5.8. Cao Nang Tep, [the only daughter of Cao Luang Tin by his Chiang Mai wife,] married Cao Cairaca, who was a nephew of Cao Luang Tin. They also joined Cao Luang Tin in Nan. They had three sons and four daughters. The sons were Cao Nai Ai, Cao Sutta, and Cao / Mano. The daughters were Cao Nang Pimpa, Cao Nang Noca, Cao Nang Lœt, and Cao Nang Li Kæo.[10]

5.9. Cao Nai Ai married Cao Nang Kham Kha, a daughter of Cao Luang Tin. They had one son, / Cao Nòi Wong.[11]

---

[1]TCRM, f° 3/5 has Rimala, but Rimla at ff° 4/1 and 4/3. She is said to have had a husband named Nai Sin, by whom she had three daughters: Nang Sri Ka; Nang Tip Duang (who went to live in Ava); and Nang Bua Tip (f° 4/1).

[2]TCRM, f° 4/1, says she was the mother of Nai Nòi Ano = Cao Paña Suliyaphong.

[3]TCRM, f° 3/5-4/3, seems to indicate five children—four daughters and one son—by his Nan wife (though the text is very difficult): Nang Rimala, Nang Yòt Manola, Nang Sukhanta, Nang Kham Kha, and [Cao] Cintalaca.

[4]The word "Nan" in this name and in many of those that follow is an honorific title borne by those who have been Buddhist monks, and is roughly equivalent to the title "Maha" common in central Thailand. Older texts, like TCRM, write it as "khanan."

[5]Illegible in MS.; restored from TCRM f° 8/5.

[6]TCRM f° 8/5 concludes with another listing of Aliyawong Wanthòk's six sons: Mongkhonwalayot, Nai Khwa, Nai Nòi Tepin, Nai Nòi Tat, Nai Nan Som, and Nai Nan Mahawong.

[7]The printed text skips a full line in this paragraph. TCRM, ff° 4/5-5/1, appears to list five children by his wife from Müang Lam (Ram): Cao Na Khwa, Cao Na Sai, Cao Sri ++n, Cao Latchawong, and Cao Paña Sommana.

[8]TCRM, f° 5/1-2, lists Nang Sri Mahamaya and Nai Khanan Mahawong as the children of Paña Manglæ.

[9]TCRM, f° 5/2-3, says that Paña Nalin had just one daughter (unnamed), who was the mother of Nai Kæo Manut.

[10]TCRM, f° 5/3-4, agrees on Cao Cailaca (who it says was a nephew/grandson of Cao Luang Tin) and lists the children as Cao Paña Nai Ai, Cao Sutta, Cao Paña Mano, Nai Pima (has to be Nang Pimpa), Nang Ca (Noca), Cao [Nang] Lœt, and Nang Si Kæo.

[11]TCRM, f° 5/4-5, says that Nòi Wong served as Cao Pa Müang Kæn (Kæo?), and that he was the husband of Nang Kham Piu.

5.10. Cao Sutta married a lady from the Lem family, Nang Kannika. They had one son, Cao Nòi Attawalapanño, who was termed a royal prince [*cao fa*].[1]

5.11. Cao Mano, third son of Cao Tep, married a lady from Müang Thœng. They had one son and / one daughter. Their son was named Cao Suliya Kang Wiang, and the daughter Cao Nang Kham Piu.[2]

5.12. Cao Nang Pimpa, daughter of Cao Tep, married Cao Nalin, son of Cao Luang Tin. They had two children.[3] Later she deserted Cao Nalin and took a new husband, breaking with her siblings. Her relatives forbade the marriage, but the lady would not listen. They had a son, /128/ Nai Nòi Kantha. When he was grown up he was strong and brave in battle. It is said that when he died he became a ghost called "Three-Eyed Khanta" who haunted the palace.[4] So it is said.[5]

5.13. Cao Nang Noca and Cao Nang Si Kæo had no children.[6]

5.14. Cao Nang Lœt married Cao Mahapom of Müang Thœng. They had three daughters and five sons. The eldest son was Cao Mahawong, who later ruled Nan. The second son was Cao Müang Kæo, the third was Cao Pimpisan, the fourth was Cao Nan / Wuttana, who became ruler of Thœng, and the fifth was Cao Suliya Cò Fa. Their daughters were Cao Nang Ubonwanna, Cao Nang Siwanna, and [Cao] Nang Cantima. This branch of the family was very numerous.[7]

5.15. The son of Cao Aliyawong Wantòk / by his Müang Lam wife was Cao Somana who later became ruler of Nan. He had a son named Cao Acittawong, who [also] became a ruler of Nan.[8] Acittawong had two brothers by a different mother. They were Cao Nan Kai Kæo and Cao / Butsalot who later became ruler of Müang Kæn.[9] Their sister was Nang Pæng Müang.[10]

5.16. The son of Cao Sutta who was named Cao Attawalapanño later became the seventh ruler of Nan. His first wife was Mæ Cao Kham Nòi of the Lem family, /129/ that is, a daughter of Paña Han. They had two sons and three daughters. The sons were Cao Mahayot who later was the Cao Latcawong and

---

[1]TCRM, f° 5/5, calls him simply Cao Noi Atta, but identifies him definitely as the fifth ruler. The "Lem family" is elsewhere the "Lim" family, and probably is to be associated with Müang Lim, at present-day Tha Wang Pha.

[2]TCRM, f° 6/2, calls him Cao Paña Mano, and lists his children as Nang Kham Piu and Cao Khanan Suliya Kang Wiang.

[3]TCRM, f° 6/2-3, says their children were Nang Sukhonta and Nai Nakkasena.

[4]TCRM, f° 6/3-4, concurs, and says the evil spirit haunts the palace "to the present" (1850, the date of the original compilation, or 1879, the date of the copy).

[5]This is a very rare historiographical comment, "so it is said." Is the author distancing himself from his composition? The comment does not appear in TCRM.

[6]TCRM, f° 6/4, concurs.

[7]TCRM, ff° 6/4-7/4, lists the children apparently in birth order: [Nang] Upbalawanna (Ubonwanna), Nang Si Wanna; Khanan Mahawong, who was later ruler; Nai Müang Kæo, Nai Noi Pimmasan, Nai Khanan Wutana, Cao Cò Fa, and Nang Cantima. The listing closes with the identical phrase about the size of this branch of the line.

[8]TCRM, f° 4/2, indicates that Acittawong's mother was Nang Sukhantha. That Cao Sommana was his father is noted at f° 4/5.

[9]Not located.

[10]TCRM, f° 5/1 mentions only Nai Khanan Buttalot, son of Cao Paña Sommana by another mother.

then became the ninth ruler of Nan, and another son who died.[1] Their first daughter was Mæ Cao Paphawadi, their second / Mæ Cao Mi, and their third Mæ Cao La (also known as Mæ Cao Kæo).[2]

5.17. The second wife was Mæ Cao Wæn of a Chiang Sæn family. By this wife there was one daughter and six sons. The daughter was Mæ Cao Siwanna. Their sons were: Cao Tong Kæo, Cao Sæn Müang, Cao Kham Lü; Cao Nan Mahawong, who died at Nakòn Sawan; Cao Suliya Hai, and Cao Nan Caiya.

5.18. His third wife was Mæ Cao Khòt Kæo. She was childless.

5.19. His fourth wife was Mæ Cao Khan Kæo of Chiang Khæng, that is, a daughter of Cao Fa Wæn of Chiang Khæng. There was a son by this wife, Cao Nòi / Anantayot, who later became the twelfth ruler of Nan with the name of Anantawalalitthidet, Lord of Life, and a daughter, Mæ Cao Tòm.[3]

5.20. Mæ Cao Siwanna[4] married Cao Mahayot of Chiang Khong. /130/ They had five daughters and four sons. They were Cao Nan Tep; Cao Canta, who became Cao Wang Khwa [Prince of the Right Palace]; Cao Nan Mahacai, and Cao Mahawong. The daughters were Mæ Cao Supan, / Mæ Cao Kannika, Mæ Cao Suthamma, Mæ Cao Kham Pæng, and [Mæ] Cao Yòt La. Mæ Cao Yòt La later became chief queen of Cao Suliyaphong Phalittadet, the / thirteenth ruler of Nan.

5.21. The first son of Cao Nang Lœt was Cao Mahawong, who was the eleventh ruler of Nan. (His family will be treated below.) The second son was Cao Müang Kæo, who took a wife from Chiang Lom. / They had a son named Cao Nan Mahayot.[5]

5.22. Nang Lœt's third son was Cao Nòi San, who died.[6] The fourth son was Cao Nan Wuttana, who became ruler of Müang Thœng.[7] The fifth son was Cao Suliya Cò Fa, who married Mæ Cao La, daughter of the Cao Fa, and his son was Cao Nòi Kittiyot.[8]

5.23. Her first daughter, Mæ Cao Ubonwanna, had a son named Cao Pa Müang Nòi. Her second daughter, Mæ Cao Siwanna, /131/ married Cao Suliya Kang Wiang, and had two daughters, Cao Yòt Lila and Cao Pia.[9] Her third daughter, Mæ Cao Cantima, married Cao Nòi Kang. They had one son, Cao

---

[1]TCRM, f° 6/1, says this was Nai Nòi Manolot.

[2]TCRM, ff° 5/5-6/1, seems very confusing. As best I can read it, the children of the first wife were sons Cao Paña Mahayot and Nai Nòi Manorot. The children of his later wives are not listed.

[3]TCRM f° 6/1 simply lists Anantayot as the child of Attawala, without specifying his mother, and notes that he is "the Cao Paña Hò Na today," i.e., the heir-apparent. As Anantayot became ruler in 1857, the date of this MS. cannot be later than this. The date given at the head of the MS. is CS 1212 (AD 1850/51).

[4]There are at least two women by this name, which is confusing.

[5]TCRM f° 7/1 adds "of Müang Thœng."

[6]TCRM f° 7/2 says Cao Nòi Pimmasan, who had a son named Cao Khanan Atta.

[7]TCRM f° 7/2 says Khanan Wutana had two children, Nai Khanan Thammalangka and Nai Müang In.

[8]TCRM f° 7/3: Cao Cò Fa took a wife named Si Kæo, daughter of Cao Atthawalapanña, and had one son, Nai Nòi Khattiya.

[9]TCRM f° 6/5 concurs: Yòt Lila and Pia. (Both are termed "nai," but this text calls even queens "nai."

Canta.[1] This branch of the family / (of Cao Mahapom of Müang Thœn and Cao Nang Lœt) became very numerous.

5.24. About the branch of Cao Aliyawong Wantòk, his first son by the Chiang Mai wife was Cao Cantapacot, who became the sixth ruler of Nan / under the name of Cao Mongkhon Walayot. His first wife was ... [name missing]. They had one son, Cao Nan Pinat Fai Kæo, and a daughter, Mæ Cao Kiang Kham. His second wife was ... [name missing]. They had one son, Cao Khamtan, and a daughter, Mæ Cao ... [name missing], who married the ruler of Müang Thœng.[2]

[Cao Mongkhon Walayot (or Cantapacot) had four brothers: Cao Witun, Cao Tepin, Cao Nòi Tui, and Cao Mahawong.]

5.25. Cao Witun was Cao Na Khwa, and later became the fifth ruler of Nan. He had one son, Cao Atta.

5.26. Cao Tepin had one son, / Cao Lattana Huamüang Kæo, and one daughter, Mæ Cao Sing Sòi.[3]

5.27. Cao Nòi Tui married a lady from Ban Kæm in Müang Pua.[4] They had two sons, Cao Nan Ya and Cao Nan Nantacai, also called /132/ Cao Som. The latter became Cao Hò Na.[5]

5.28. Cao Mahawong married a lady from the Chiang Lom line. They had one son, Cao Nòi Cawana, and two daughters, Mæ Cao Nang Nanta and Mæ Cao Nang Cai Kham.[6] Mæ Cao Nang Nanta married a commoner. They had two sons, Nòi Tep / and Nòi Tip Duang. Mæ Cao Nang Cai Kham [also] married a commoner. They had one son, Compu, and one daughter, Nang Sisopa, who became the wife of Cao Paña Rattana.[7]

5.29. These were the descendents of Cao Aliyawong Wantòk and his Chiang Mai wife.

---

[1]TCRM f° 7/3-4: she married Nai Nòi Kang and had one son, Nai Canta Nòi.

[2]TCRM f° 7/5 has the same information, but supplies none of our missing names: he had two children by his (unnamed) first wife—Nang Kiang Kha and Cao Khanan Pinta—and two by his second wife—Nai Khamtan and an unnamed daughter who was the wife of the ruler of Thœng.

[3]TCRM f° 8/1 seems to conflate Witun and Tepin: it literally reads, "Na Khwa, who was the father of Nai Nòi Tepin, took a wife and had children Cao Paña Rattana Hua Müang Kæo [and a] younger sibling Nang Sing Sòi.

[4]This village is located immediately adjacent to the modern town of Pua, on the east side.

[5]TCRM f° 8/1-2: "Nai Nòi Thatda took a wife from Ban Kæm in Müang Pua and he had as children Nai Nòi Wiya [and] Nai Khanan Ya—that Nai Khanan was the Cao Hò Na who died at the mouth of the Samun—and Nai Khanan Som."

[6]TCRM f° 8/2 does not specify the origins of his wife. His children were Nòi Nanta, Nai Khanan Cawana, and Nang Cai Kham.

[7]TCRM f° 8/2-3 is very confusing here. What it appears to say is that [she—the nearest antecedent is Nang Cai Kham] "took a husband and had as children Nai Nòi Tep (now deceased); Nang Tip Duang, who took a husband and had as child Nai Cumpu, father of Si Wanna; Nang Si Sopa, his younger sibling, became the wife of Cao Paña Rattana (now deceased)."

CHAPTER SIX

THE FIRST SIX RULERS, AD 1727-1786

6.1. Here we will / tell of the lineage of Cao Paña Luang Tin Mahawong of Chiang Mai, who came then to rule Nan. The sages regard him as the first of the lineage. We have enumerated the different / branches of this great family, which are numerous and widespread.

6.2. Cao Luang Tin ruled Nan for twenty-six years [from 1088] and died in the *luang met* year, on Thursday, the eighth day of the waning moon of the seventh month.[1] His son, Cao Aliyawong, then ruled. In the *ka lao* year, CS 1115, Cao Aliyawong, with the members of the family and the councillors and elders, /133/ arranged the funeral.[2] He was the first of the ruling line, and the fifty-first ruler from the time of Cao Khun Fòng.

6.3. In the *kap set* year, CS 1116, on the fourteenth day of the waxing moon of the eleventh month, Min Sam Luang Min Than Lwin brought an order / from the king of Ava appointing Cao Aliyawong Wan Tòk, the eldest son of Cao Luang Tin, to rule as governor of Nan.[3] He had ruled seven years when, in the *kot si* year CS 1122,[4] all of / Lan Na Thai, including Chiang Mai and Chiang Sæn, revolted against the king of Burma.

---

[1]The closest *luang met* year was CS 1113 (AD 1752/53). PTMN f° 151/1 concurs on death date, but says he ruled 27 years. PMN&TY f° 1/2 concurs on 26 years, and says he died on Thursday the 8th waning of the 7th month in CS 1113. Thursday 7 April 1752 was a 7th waning.

TCH/TC states that Paña Ti ruled "from 1071 to the *ka lao* year CS 1115, when he died." That was a *ka lao* year. This somewhat aberrant text then lists the succeeding rulers in the following order:

Fa Ai, 3 years, CS 1115-1118
Paña Kan, 8 years, CS 1118-1126
Fa Mano, 11 years, CS 1126-1136, fleeing to Thœng in 1140
Caofa Attacaiyalaca, also called Sumana, ? years, CS 1140-1187.
Caofa Atta, 11 years, CS 1187-1197.

This is very confused, and the other more detailed accounts are to be preferred.

TPMCM, p. 83, indicates that, soon after the *müang met* year 1089, a certain Thammapanña of Nan attacked Chiang Mai, and was killed in a battle at Pa Sang (south of Lamphun). Six years later, in the *tao cai* year 1095, Phræ and Nan, together with Lampang, Fang, Müang Sat, Chiang Khong, and Thœng, were placed administratively under Chiang Sæn.

[2]AD 1753/54. PTMN f° 151/1: funeral in CS 1114, a *ka lao* year (AD 1752/53). PMN&TY f° 1/3 agrees on 1115 for the funeral.

[3]Saturday 3 August 1754. PTMN f° 151/2: Friday the full-moon day of the 11th month in CS 1116, a *kap set* year (AD 1754/55). He is here termed Aliyawongso; also in PMN&TY f° 1/4. Min Sam Luang is probably Min Than Lwin in Burmese.

[4]AD 1760/61; confirmed in PMN&TY f° 1/4.

6.4. In the *luang sai* year, CS 1123, a Burmese army of thirteen thousand men under the command of Amyakamani arrived in Chiang Mai on the eighth day of the waxing moon of the third month.[1] The Burmese besieged the city for five months and fourteen days and then Chiang Mai surrendered. After having subdued Chiang Mai, three Burmese armies went to Lampang, Phræ, and / Nan. They made their base at the head of the city, where they stayed during the rainy season. While there, the Burmese imposed a head tax of 500 *bat* weight of gold on all married couples.[2] In the *tao sanga* year, CS 1124, on the fifth day of the waxing moon of the third month,[3] the three Burmese armies withdrew to Ava.

6.5. In CS /134/ 1125, a *ka met* year,[4] four Burmese armies of 4,000 men [each?], under the command of Maha Mingaladok Gyi, gathered up the forces of Lan Na Thai, and then took Luang Prabang.[5] On the sixth day of the waxing moon of the eighth month,[6] the Burmese army left Luang Prabang and encamped / at Wat Luang Pabat in Lampang[7] for the rainy season. There they collected forces from the fifty-seven[8] domains of Lan Na Thai. Then, on the fifth day of the waxing moon of the third month in the *kap san* year, CS 1126,[9] the Burmese and Lan Na Thai armies left for Ayudhya. / As for Nan, Cao Aliyawong appointed his nephew, Cao Nai Ai, to lead the Nan unit under Maha Mingaladok in going to the South Country.[10]

6.6. During this period, all of Lan Na was oppressed by the Burmese, who took away all the horses, stripped the country of valuables, / and carried away countless prisoners. By the *dap lao* year, 1127,[11] the nobles and people of Lan Na could stand it no longer, / and together revolted against the Burmese, after Cao Nai Ai had gone South with the Burmese army.[12]

6.7. In the *lwai set* year, CS 1128,[13] the Burmese general—the "Great Demon"—heard about the uprising in Lan Na Thai, and came with his army from Laos /135/ to subdue Lan Na on the eleventh day of the waning moon of the

---

[1] Friday 4 December 1761. PMN&TY f° 1/5. The Burmese chronicle terms him Abayagamani. Cf. "Intercourse between Burma and Siam," *Selected Articles from the Siam Society Journal* 6 (Bangkok, 1959): 17.

[2] As in PMN&TY f° 2/1.

[3] Sunday 21 November 1762. PMN&TY f° 2/2.

[4] AD 1763/64. PMN&TY f° 2/2-3.

[5] "Intercourse," pp. 18-19, says the army was composed of 18 regiments with a total of 100 elephants and 20,000 men, under the command of Nemyo Thihapate. The Lao sources do not mention the Burmese invasion of Luang Prabang. See Sila Viravong, Cao Khamman, and Le Boulanger.

[6] Monday 18 April 1763. PMN&TY f° 2/3 says Friday.

[7] Wat Pathat Lampang Luang? This seems a logical place, as it is somewhat higher ground, southwest of the modern city of Lampang.

[8] The usual Burmese phrase is the "57 *khayaing*," or 57 *müang*. The text says 27. PMN&TY f° 2/4 clearly says 57, as the Chiang Mai Chronicle (manuscript) does.

[9] Wednesday 28 November 1764. PMN&TY f° 2/4 clearly states the 3rd waxing of the 3rd month.

[10] PMN&TY f° 2/5: Cao Na Aliya went with the Burmese forces.

[11] AD 1765/66.

[12] PTMN f° 151/2-3 says CS 1128, a *lwai set* year (= AD 1766/67). PMN&TY f° 3/1-2 has CS 1127, but the date occurs at the end of the line and the year name is broken off.

[13] AD 1766/67. PMN&TY f° 3/3 concurs.

eleventh month.[1] The Burmese encamped at the mouth of the Ngao on the twelfth day of the waxing moon of the eleventh month.[2] Cao Luang Aliyawong of Nan raised an army and came with his force and attacked the Burmese at the mouth of the Ngao, north of Nan, and the Burmese were defeated and withdrew.

6.8. When the king of Ava[3] learned that all Lan Na Thai / was in rebellion in the *müang kai* year, CS 1129, he sent an army of ten thousand under General Ase Wungyi to Chiang Mai to put down the rebellion on the tenth day of the waxing moon of the third month.[4] Paña Caban of Chiang Mai and Pa Müang Cai of Lamphun / gathered three thousand men[5] of the two cities and waited for the Burmese at Lamphun. The Burmese army besieged Lamphun from the eleventh day of the waxing third month[6] to Thursday, the fourteenth day of the waning fourth month before / it surrendered.[7] Paña Caban was captured, while Pa Müang Cai escaped to Yunnan, where he remains to the present day.[8]

6.9. After having defeated Lamphun, the Burmese went to / Lampang, Phræ, and Nan. They reached Nan on the first day of the waning fifth month[9] and took the city. The officials fled to Laos[10] and remained there for the rainy season, returning to Nan as before in the *pœk cai* year CS 1130.[11]

6.10. Cao Nai Ai, nephew of Cao Luang Aliyawong of Nan, /136/ went to Ayudhya[12] with the Burmese army which succeeded in defeating Ayudhya in the *müang kai* year, CS 1129.[13] After the defeat of Ayudhya, the Burmese sent Cao Fa Dok Düa,[14] the king of Ayudhya, back to Ava, travelling by way of Martaban and Tavoy. Cao Nai Ai / accompanied him and on arrival in Ava was received in audience by the king of Ava.[15]

---

[1]Sunday 31 August 1766. PMN&TY f° 3/3 says he brought only 500 men.

[2]Sunday 17 August 1766. PTMN f° 151/4 writes Plak Ngao, which is usual form for many Nan manuscripts. The Ngao, flowing from the northwest, empties into the Nan River 12 miles north of Nan.

[3]PTMN f° 151/4 and PMN&TY f° 3/4 have, here and elsewhere, Awa, where the Thai usually write Angwa.

[4]PMN&TY f° 3/4-5 concurs. Tuesday 1 December 1767.

[5]PMN&TY f° 4/1 says 1 thousand.

[6]Wednesday 2 December 1767.

[7]Monday 18 January 1768.

[8]PMN&TY f° 4/2-3. This sentence indicates that the source(s) used by *Sænluang* Ratchasomphan date from no later than about 1825. This seems careless of him.

[9]Thursday 4 February 1768; however, PTMN f° 151/4-5 has the basic story, but has the city of Nan fall to the Burmese on the 6th waning of the 5th month—or is this simply a mistaken transcription? It might be read as Friday, the 1st waning of the 5th month. PMN&TY f° 4/3-4 concurs on the 1st waning of the 5th month, a Friday.

[10]PTMN f° 152/1 and PMN&TY f° 4/4: they went to Laos by way of Bò Wa, one of the salt wells in the upper valley of the Wa River.

[11]AD 1768/69.

[12]PTMN f° 152/2 has Ayothiya.

[13]PTMN f° 152/2 and PMN&TY f° 4/5 have the same date. AD 1767/68.

[14]PTMN f° 152/3 has Pa Cao (King) Dok Düa, not Cao Fa (Prince).

[15]PMN&TY f° 4/5-5/2.

6.11. In that *müang kai* year,[1] a large Hò[2] army of 90,000 men invaded / Ava. When they reached Hsenwi, the king of Ava sent Cao Nai Ai with a force to meet the invaders. / The Hò were defeated and withdrew to the Gold and Iron Bridges.[3] Cao Nai Ai returned, and had an audience with the king of Ava. The king issued an order / naming Cao Nai Ai as governor of Nan. Taking leave of the king, Cao Nai Ai returned to Nan in the tenth month of CS 1130, a *pœk cai* year.[4]

6.12. Cao Luang Aliyawong, / who had ruled for fifteen years, turned his office over to his nephew on the eighth day of the waning tenth month in CS 1130, a *pœk cai* year.[5] Cao Aliyawong was the second ruler of the line [of Cao Luang Tin], and the / fifty-second from Cao Khun Fòng.

6.13. After having ruled Nan for seven months, Cao Nai Ai went to Laos on public affairs. He suddenly became ill at Ban Pò and there / died.[6] He was the third ruler, the fifty-third[7] from Cao Khun Fòng.

6.14. On the tenth day of the waxing tenth month, CS 1131,[8] Min Sam / Luang bore an order appointing Cao Nan Mano, younger brother of Cao Nai Ai, as governor of Nan. Cao Nan Mano had ruled six years when, in the *kap sanga* year, CS 1136,[9] Paña / Caban of Chiang Mai, the governor of Lamphun, and the governor of Lampang joined in revolt against the Burmese in Chiang Mai. They asked for forces from Ayudhya[10] to fight the Burmese governor and *chakhai*[11] in Chiang Mai.[12] The Burmese were defeated and withdrew.[13] At that time Cao Nòi Witun, i.e. the Cao Na Khwa, /138/ son of Cao Aliyawong, was in the Burmese service in Chiang Mai. The Ayudhya forces captured Cao Nòi Witun in Chiang Mai and took him to Lampang, and then appointed him governor of Nan in the *kap sanga* year, CS 1136.[14] On the thirteenth day of the waxing fifth month he reached Nan.[15]

---

1 PTMN f° 152/3 gives the year as CS 1130, a *pœk cai* year, = AD 1768. The nearest *müang kai* year was 1129 (AD 1767/68).

2 Hò (Haw) usually refers to Yunnanese Chinese; but here the reference is simply to Chinese.

3 On the Chinese invasion of Burma, see G. E. Harvey, *History of Burma* (London, 1925; reprinted 1967), pp. 253-58.

4 16 June-15 July 1768. PTMN f° 153/1 simply says the 10th month, implying the *pœk cai* year stipulated above. PMN&TY ff° 5/5-6/1.

5 8 July 1768. PTMN f° 153/2 does not mention this event here.

6 PTMN f° 153/2 and PMN&TY f° 6/1 agree, and have no additional details.

7 MS. mistakenly writes "fifty-first."

8 Thursday 13 July 1768. PMN&TY f° 6/1 adds that it was a *kat pao* year.

9 AD 1774/75. PTMN f° 153/2-3 says the *kap sanga* year CS 1131; but 1131 was a *kat pao* year. The nearest *kap sanga* year was 1136. The copyist of PTMN might have skipped a line here. PMN&TY f° 6/2 has the full text.

10 Actually Thonburi, of course.

11 Probably a *sitkè*, usually the deputy to a governor who dealt with military and police functions.

12 PMN&TY f° 6/3-4 agrees.

13 PTMN f° 153/3 and PMN&TY f° 6/4 say the Burmese were defeated in Chiang Mai on the 14th day of the 4th month. Sunday 15 January 1775.

14 AD 1774/75.

15 15 February 1775. PTMN f° 153/4 says he reached Nan on the full-moon day of the 5th month in "that year." PMN&TY ff° 6/5-7/1 says he was appointed on the 13th waxing of the 5th month and replaced his predecessor the next day, on the full-moon day.

6.15. When Cao Witun reached Nan, Cao Luang Manolot handed over all of Nan to him to rule, in the fifth month of that year. Cao / Luang Mano had ruled for six years when he handed over to Cao Witun. He was the fourth ruler, and the fifty-fourth from Cao Khun Fòng.

6.16. On the first day of the seventh month,[1] / the Burmese invaded Nan by way of Sala Pak Ngao.[2] Cao Luang Witun took his family and retainers and fled to Ban Calim Ta Pa,[3] where he gathered a force and returned to Nan to fight and defeat the Burmese. /

6.17. In the *dap met* year, 1137,[4] Cao Witun and Cao Aliyawong moved with their families and retainers and labor from Ban Calim [Ta Pa] to Ban Na Pang,[5] where they remained for the rainy season. Later, Cao Witun went to Lampang, /139/ while on the sixth of the waning sixth month,[6] Cao Aliyawong and Cao Cantapacot[7] and their families and labor fled Ban Na Pang and went to Viang Can.[8] Later, Cao Luang Witun went to Lampang.

6.18. In the *kat kai* year, CS 1141,[9] / a large army from Ayudhya[10] attacked Viang Can,[11] which fell to the invaders on the fourth of the waning twelfth month.[12] The king of Viang Can escaped to Müang Kæo.[13] The Siamese captured Cao Nantasen,[14] son of the ruler of Viang Can, and Nang Khieo Khom, a daughter of the king of Viang Can, and many prisoners, whom they took to the South Country.[15] At that time, Cao Aliyawong and his family and labor from Nan who had fled to Viang Can were also taken to the South Country. In the *luang pao* year, CS 1143, on Saturday, the first day of the waning third month,[16] Cao Paña Aliyawong, father of Cao Luang Witun, died in the South Country.

6.19. As for Cao Nan Mano, / after he turned over the governorship to Cao Witun, he moved to Phræ and later returned to Ban Cang Pa,[17] where he stayed for a year. In CS 1139, a *müang lao* year, on Friday, the fourteenth day of

---

[1]PTMN f° 154/1 and PMN&TY f° 7/1 concur. 1 April 1775.

[2]AD 1775/76. PTMN f° 154/1 explicitly states that the Burmese took Nan. Again, the mouth of the Ngao River.

[3]PTMN f° 154/1 and PMN&TY f° 7/2: south of Ban Calim; no mention of Ta Pa. Calim is on the Nan River, in the extreme north of Uttaradit province.

[4]PTMN f° 154/2 and PMN&TY f° 7/3 concur. AD 1775/76.

[5]Ban Na Pang is approximately 4 km. south of Cæ Hæng.

[6]Sunday 10 March 1776. PTMN f° 154/3 and PMN&TY f° 7/4 concur.

[7]PTMN and PMN&TY refer to this prince only as Cao Paña Witun.

[8]PTMN f° 154/3: Müang Cantabuli Lan Cang; i.e., Vientiane in Laos.

[9]AD 1779/80. PTMN f° 154/4 and PMN&TY f° 7/5 concur.

[10]Siamese; Thonburi.

[11]For this invasion, see David K. Wyatt, "Siam and Laos, 1767-1827," *Journal of Southeast Asian History* 4, 2 (September 1963): 19-21.

[12]PMN&TY f° 8/1 concurs. Wednesday 29 September 1779.

[13]Here, Vietnam clearly is meant.

[14]Cao Nantasen ruled as king of Vientiane under Siamese suzerainty from 1782 to 1792.

[15]PTMN ff° 154/4-155/1 and PMN&TY ff° 7/5-8/2 are the same.

[16]Saturday 1 December 1781. PTMN f° 155/1-2 and PMN&TY f° 8/3-4 state that he died in the *luang pao* year CS 1143 on Saturday, the 1st waning of the 3rd month, and that his funeral was on Saturday the 14th waning of the 3rd month. Has to be Friday 14 December 1781.

[17]Not identified.

the waning seventh month,[1] he moved to Na Tan in Laos.[2] In that same year, /140/ Cao Witun returned from Lampang to Nan, and then moved to Müang Uan,[3] where he stayed for a year.

6.20. In the *pœk set* year, 1140,[4] the governor of Lampang brought his army to Müang Ngua[5] and sent for Cao Witun. He accused Cao Witun of being unfaithful to the / king of the South Country. When Witun came to Ngua, he was arrested with his family and sent to the South Country, where he died.[6]

6.21. Paña Witun, i.e. Cao Na Khwa, was the second brother of Cao Cantapacot. Their mother was a Chiang Mai princess. Cao Cantapacot accompanied his father, / Cao Aliyawong, when his father fled to Lan Cang, and later went to the South Country with him. Cao Witun ruled Nan for five years, then left for the South Country in the [*pœk*] *set* year, CS 1140.[7] He was the fifth ruler in the line, and the fifty-fifth from Cao Khun Fòng.[8]

6.22. During this period the whole of Lan Na Thai was in a state of turmoil. Nan was practically deserted, lacking even rulers. In that very year, /141/ Cao Paña Mano brought his family from Na Tan in Laos and settled down at Müang Ngua for a year.[9]

6.23. In the *ka kai* year, 1141, on the fourth day of the waxing fifth month,[10] the governors of Sawankhalok and Lampang brought an army to Müang Ngua with the intention of / rounding up Nan people and taking them to the South. Paña Mano and the governor of Lampang together resisted the armies and caused them to withdraw. In that same year, Paña / Mano moved his family and labor to Dòi Pu Piang Cæ Hæng and settled down at the foot of the hill on the west side. He cleaned up Wat Cæ Hæng, which by now was overgrown with scrub and vines. He expanded the uposot / by adding a room to it. He tore down the main gate on the western side, in order to rebuild it. Before the gate was finished, the combined armies of the Burmese and the ruler of Müang Yòng[11] captured / Nan, on the eighth day of the waxing sixth month,[12] and took

---

[1]PTMN f° 155/3 and PMN&TY f° 8/5 concur. Sunday 26 April 1778. Two days earlier?

[2]PTMN f° 155/3 gives same name.

[3]Uan is 20 km. south of Pua. All the material in this paragraph is in PMN&TY ff° 8/5-9/1.

[4]AD 1778/79. PTMN f° 155/4 concurs.

[5]The location of this place is problematic. An incident below, in §7.21, suggests a location close to the Cæ Hæng Reliquary, while local people insist that Müang Ngua was in the extreme south of Nan, at modern Na Nòi, south of Wiang Sa.

[6]PTMN f° 156/1 and PMN&TY f° 9/2: he was sent first to Lampang, and then to the South.

[7]AD 1778/79.

[8]This paragraph has no parallel in PTMN or PMN&TY. It may be regarded as a typical example of the type of insertions that *Sænluang* Ratchasomphan made in compiling the Nan Chronicle.

[9]PMN&TY f° 9/3 gives a date for this move: same year; 5th waning of the 4th month.

[10]No date is given in PTMN f° 156. PMN&TY f° 9/4 concurs on date. Wednesday 9 February 1780.

[11]Yòng is often mentioned below. It is located in the extreme northeastern tip of Burma, east of Keng Tung.

[12]PMN&TY f° 10/2-3 concurs on date. Monday 13 March 1780. No date is given in PTMN.

the people of Nan to Chiang Sæn. Paña Mano and his family also were taken, on the sixth day of the waning of the seventh month, in the *kat kai* year, CS 1141.[1]

6.24. In 1142, / a *kot cai* year, on the eleventh day of the waning sixth month,[2] the armies of Paña Caban of Chiang Mai, the governor of Phræ, the governor of Lampang, and the Lao of Luang Prabang marched an army to the mouth of the Kok [River][3] and encamped there.

6.25. The Myowun, Burmese governor of Chiang Sæn, and the army of Lampang-Chiang Mai fought / for a month. The Chiang Sæn forces could not withstand the invaders, and the city fell on the morning of Sunday, the sixth day of the waning seventh month.[4] The people of Chiang Sæn evacuated to Müang Pu Piang. Cao Mano and his family and labor also went with the Chiang Sæn people. They stayed there one rainy season, and then the Burmese drove all the families and labor and all the Chiang Sæn people back to / Chiang Sæn to re-establish the town and villages. Cao Mano also brought his families and labor back to the town of Chiang Sæn with all the Nan people.

6.26. In CS 1144, a *tao yi* year, on the fifth day of the waxing third month,[5] the Burmese issued an order moving Cao Mano and his family and labor of Nan and Thœng, who were in Chiang Sæn, to Thœng, where they stayed for three years. In the *kap si* year, CS 1146, on Thursday, the second day of the waning eighth month,[6] at midnight, /143/ Cao Mano died in Thœng. His funeral ceremony was held on the fourteenth day of the waxing ninth month.[7]

6.27. In that same year, the Myowun of Chiang Sæn sent to Thœng for Cao Attawalapanño, the son of Cao Sutta and nephew of Cao Mano,[8] / and made him governor of Nan. At that time, the Myowun sent Sæn Caipakan to report to the king of Ava, who consented / to the appointment.[9] Cao Attawalapanño accepted the position, but remained at first at Thœng.

---

[1]PMN&TY f° 10/3 concurs on date. Tuesday 25 April 1780. PTMN f° 157/1-2 says they were taken from Ngua on the 3rd waning of the 7th month. Note that the first line of this paragraph gives the year as *ka kai*, while the last line gives it as *kat kai*. The correct year is CS 1141 *kat kai*.

This particular war, including its extension into Nan, is vividly described in the lengthy poem published as *Phama rop Thai* (Chiang Mai, 1989).

[2]Tuesday 20 March 1781. PTMN f° 157/2 and PMN&TY f° 10/4.

[3]Clearly, in the region of Chiang Sæn. The Kok River flows from the region of Fang through Chiang Rai to empty into the Mekong above Chiang Sæn.

[4]14 April 1781, which was a Saturday. PMN&TY f° 10/5 concurs on date. PTMN f° 157/2 says they marched on Chiang Sæn, and that Chiang Sæn fell on Monday, the 9th waning of the 7th month (Tuesday 17 April 1781). The PTMN and PMN&TY also add that in the *luang pao* year CS 1143, Myowun Sitkè (our source writes "Mayuwan Chakhai") was re-established in Chiang Sæn as before; and also adds that the rulers of Chiang Khong and Chiang Rai returned to their cities.

[5]PTMN f° 157/4 gives the year, but not the day and month. Monday 9 December 1782.

[6]PMN&TY f° 11/3-4 concurs on date. Thursday 7 May 1784. PTMN f° 157/4 gives a variant date: Thursday the 10th waning of the 8th month (Friday 15 May 1784).

[7]Wednesday 3 June 1784; if Tuesday then 2 June. PMN&TY f° 11/4 concurs on date. PTMN f° 158/1 says Tuesday the 14th of the 9th month for the funeral, and merit-making on the 2nd waning of the 9th month (Saturday 6 June).

[8]PTMN f° 158/2.

[9]PTMN f° 158/3 gives a slightly different version, saying that the Burmese king approved the appointment and consented to his staying in Thœng.

6.28. In 1145, a *ka mao* year,[1] Nan was completely deserted. / It had no ruler to care for it, and most of the people had evacuated the town, fleeing into the jungle and mountains.

6.29. The senior prince, [i.e. Cao Cantapacot,][2] / son of Cao Aliyawong, was then in the South Country. The king of the South made him governor of Nan with the title of Cao Paña Mongkhonwalayot, on Thursday, the first day of the waxing fifth month in the *ka mao* year, 1145.[3] The new governor went up and stayed at Ta Pa.[4]

6.30. In the *dap sai* year, 1147,[5] the king of Ava / sent a huge army to take Ayudhya[6] by way of Martaban and Tavoy.[7] Another army of ten thousand men, under the Pagan prince was sent to Lan Na Thai by way of Chiang Sæn. / On Saturday, the eleventh day of the waxing fourth month,[8] this army reached Thœng, and after sweeping up the Thœng people, moved on to Nan and Phræ. Chiang Mai and Lampang suffered the same fate. The governors of Nan and Phræ surrendered without fighting. / Thœng also submitted to the Burmese. Chiang Mai and Lampang did not submit, and were besieged. The Burmese royal army that came by way of Martaban and Tavoy failed to take / Ayudhya and had to withdraw to Ava.

6.31. The Burmese army in Lan Na Thai, under the Pagan Prince, failed to take Chiang Mai and Lampang. When the commander learned that the Burmese royal army in the South also had failed to take Ayudhya, he and his northern army withdrew. They swept up and took / with them to Chiang Sæn a large number of Phræ and Nan people.

6.32. In CS 1148, a *lwai sanga* year, on the second day of the waning eighth month,[9] the Pagan Prince took his army out of Chiang Sæn and returned to Ava. In that same year, on the full moon of the fifth month,[10] /145/ the governor of Phræ, with all the cities in the North, including Müang Yòng, rose against the Burmese at Chiang Sæn. The Myowun of Chiang Sæn[11] was defeated and fled to Chiang Rai. The governor of Chiang Rai arrested him and sent him to Lampang. The governor of Lampang sent him to the South Country, where he later died.[12]

6.33. In the same year the ruler of Lampang sent an army to Chiang Sæn and captured the governor of Phræ and sent him to the South Country. During

---

[1]AD 1783/84. PTMN f° 158/4 states this condition rather more fully, saying that the *müang* was deserted, without rulers, the *khunsæn* and *khunmün* and people having fled to the forest.

[2]The MS. says *cao ton mî âyu*—"the prince who had age."

[3]Friday 23 January 1784; if Thursday then 22 January. PTMN f° 159/1 curiously has CS 1146, a *ka mao* year; but 1145 was *ka mao*. The ruler's father here is named Aliyawongsa.

[4]Apparently Tha Pla, the northernmost district town in Uttaradit province. PMN&TY f° 12/1-3 calls him *nai nan* Cantapacot.

[5]AD 1785/86. PTMN f° 159/2 and PMN&TY f° 12/4 concur.

[6]PTMN f° 159/2: Müang Rattanakosin Ayothiya.

[7]PMN&TY f° 12/4-5 says Martaban and Tavoy; but PTMN f° 159/2 only says that the Burmese went by way of Tavoy.

[8]Tuesday 10 January 1786—three days ahead! Saturday 7 January?

[9]PMN&TY f° 13/5 concurs on date. Sunday 14 May 1786. No date in PTMN.

[10]Friday 2 February 1787. PMN&TY f° 13/5. PTMN f° 160/1: in the *müang met* year CS 1149.

[11]PTMN f° 160/2 names him: Phawæ Warawa(?).

[12]PMN&TY f° 14/1-2.

this year, on the sixth day of the waxing second month,[1] the Burmese king sent a large army to Chiang Sæn. / It was based at Ban Dai Ta Pæ.[2] The ruler of Lampang quickly gathered up Chiang Sæn people and took them to Thœng and then fled back to Lampang. The ruler of Müang Yòng took his family across the Khong River and stayed at Müang Pukha.[3] The governor of Nan and all the people of Nan and Thœng / left Thœng and on the thirteenth day of the waxing second month[4] went to Nan, where they arrived on the fourth day of the waxing seventh month.[5] They camped at Ban Tüt along the Nan River west of Pu Piang Cæ Hæng.[6]

6.34. At this time, Cantapacot, i.e., Cao Mongkhonwalayot, / was staying at Ta Pa.[7] Cao Somana, his younger brother, was living at Wiang Pò, that is, Wiang Sa.[8] One day Cao Attawalapanño, son of Cao Mongkhonwalayot, accompanied by his men, decided to visit his uncle, Cao Somana. /146/ At that time, there was a noble who was close to the family of Cao Attawalapanño who said that the visit he intended to make should be stopped, because it was [astrologically] an inauspicious time and because it would cause great trouble. The officials similarly advised him not to go, / but he would not listen. He got into a boat to go to his uncle's home at Wiang Sa.

6.35. When he arrived at his uncle's place, the uncle, Cao Somana, was busy beating iron [at the forge]. When Cao Somana saw his nephew coming, / he said to himself, "He belongs to the North and I belong to the South. If he wanted to capture me, why did he not let me know in advance?" He then told his nephew not to approach him. He warned him twice, and thrice. His nephew shouted that he was just paying a visit, and harbored no bad intentions, / and continued to walk towards his uncle.

6.36. When Cao Somana saw his nephew coming nearer, he grabbed a gun and shot at his nephew. The gun misfired. Cao Somana tried to fire a second and third time, but the gun would not fire. When Cao Attawala realized that his uncle intended to kill him, he picked up a spear, / and Cao Somana started to run away. The nephew gave chase. The uncle ran to the river and then jumped in. He would have drowned had not his servant jumped in to rescue him /147/ and took him to the opposite bank and helped him to escape. The nephew gathered his men and returned home.

---

[1]15 November 1787. PMN&TY f° 14/3 concurs. PTMN f° 160/3 simply says the 2nd month.

[2]PTMN does not have this location.

[3]PMN&TY f° 14/4 concurs on all details. PTMN does not here mention the ruler of Yòng; but see below. The context suggests Muong Luong Phukha, in Laos.

[4]22 November 1787. PTMN f° 160/4 and PMN&TY f° 14/5 say they arrived on the 4th waxing of the 3rd month.

[5]Wednesday 9 April 1788. Did they really take five months to make this trip?

[6]PTMN f° 161/1 inserts something else here: To paraphrase, as for Müang Thœng, there was Cao Poma at the head, Müang Salao had Cao Nai Noi Cai, and the men of Thœng and Salao. These also came to Nan. PMN&TY ff° 15/4-17/1 has something completely different, involving repairs to the Cæ Hæng Reliquary. Ban Tüt has to be Ban Muang Tüt, which is on the city map.

[7]On the Nan River in present-day Uttaradit province. The strange story that follows is not in PTMN.

[8]Wiang Sa, the major district town of the southern part of Nan. This seems to be the definitive point in arguing for the identity of Müang Phò and Wiang Sa.

6.37. In that same year, Cao Attawala took his men and called on his [other] uncle, Cao Mongkhonwalayot, at Ta Pa / and respectfully told him about what Cao Somana had done. Paña Mongkhonwalayot, by then an old man, advised his nephew not to be disrespectful of his uncles. He said, "Please, Nephew, disregard what your uncle has done; first, for the sake of our Nan's future welfare and prosperity. I intend to turn it over to you to rule and care for at the appropriate time. Second, I am getting old and have been ruling for two or three years already, but the domain is still chaotic and unstable." Hearing this advice, Cao Attawala was pleased, and forgave his uncle, Cao Somana. He took leave of Cao Mongkhonworayot, and went to live in Ban Tit Bun Hüang.[1]

6.38. Cao Mongkhonwalayot ruled Nan for four years. In the *lwai sanga* year, CS 1148,[2] he handed over the country /148/ of Nan to his nephew, Cao Attawalapanño. He was the sixth ruler, the fifty-sixth from Cao Khun Fòng.

---

[1]This is clearly an important area of Nan, located on the east side of the Nan River, roughly to the southeast of the center of the modern city; and the name is perpetuated in the name of the temple. See below. The story above (§§6.34-37), which I refer to as the "Mexican stand-off," was translated with the help of Aroonrut Wichienkeeo. The translation remains somewhat free.

[2]AD 1786/87.

CHAPTER SEVEN

THE FIRST "KING" OF NAN, AD 1786-1810

7.1. After having ruled Nan in place of his uncle for one year, / Cao Attawalapanño went with his officials and retainers on the thirteenth day of the waning moon of the ninth month in the *pœk san* year, CS 1150,[1] to pay homage to the king [in Bangkok]. The king was pleased to appoint Cao Attawalapanño / as ruling prince of Nan, and also appointed Cao Samana, his uncle, younger brother of Cao Mongkhonwalayot, as Prince of the Front Palace (*Cao Paña Hò Na*).[2]

7.2. Having accepted appointment as ruler of Nan, Cao Attawalapanño / took leave of the king and returned with his officials and retainers. On the ninth day of the waxing moon of the second month[3] he arrived at Müang Ngua,[4] and remained there for a time. The [lower-ranking] officials welcomed him [to the principality] by meeting him at Müang Ngua with a stately procession, [and escorted him to Nan] / on the sixth day of the waning moon of the second month.[5] When he reached the city he stopped at Tung Tan Cang at its northern corner to cast the Cao Tan Cai image of the Lord Buddha. On the evening of the eighth day of the waxing moon,[6] the monks were invited to perform the ceremonies (*buddhâbhiseka*) appropriate to the casting of a new image. The next morning /149/ he presented food alms to the monks, and then proceeded to Ban Tit Bun Hüang,[7] [where he took up residence] in the *kòng ngai* watch.

7.3. On Tuesday, the fifth day of the third month,[8] he moved to Müang Ngua with his family, elephants, horses, officials, and retainers, after having formally given Ban Tit Bun Hüang / to its officials, headed by Cao Pa Müang

---

[1]PTMN f° 161/2 and PMN&TY f° 17/1 concur. Tuesday 1 July 1788.

[2]PTMN f° 161/2-3 and PMN&TY f° 17/2 do not mention the appointment of Samana/Sumana.

[3]PTMN f° 161/3 and PMN&TY f° 17/3 concur. 7 November 1788,

[4]Just where is Müang Ngua? I now believe that my "Assault by Ghosts" article is wrong; that Ngua was in the southern part of Nan, perhaps as far south as the modern Na Nòi district, where Somchet Vimolkasem would put it. I am persuaded to this change of mind by internal evidence within the chronicle. In particular, it would not take four days for Cao Attawala to travel from Ngua to Ban Tit Bun Hüang if Ngua were near Nan itself (§7.4). Ngua cannot be at Wiang Sa because §7.20 says that the ruler traveled from Ngua to Wiang Sa.

[5]PTMN f° 161/3 concurs. 19 November 1788.

[6]PTMN f° 161/4 concurs. 21 November 1788.

[7]PTMN f° 162/1: Ban Thit S(r)i Bun Hüang.

[8]PTMN f° 162/1 and PMN&TY f° 17/3 concur. Wednesday 3 December 1788.

Kæo, Nai Cai Kæo, and Nai Duang Tip. These officials, with their labor force, were to maintain the old *wiang* as the chief northern province of Nan.[1]

7.4. In the *kat lao* year, CS 1151, on the fifth day of the waxing moon of the second month,[2] / Cao Attawala left Müang Ngua and returned to Ban Tit Bun Hüang, where he arrived on the ninth day of the waxing moon.[3]

7.5. In the preceding period, the country of Nan had been deserted. Bandits and thieves had destroyed the cetiya of Wat Cæ Hæng, / even having taken the golden umbrella (*chatra*) from the spire of the cetiya. When Cao Attawala saw the shameful sight he felt it was a great dishonor to the religion.[4]

7.6. In that same *kat lao* year, 1151, on the fourteenth day of the waxing moon of the second month,[5] Cao Attawala brought the officials and / people to clean the temple grounds. Two days later, in the *kòng ngai* watch, they began [re]constructing the main gate, which was finished three days later. On the eleventh waning,[6] they erected scaffolding on the cetiya, /150/ finishing it in the *kòng læng* watch of the same day. He had the iron core of the top of the cetiya brought down and repaired, and made it one cubit longer.[7] After the iron rod had been put back atop the cetiya, on Tuesday the seventh day of the third month[8] he assembled the smiths / and craftsmen and told them to make the new umbrella with nine tiers: the old one had only seven tiers. He then had a very beautiful swan (*hamsa*) made, which bore the nine-tiered umbrella in its beak. When all was finished, on the twelfth waxing of the third month,[9] he invited altogether / 73 monks and 114 novices to receive food offerings presented by the officials and people, and to chant the scriptures, on Wednesday, the full-moon day of the third month.[10] At noon, the swan with the nine-tiered umbrella in its beak was hoisted to the top of the cetiya. / That evening the [renovated] reliquary was rededicated (*buddhâbhiseka*). The next morning the food offerings were repeated.

7.7. On that day, when the parasol was being installed atop the cetiya, / seven miracles were manifested: four vultures flew over the cetiya; the sound of the flight of a peacock was heard /151/ but no peacock was seen; a snake followed Cao Attawala into the enclosure of the cetiya and then disappeared; when the swan was raised, all clouds disappeared and the sky was pure and crystal-clear; a star was shining at noon and everyone saw it; heavy rain fell, extremely hard and dense, but no one could touch it or / get wet from it; and it rained for

---

[1]PTMN f° 162/3: *pen huamüang fai nüa tam kala kon.* This reference reinforces the idea that Ngua is to the south.

[2]PTMN f° 162/3 concurs. Friday 23 October 1789.

[3]PTMN f° 162/3 concurs on date (second month). 27 October 1789.

[4]This paragraph is in PTMN f° 162/3-4, in much the same words.

[5]PTMN f° 163/1 and PMN&TY f° 17/5 concur. Monday 1 November 1789.

[6]PTMN f° 163/2 concurs. Friday 13 November 1789.

[7]About the measurements: a cubit is an ancient linear unit based on the length of the forearm varying in extent, but usually from 17 to 21 inches; the *khüp* is the distance from the tip of the middle finger to the thumb when the hand is spread flat, roughly one-fourth of a meter; and the *niu* is a Thai inch, a finger joint. McFarland, pp. 792, 203, 460.

[8]PTMN f° 163/3 and PMN&TY f° 18/2-3 concur. Tuesday 24 November 1789.

[9]PTMN f° 164/1 concurs on date; also on numbers of monks and novices. Sunday 29 November 1789.

[10]PTMN f° 164/1 and PMN&TY f° 18/4 concur. Wednesday 2 December 1789.

two days.[1] On witnessing these marvels, never before seen, Cao Attawalapanño was in a state of indescribable ecstasy and supreme happiness. / He invited the abbot (*kuba*) of Wat Lòng La,[2] whose name was Aliyawangso, to become abbot of Wat Cæ Hæng.[3]

7.8. Now we will tell about the governor of Müang Yòng.[4] In CS 1149, /152/ without thinking about his own country, he made a mistake by collaborating with the governor of Phræ, who was revolting against the [Burmese] governor (*myowun*) of Chiang Sæn. In that year, on the sixth of the second month,[5] the Burmese army came to Ban Kum in Chiang Rai by way of Ban Dai Ta Pæ. At that time, the governors of Chiang / Khong, Chiang Rai, and Nan evacuated their families and retainers to take refuge with the South. The governor of Yòng, however, did not come down, but took his family and retainers across the Khong River to Müang Luang Pukha.

7.9. When the Burmese army arrived in Chiang / Sæn, the Cao Na Khwa of Chiang Sæn brought his family and retainers back to Chiang Sæn with the Burmese. The Burmese, however, waited and did not go to fight the rebels, the men of the governor of Yòng, for the Burmese realized that the governor of Yòng / was a subject of the king of the South, but his son was still at the court of the Burmese king. The governor of Yòng, however, was determined to revolt against the Burmese. / The Burmese commanders awaited events [at Chiang Sæn], but the governor of Yòng would not come down and fight.

7.10. Finally, in the *kot set* year, CS 1152,[6] the Burmese marched against the army of the governor of Yòng. Paña Yòng's army was defeated, and he fled by way of Laos [Luang Prabang], heading for Müang /153/ Thæng.[7] The Burmese followed the defeated army and captured Paña Yòng. They were taking him to Ava, but he died along the way. The rest of the Yòng forces, including Paña Si, Raja Prap Lok, and / Thao Han, escaped to Nan. Altogether, there were 585 families who arrived at Bò Mang[8] in that year, on the third waning of the eleventh month.[9] All ended up in Nan [town].

7.11. In the *luang kai* year, CS 1153, on the sixth day of the seventh month,[10] the / governor of Chiang Khong moved his family and all his

---

[1]PMN&TY f° 18/5, and PTMN f° 164/3-165/2 say only six miracles and list six, though the head of this paragraph says seven. PTMN says the four vultures were incarnations of the four guardian spirits of the world.

[2]PTMN f° 165/2: Wat Lòng Ha. Not identified.

[3]PTMN f° 165/3 adds that the new abbot repaired the large *vihara*, which had fallen down.

[4]This same story appears in PMN&TY f° 20/2 ff.

[5]PMN&TY f° 20/3 concurs. Thursday 15 November 1787.

[6]PTMN f° 165/4 concurs. AD 1790.

[7]MS: Müang Thæng Nakòn Lok. PTMN f° 165/4 states that the ruler of Yòng fled by way of Müang Luang [Prabang?], saying that he was going to Müang Thæng Kolalok, i.e., Dien Bien Phu.

[8]PTMN f° 166/1-2 writes Bò M(l)ang, one of the salt wells; = Bò Klüa Tai village today. See also Walailak Songsiri, "Chum chon boran thi Ban Bò Luang," *Muang Boran* 17, 3 (July-Sept. 1991): 55-61; and Walailak Songsiri, "Bò klüa müang Nan thi Ban Bò Luang," *Muang Boran* 18, 1 (Jan.-Mar. 1992): 41-49.

[9]PTMN f° 166/2 and PMN&TY f° 21/4 concur. Saturday 28 August 1790.

[10]This is a rare problem date in this section. The text says 1151, which was a *kat lao* year. 1153 was the nearest *luang kai* year. PTMN f° 166/2 and PMN&TY f° 21/4 both have the *luang kai*

manpower from Müang Kæn Tao to Müang Nan by way of the southern frontiers. These consisted of 505 families.[1]

7.12. In the *tao cai* year, / CS 1154, around noon on Sunday, the eighth day of the waning moon of the eighth month,[2] Cao Attawalapanño[3] and his officials[4] and elders began the construction of the cetiya at Wat Na Lap[5] in Müang Ngua.[6] / This work was new construction, not just the restoration of an old cetiya, and was undertaken in order to fulfill a vow he had made. It was completed on Wednesday the full-moon day of the third month,[7] and was duly dedicated with a ceremony.

7.13. In the same year, Cao Mongkhonwalayot /154/ and the uparaja of the Front Palace, with their families, officials, and labor, two hundred in all, moved back to the old city, Ban Tit Bun Hüang, on Sunday, the eighth day of the sixth month.[8] As soon as they arrived, Cao Attawalapanño, accompanied by the princely family and their officials and people, presided over by the abbot of Wat Si / Bun Hüang, began the construction of a *vihara*. At that time, the ruler and the abbot (*kuba*) of Wat Luang Cæ Hæng discovered that the Buddha image of Wat Cæ / Hæng was damaged. The ruler thus had all the officials and people, headed by the abbot of Wat Cæ Hæng, repair and refinish the image. /

7.14. In the *ka pao* year, CS 1155, on Thursday, the eleventh day of the second ninth month, a *kap yi* day,[9] the *camlòng* wood finial which served as a reminder of the presence of a hair relic of the Lord Buddha in the Pu Piang Cæ Hæng Reliquary, which had been enshrined there by Pa Maha Ananda Thera, broke off at the top and fell down against the lower portion of the cetiya, breaking off some of the decorative figures on the octagonal levels, and then fell further down, doing more damage /155/ on the rectangular levels and to the base, down to the ground. Furthermore, the small *vihara* of the Cao Tan Cai image was also struck and damaged. ...[10]

---

year CS 1153, with the same day and month. This has to be the seventh month at the *end* of the year, rather than the seventh month, with which the year begins. Thursday 29 March 1792.

[1]Number not given in PTMN.

[2]PTMN f° 166/3 and PMN&TY f° 22/1 concur. Sunday 14 May 1792.

[3]PTMN usually writes Cao Attawalalatcapanño.

[4]PTMN f° 166/3 adds: and all the *yuwarat*—apparently the royal children.

[5]PTMN f° 166/4 and PMN&TY f° 22/1 spell this with an L, while MS1 spells it with an R.

[6]PMN&TY f° 22/1-3 details the relics deposited in the cetiya.

[7]PTMN f° 166/4 concurs. The date converts to Thursday 30 November 1792. If we take the weekday as determining, the date was 29 November 1792. Most of the dates in 1793 and 1794 are off by one day, suggesting perhaps that local calendrists neglected making this year a Type B year (with 30 days in the 7th month). Such a possibility is hardly far-fetched: the *Chotmaihet hon* (Prachum phongsawadan, pt. 8; Kaona edition, v. 4, pp. 91, 92, and 98) gives three instances when the court astrologers handled Type B years incorrectly over a fourteen-year period!

[8]PTMN f° 163/3 concurs. Monday 19 February 1793; or Sunday 18 February.

[9]Friday 19 July 1793; or Thursday 18 July. PTMN f° 167/3 and PMN&TY f° 22/4 both very interestingly agree on Thursday, the 11th day of the *second* tenth month, a Thai *kap yi* day (11 July 1793; thanks to J. C. Eade). There is one published inscription from Nan from this year (23 June 1793): MNBPS, pp. 262-264. It is on the base of a Buddha image at Wat Si Bun Hüang, and includes the ruler's name as Cao Attawalawongsa. It specifies the first of two months named Asadha.

[10]I have been forced to paraphrase here, as the text is exceedingly obscure.

7.15. In that same year, on Saturday, the fourteenth day of the second month, in the second lunar mansion,[1] in the *kòng ngai* watch, Cao Attawalapanño accompanied his officials and people from Müang Ngua to Ban Pò at the mouth of the Sa River / and cleaned up the site for a new city. On Saturday, the fourth day of the fourth month, in the twentieth lunar mansion, in the *tut cao* watch,[2] the ruler erected a wooden palisade for the new town at Wiang Pò,[3] at the mouth of the Sa. In the *kap yi* year, CS 1156, on Wednesday, the second day of the eighth month, fourth lunar mansion,[4] at noon, he brought / his family and all his officials and labor to the mouth of the Sa.

7.16. Once established at Wiang Pò there, he started to build a dam across the Sa River, as the Sa dam and system of paddy fields there had been abandoned when the Lao had swept up / the Nan people there 213 years earlier.[5] He therefore decided to repair the dam and restore the rice plain as before.

7.17. Also in that year he led an army, with the governor of Phræ, to invade Mæ Huak in Chiang Sæn.[6] On the second day of the third month /156/ in that year,[7] Cao Attawalapanño accompanied his officials and people from Wiang Pò and settled down at Pu Piang Cæ Hæng. Together with the Sangha, headed by the abbot of Wat Cæ Hæng, he restored the Pa Maha Jina cetiya, which had been damaged earlier. These meritorious works lasted for six days, from the fifth day of the third month, until completion.[8]

7.18. The *vihara* of the Tan Cai image, which was damaged, he led the officials / and people to repair completely.[9] On Thursday, the full-moon day of the sixth month,[10] the ruler organized the consecration of the reliquary, and made merit on that day. On the eighth day of the waning moon of the seventh month,[11] / he led his officials and people from Ngua to consecrate Wat Si Bun Hüang.

7.19. On the full-moon day of the eighth month, in the new year, 1157, a *ka / mao* year,[12] he assisted in the dedication of the main Buddha image at Wat Cæ Hæng.

---

[1]PTMN f° 168/3 concurs on date and lunar mansion. Sunday 17 November 1793; or Saturday 16 November.

[2]PTMN f° 168/4 concurs on date and lunar mansion. Sunday 5 January 1794; or Saturday 4 January.

[3]PTMN f° 168/4 says Ban Phò, but later has Wiang Phò. There can be no doubt that Ban Phò/Wiang Phò has to be associated with Wiang Sa, which is at the mouth of the Sa River.

[4]PTMN f° 169/1 concurs. Thursday 1 May 1794; or Wednesday 30 April. The fourth lunar mansion (*rœk*) was on the Thursday.

[5]This reference is problematic. CS 973 seems to have been the last previous Lao attack, but the reference here would suggest an attack in CS 944 (AD 1582).

[6]Not mentioned in PTMN. Place-name read with the assistance of Harald Hundius. Is the valley of the Mæ Luak (river) suggested?

[7]PTMN f° 169/2-3 concurs. Monday 24 November 1794.

[8]PTMN f° 169/4 concurs. 27 November-1 December 1794.

[9]The Tan Cai image apparently is located at Wat Cæ Hæng.

[10]PTMN f° 170/1-2 concurs. Friday 5 March 1795.

[11]PTMN has the information, but not the date. Sunday 12 April 1795, which was Songkan (New Year's).

[12]PTMN f° 170/3 is somewhat at variance with our text here. Sunday 3 May 1795. There is an inscription on a manuscript chest dated Tuesday, the full-moon day of the 1st month of CS

7.20. On the second day of the [waning] eighth month, with his subjects, nobles, and officials he began the construction of a library for the sacred writings /157/ at Wat K[l]ang Wiang in Müang Sa.[1] There, in a cetiya 9 fathoms 1 elbow high[2] he enshrined twenty images of arahats and a crystal image of the Lord Buddha. Then, on Tuesday, the third day of the waxing moon of the fifth month, in the *kòng læng* watch,[3] the ruler left Ngua and settled / in Wiang Sa, leaving Ngua in the hands of Cao Mongkhonwalayot and Nai Aliya.

7.21. On reaching the ninth month in that year 1157,[4] there was a strange occurrence at Müang Ngua. It was a warning to the people from the *devas*. It took the form of ghosts going around the city assaulting monks and people. After these beatings they dropped written messages, saying that they had come from the *deva* guardians of the cetiya of the Cæ Hæng Reliquary, and that the cetiya containing the holy relics was now in a very bad state of disrepair and that no attempt had been made to restore it to its original condition. The holy shrine had to be restored to its beauty as when it was first built, and the *devas* would continue annoying and assaulting until it was rebuilt and made as beautiful as when it was first built. "When the shrine has been repaired and made beautiful, we will cease annoying and tormenting you," the messages said.

7.22. Cao Mongkhonwalayot then went to Cao Attawalapanño, the ruler, and told him about the occurrences in Müang Ngua and the warning of the *deva* guardians of Wat Cæ Hæng. Cao Attawala appointed his uncle Cao Mongkhonwalayot, Nai Aliya, and several monks to supervise the work of reconstruction. Thereupon, in the second month, Cao Paña Mongkhonwalayot, the uncle, accompanied by the princes and their men, and by the leading monks of Müang Ngua, began the construction and restoration of the Holy Reliquary of Pu Piang Cæ Hæng. The work took five months to complete. On Tuesday, the eighth day of the sixth month,[5] Cao Attawalapanño performed the ceremony of placing the finial atop the cetiya. When the restoration was completed there was a celebration. The ghosts that had been tormenting the monks and the public disappeared.

7.23. In the *muang sai* year, CS 1159, Cao Attawalapanño took his nobles and officials and started to build the *vihara* of Wat Bun Yün at Wiang Sa on Saturday, the fifth day of the ninth month, a *kot sanga* day, in the *tut mai* watch.[6] In

---

1157 (Tuesday 27 October 1795; the month being given in Keng Tung style) from Wat Bun Yün in Wiang Sa. MNBPS, pp. 265-268. The manuscript chest, which is unusually beautiful, is pictured in color on page [13].

[1]This has to be Wat Bun Yün in Wiang Sa. For a fine description of this temple, see *Sathapattayakam Phayao læ Nan* (Chiang Mai, 1989), pp. 96-107, 190-204. It is tempting to read the inscription noted in the preceding footnote as referring to this library. Wat Bun Yün is mentioned below.

[2]55 feet, or 19 meters.

[3]PTMN f° 170/4-171/1 concurs. Tuesday 12 January 1796.

[4]19 May-16 June 1795. PTMN f° 171/1 gives the whole story in wording very close to that employed here. This curious episode is the subject of David K. Wyatt, "Assault by Ghosts: Politics and Religion in Nan in the 18th Century," *Crossroads* 4, 2 (1989): 63-70.

[5]PTMN f° 172/2-3 concurs. Monday 15 February 1796; or 16 February 1796.

[6]PTMN ff° 172/4-173/1, where this is called Wat Luang Bun Yün, and the date is given simply as CS 1160, a *pœk sanga* year. This date has to be corrupt. The only *kot sanga* day that fell on a Saturday that year was in the 8th month (Northern), 21 April 1798.

CS 1160 the work continued. He appointed Mün Sap as chief carpenter of the work.[1]

7.24. In the *kat met* year, CS 1161, on the second day of the waning moon of the sixth month,[2] the ruler /159/ conscripted 4,963 people and 434 of the princes and officials, altogether 5,397 people, to repair the Samun irrigation dam, beginning on the fifth day of the waning moon of the sixth month.[3] After fixing the dam, 2,481 irrigation ditches were laid out. This dam had been neglected for 219 years,[4] ever since the Lao had swept up the Nan population. The work took fifteen days. / Ever since, the irrigation system has worked to make the rice plain productive, to the present day.[5]

7.25. On Tuesday, the second day of the second month in the *kot san* year, CS 1162,[6] in the *tut cao* watch, Cao Attawalapanño had the people clean up the old city of Nan. On Wednesday, the seventh day of the fifth month, a *kap yi* day, at noon, in the 22nd lunar mansion, / called Samana,[7] he had a standing image of the Buddha cast at Wat Luang Bun Yün. On Wednesday, the fifth day of the seventh month, a *tao cai* day, in the 24th lunar mansion, called Mahadhana,[8] it was completed, and he had it gilded with 4950 pieces of gold leaf.

7.26. In the *lüang mao* year, CS 1163,[9] Cao Attawalapanño visited the king [in Bangkok] to ask his permission to move the seat of the government back to the old city, and the king acceded to his request.

7.27. In the same year, on the tenth day of the second month,[10] in the *müt tük* watch, /160/ there was a great earthquake. The crystal ball atop the cetiya of Cæ Hæng came loose and fell down. The tips of the cetiya of the Sutep reliquary in Chiang Mai, the great reliquary of Lamphun, the reliquary of Lampang, and the reliquary of Wat Cò Hæ in Phræ also were broken, while the roof of the great *vihara* of / Phayao in which the Pa Cao Ton Luang image is enshrined collapsed.[11] On the fourteenth waning there was another earthquake.[12]

---

[1]PTMN f° 173/1 has Mün S(r)i Sap Cang as the chief carpenter, and Sæn Cittapañña as another head craftsman.

[2]PTMN f° 173/1 concurs on the date, as well as on the numerals in the sentence following. Friday 14 March 1800.

[3]PTMN f° 173/2 gives a somewhat fuller date: Tuesday, the fifth day of the waning moon of the sixth month. 17 March 1800.

[4]Though the rest of this episode is in PTMN, this particular backward reference is not. It is at variance with the reference above (§7.16) to an attack 213 years before CS 1156, i.e., in CS 944: the reference here calls for an attack 219 years before CS 1161, i.e. in CS 943 (counting current, not elapsed, years).

[5]The dam is still functioning, now under the auspices of the Royal Irrigation Department.

[6]PTMN f° 173/4 concurs. Sunday 19 October 1800.

[7]The reference to further work at Wat Bun Yün does not occur in PTMN. Tuesday 21 January 1801 was a *kap yi* day. That day was in the 27th lunar mansion, however.

[8]Thursday 19 March 1801; or 18 March 1801.

[9]PTMN f° 174/1 gives the year as *luang lao*: AD 1801/02.

[10]PTMN f° 174/1 concurs. Sunday 15 November 1801.

[11]On this image, see Phra Ratchawisutthisophon et al., *Müang Phayao* (Bangkok, 1984), pp. 214-32. The front cover of this book has a good photograph of the image, which is at Wat Sikhomkham. PTMN f° 174/3 mentions neither the Pa Cao Ton Luang nor Phayao; instead, it says that the Pa Wihan Luang Pa Cao Tong Iang was broken. Unidentified?

[12]PTMN f° 174/3 concurs on date. Friday 4 December 1801. This pair of earthquakes is noted in the Bangkok Astrologer's Diaries, on 3 14/ 8 1161 and 5 10/ 12 CS 1161 (Wednesday 24

7.28. Cao Attawala came from Wiang Sa to Wat Cæ Hæng[1] and had the Sangha put the crystal ball back atop the cetiya, / and repaired the damage caused by the earthquake. He then returned to Wiang Sa and stayed at Dòn Mak Ben while he had workmen clean the old city inside and out. On Thursday, the fourth day of the fourth month, in the eighth lunar mansion,[2] at noon, he began the construction of a city gate and wall. / When the work was finished, he returned to Wiang Sa. There, he fetched his family and, on Monday, the fifth day of the sixth month,[3] he went first to Dòn Cai. On a propitious day—Tuesday the thirteenth day of the sixth month, lunar mansion 20,[4] in the *tut cai* watch—he moved [back] into the old city of Nan./

7.29. On the thirteenth day of the fifth month in the *tao set* year, CS 1164,[5] Cao Attawalapanño, with a force of 3,000 men, invaded Chiang Sæn. His army combined forces with the armies of the Phraya Yommarat of the South,[6] with the kings of Vientiane and Chiang Mai, and the leaders of all the cities of the South. /161/ Altogether the forces numbered 20,000 men. They besieged Chiang Sæn, but failed to take it, and the ruler returned on the fourteenth day of the eighth month.[7]

7.30. In CS 1166, a *kap cai* year, on the thirteenth day of the eighth month,[8] Cao Attawala again joined in an expedition to take Chiang Sæn that totalled 3,000 men, including contingents of one thousand men each from Chiang Mai, Nan, and Lampang. / On Tuesday, the fifth day of the first ninth month,[9] in the *su cæng* watch, his army entered Chiang Sæn by the Din Khò Gate and took the town.[10] The Burmese governor (*myowun*) was / shot and killed in the battle. The vice-governor (*cao na khwa*) fled to Còm Fao Còm Sæo, but he was followed and captured, together with his two wives and three children. A large number of prisoners of war was taken. They were taken to / Nan and Chiang Mai. The vice-governor was taken to the South to be brought before the king, and died there. The king was highly pleased, and made Cao / Attawalapanño ruling

---

June and Sunday 15 November 1801): see *Prachum Phongsawadan*, pt. 8; Kaona ed. vol. 4, p. 98. The astrologers' diaries mention no earthquakes in CS 1162 and 1163. The *Cotmaihet hon chabap Phraya Pramunthanarak* (Bangkok, 1921), p. 25, mentions only one earthquake in CS 1162, on Friday, 1st waning of the 9th month (Friday 8 August 1800).

[1]In the third month, according to PTMN f° 174/3. December 1801.

[2]PTMN f° 174/4 concurs. Thursday 7 January 1802. That day was in the 24th lunar mansion, however.

[3]PTMN f° 175/1 concurs. Monday 8 March 1802.

[4]PTMN f° 175/1 says the *fifth* day of the sixth month, which cannot be right. Tuesday 16 March 1802.

[5]PTMN f° 175/1-2 concurs. Friday 4 February 1803.

[6]The Phraya Yommarat (Bunma Bunnag) was head of the Ministry of the Capital. On this campaign, see Caophraya Thiphakòrawong, *The Dynastic Chronicles, Bangkok Era, The First Reign*, tr. Thadeus and Chadin Flood (Tokyo, 1978), I, 247-54; and Klaus Wenk, *The Restoration of Thailand Under Rama I 1782-1809* (Tucson, 1968), pp. 85-94.

[7]PTMN f° 173/3 concurs. Wednesday 4 May 1803.

[8]PTMN f° 175/3 concurs. Sunday 22 April 1804.

[9]Very interestingly, PTMN f° 175/4 gives Tuesday, the 5th day of the waxing moon of the *first tenth* month. Tuesday 12 June 1804.

[10]The Din Khò Gate was on the southern side of the city of Chiang Sæn. There is a map of the old city in Somcit Rüangkhana, *Namchom borannawatthusathan nai amphœ Chiang Sæn cangwat Chiang Rai* (Bangkok, 1970).

prince (*cao fa*) of Nan.[1] The king loved him as his own son. The king then bestowed many presents upon the prince: a bejeweled ring, /162/ two gold tobacco boxes, two gold betel cups, a gold flat betel receptacle, a gold-handled betel knife, a gold goblet, a gold cuspidor, two silver offering trays, and many pieces of good cloth and many other things. Having received so many marks of favor from the king, / the prince then took leave of the king and returned.[2]

7.31. In that same year, on Tuesday, the fourteenth day of the fourth month,[3] Cao Attawala called up his soldiers, and on the fourth waning of the fourth month[4] led them up to the Sipsong Panna and Chiang Hung, intending to conquer the area. However, Chiang Khæng and Chiang Hung and the Sipsong Panna did not resist the Nan army, but made their submission and asked to be vassal provinces of the king of Bangkok. / Cao Attawala took Cao Nam Wong, the uncle of the ruler of Chiang Hung, and nobles of the Sipsong Panna with the governor of Chiang Khæng as leader, and the son(s) of the ruler of Pukha, together with tribute / to be presented to the king in Bangkok.[5] The king again was highly pleased with Cao Attawala and gave him many costly presents. He also gave presents /163/ to the princes and governors of his newly acquired Northern territories, including Chiang Hung. He gave to the ruling prince of Chiang Hung two male and two female elephants, 6 iron alms-bowls, 12 bundles of palm leaves [for inscribing scriptures], 6 red *saklat* cloths, 3 pieces of flowered white cloth, 6 pieces of cloth for monks' robes, 1 red woven cloth, 1 *yok nam nam kha* cloth, 1 imported *yok* cloth, 1 *kan yæng* cloth, 1 Lampang cloth, 1 green *kan yæng* cloth, 1 [Chinese-style] cloth, 20,000 pieces of mirror glass [for architectural decoration], and 12,000 pieces of gold leaf.

7.32. After having received these presents, Cao Attawala and the Northern princes took leave of the king and returned [to Nan]. Cao Attawala / then appointed the Uparaja, his own uncle, and a suite of 200 officials and men to accompany the Northern princes to Chiang Hung.

7.33. In 1167, a *dap pao* year, on the full moon day of the sixth month,[6] Cao Attawala left his capital and went / to stay on the Cang Yi plain at the foot of Pu Piang Cæ Hæng mountain. He noticed the rundown condition of the walls surrounding the cetiya of Wat Cæ Hæng. He had the south wall removed and built it anew 4 fathoms further out. He also had the main gate on the east and the west and south gates rebuilt, and expanded two of them. He repaired the

---

[1]PTMN f° 176/2-3 says that he was named *cao fa luang müang Nan*, while our 1894 text says simply *cao fa Nan*.

[2]The favor shown to Nan deserves emphasis. Note that a much larger attack the previous year had failed, and that the Burmese ceased to be a real military threat to Siam after this event. No wonder, then, that Nan was honored; and even as late as the 1920s, the ruler of Nan was a king, a *phracao*, while the ruler of Chiang Mai was only a *caoluang* (Reginald le May, *An Asian Arcady: The Land and Peoples of Northern Siam* [Cambridge, 1926], p. 171).

[3]PTMN f° 176/4 says the 15th, not the 14th. Wednesday 13 February 1805 was the 15th.

[4]PTMN f° 177/1 adds that it was a Saturday. Monday 18 February 1805.

[5]Chiang Khæng is difficult to locate. It clearly was somewhere in the wide area to the east of Keng Tung in Burma, and my guess is that it was on what is now the Lao side of the Mekong River. Very late in the nineteenth century, the ruler of Chiang Khæng moved his domain near Muong Sing, in what is now Laos.

[6]PTMN f° 178/3 concurs. Tuesday 4 March 1806.

golden petals on the north side of the cetiya, and repaired the seven-tiered umbrella.[1] He added *devaputta* images on each of the four corners.

7.34. A year later, in the *lwai yi* year, CS 1168, on Tuesday, the full-moon day of the fourth month, a *pœk cai* day, at noon,[2] he commanded 500[3] workmen to /164/ build two large naga balustrades, 68 fathoms long and 4 elbows high along the body, and with heads 10 elbows high, to line the two sides of the approach worshippers used in coming to reverence the great reliquary.[4] He also had a gallery built surrounding the cetiya, and at each corner of the enclosure erected images of a guardian deity and two subordinate deities. These works were inaugurated on the full-moon day of the sixth month.[5]

7.35. In the *müang mao* year, CS 1169, on Tuesday, the first day of the eleventh month, a Thai *luang pao* day, in the *kòng ngai* watch,[6] the cetiya to the north of the Dibbacetiya of Wat Cang Kham tumbled down. On Wednesday, the sixth day of the waning moon of the fifth month,[7] His Majesty [Attawala] again constructed the Nang Yong pavilion with three rooms. At noon on Wednesday, the twelfth of the waning moon of the sixth month,[8] / he led the faithful, from the inside and outside, to rebuild the Dibbacetiya, in which he enshrined sixteen relics. He raised it seven fathoms, and put five-tiered parasols at the four corners, each of which sheltered a Buddha image.

7.36. In the / *pœk si* year, CS 1170, on the fifth day of the twelfth month,[9] Cao Attawala left for an audience with the king in the South. When he was at the Fish Landing at Ban Fæk,[10] he saw two novices named Aliya and Panña going into the river in the morning to bathe. /165/ The two novices saw a large Chinese jar floating and turning in a whirlpool in front of a cave. The two novices brought the jar ashore and opened it. In it were found 100 hair relics, 4 pearls, 260 relics of the arahats; 60 gold votive tablets, 204 silver votive tablets, and 4 crystal images of the Lord Buddha; / a golden tree, a silver tree, a golden and a silver goblet, a golden and a silver cup, a golden pillow, 60 gold and silver coins, a golden mat, a silver mat, and many jewels and gold ornaments.[11] / Cao Attawala had a silver repository made for these objects, and a golden and a silver tree made as offerings to the holy relics. Then he invited monks to chant the scriptures and perform a ceremony in honor of the relics. Then he had these objects brought along to the king of the South.

7.37. When the king learned that the prince had obtained the hair relics, he was overjoyed and delighted. He had a procession and musicians to

---

[1] An earlier reference says a 9-tiered umbrella was added: p. 94 above (§7.6).

[2] PTMN f° 179/2 concurs. Friday 23 January 1807 was the *pœk cai* day in the stated month.

[3] PTMN f° 179/2 says 400 workmen. Otherwise its figures agree with those given here.

[4] The modern (1992) balustrade is 100 meters long (50 fathoms). The description of the nagas at the end sounds about right.

[5] PTMN f° 179/4 concurs. Monday 23 March 1807.

[6] PTMN ff° 179/4-180/1 concurs. Tuesday 4 August 1808, which was a *lüang pao* day.

[7] PTMN f° 180/1 gives 3rd waning, not sixth.

[8] PTMN f° 180/2 concurs on the date, but does not give the month. Wednesday 24 March 1808.

[9] PTMN f° 180/3 concurs. Friday 27 August 1808.

[10] Müang (or Ban) Fæk appears on the McCMap, near the present border between Uttaradit and Nan provinces, just above Carim on the Nan River, on the west bank.

[11] PTMN f° 181/1 ff. has the same story, with the same figures mentioned.

accompany the holy objects on golden vessels to the palace, and had a ceremony of celebration performed when they entered the palace. /166/ With candles the king invited the hair relics into the temple in Bangkok. He expressed even greater pleasure with the prince than before, and in gratitude bestowed upon him many valuable presents. The prince conferred with the king, / then took his leave, and His Majesty returned to Nan on the eleventh day of the fifth month.[1]

7.38. Upon his arrival back in Nan, he invited the royal family, the *khun sæn* and *khun mün*, and all the people of Nan, within and without the city, everywhere in Nan,[2] to build stalls and decorate them in the plaza of the city. In the stalls were to be placed articles to be given to the monks as gifts. [For three days,] from the twelfth day of the sixth month,[3] at the ruler's command there were plays, singing and music, and other entertainments. On the full-moon day[4] the gifts were taken to Wat Cæ Hæng, where 463 monks and 863 novices from 139 temples[5] were invited to receive them. Altogether there were 1,326 monks and novices, and each was presented requisites. After this, many rockets were fired and at night there were fireworks. The celebration continued for three days.[6]

7.39. In the *kot sanga* year, CS 1172, on the tenth day of the twelfth month,[7] Somdet Cao Fa Attawalapanño went to Bangkok for the funeral ceremonies for / the late king.[8] Before the ceremonies, on the fourth day of the waning moon of the second month,[9] near dawn, he suddenly became ill and died there.

7.40. His Majesty the king [Attawalapanño], when the king of Ava had consented / to his appointment as governor of Nan, stayed first at Thœng for three years. Then, in the *lwai sanga* year, ... he moved from Thœng to Nan, ... and first stayed at Ban Tit Bun Hüang. Then he went to see Cao Mongkhonwalayot at Ta Pa, to ask him about bringing Nan under the king of Siam. His uncle was pleased with this idea of his nephew, and relinquished the administration to Cao Attawalapanño, who then returned to Ban Tit Bun Hüang for a year. On the thirteenth day of the waning moon of the ninth month in the *pœk san* year, CS 1150,[10] he had gone to the South for an audience with the king. The king was pleased with Cao Attawala's request to put Nan under the

---

[1]PTMN f° 183/2 says the fourth month, not the fifth. Friday 28 January 1809. The only Bangkok reference I can find to this event says that "relics came from Nan" on Sunday 3 December 1837; but the source is not always reliable (*Cotmaihet hon Phraya Pramunthanarak*, Bangkok, 1921, p. 52). There is nothing in the First Reign chronicle concerning the relics.

[2]Interestingly, the word *cangwat* is used here, though not in PTMN f° 182/3. The word is used frequently in the addendum.

[3]Sunday 27 February 1809.

[4]Wednesday 1 March 1809.

[5]PTMN f° 182/4 says 169 temples. Otherwise its numbers all agree with those given here.

[6]PTMN ends here, at f° 183/2. The notes that follow from the PTMN are all from the early portion of the text.

[7]PTMN f° 1/1 concurs. Saturday 8 September 1810.

[8]The cremation of King Rama II took place in Bangkok only in early 1811. See Caophraya Thiphakòrawong, *Phraratchaphongsawadan Krung Rattanakosin ratchakan thi 2* (Bangkok, 1961), pp. 25-30.

[9]PTMN f° 1/1 says he died on the 9th waning (Tuesday 20 November), not the 4th. Thursday 15 November 1810.

[10]Tuesday 1 July 1788.

suzerainty of the South /168/ and his military cooperation with Lampang and Chiang Mai, and he elevated Cao Attawala to the rank of Cao Paña Nan. Seventeen years later he led the combined forces of Nan, Lampang, and Chiang Mai which successfully invaded Chiang Sæn and brought it under the / government of the South. The king was pleased, and made him Somdet Cao Fa Luang Müang Nan. Five years later he died .... / He was under Burmese rule and stayed in Thœng for three years, and was under the king of Siam for twenty-two years; altogether twenty-five years. He was the seventh ruler of Nan in the line [of Cao Luang Tin Mahawong,] and fifty-seventh[1] / from Cao Khun Fòng.[2]

---

[1]MS. says 54th.

[2]The ellipses in this final paragraph mark redundant repetitions.

CHAPTER EIGHT

CAO SUMANATEWALAT, AD 1810-1825

8.1. In that *kot sanga* year, CS 1172, on Thursday, the tenth day of the third month,[1] [after the death of Cao Attawalapanño,] when the Uparaja, his uncle, who had acted in the interim, had taken over the office [of governor], he was visiting the Cao Khao Kæo Reliquary.[2] / The king's representative, Paña Cantathip brought him a letter of appointment from the king of the South. He was officially appointed Cao Paña Nan with the name Cao Sumanatewalat Cao Paña Nan.

8.2. Informed that he had received the principality, on /169/ the third day of the waning moon of the sixth month[3] he went to pay attendance upon the king in the South, son of his predecessor, reaching Bangkok on the fourth day of the waning moon of the seventh month.[4] On the sixth day of the waning moon of the seventh month, in the *luang met* year, CS 1173, at the new year,[5] the king presented [Cao Sumana] with the regalia of a ruling prince: a gold *phra sri* tray, / two golden goblets, two gold tobacco boxes, a gold betel receptacle, a gold-hilted dagger, a gold razor (?), a gold ewer, a gold cuspidor, two rings set with precious stones, a richly decorated long-handled parasol, a [firearm of some sort], two sporting guns, / three ... (?), one silk cloth with a gold royal pattern, four silk *phanung* [cloths for covering the lower body], one *pha phok riu thòng* cloth, one gold-flowered *süa cip eo phu* cloth, one robe with gold flowers, two *hum phræ*, and two silver offering trays. After conferring with the king, [Cao Sumana] / took leave, and reached Nan on the seventh day of the second ninth month.[6]

8.3. In that same year, on the twelfth day of the waning moon of the sixth month,[7] Cao Sumanatewalat led all his troops and forces to attack Müang La

---

[1]PTMN f° 1/2 concurs. Thursday 6 December 1810.

[2]The formal name of this temple today is Wat Phrathat Cao Nòi; located atop the small hill immediately to the southwest of the city.

[3]PTMN f° 1/4 says the 6th waning of the 6th month (Friday 15 March). Tuesday 12 March 1811.

[4]Friday 12 April 1811, the day before Songkran.

[5]PTMN f° 2/1 concurs on date. New Year (Songkran) that year was on the fifth waning of the fifth month (Southern style, 7th month Northern style). The 6th waning would have fallen within the new-year period. The 5th waning was Saturday 13 April 1811.

[6]PTMN f° 2/4 concurs. There are real problems here: according to the calendar, that year was an A-type year (regular), without an added month.

[7]PTMN f° 2/4 concurs. Monday 9 March 1812.

and Müang Pong,[1] and then made his base at Ta Khi Lek. There he / subsequently had a *vihara* built. On Saturday, the twelfth day of the ninth month in CS 1174,[2] the officers he had left behind there completed the *vihara*. When he returned to Nan in the third month,[3] he brought with him /170/ 6,000 prisoners from Müang La, Müang Pong, Chiang Khæng, and Müang Luang Pukha. In the *ka lao* year, CS 1175, he left his army and went to Nan, arriving in the eighth month.[4]

8.4. In the twelfth month,[5] he escorted the provincial rulers to / audience with the king in Bangkok. After conferring with the king, he took leave and escorted the princes and officials back to Nan, where they arrived in the fourth month.[6]

8.5. On the full-moon day of the sixth month[7] of that year, he [built and] dedicated the / ordination hall on the north side of Wat Cang Kham.

8.6. In the *kap set* year, 1176, at the full moon of the eighth month,[8] Cao Sumanatewalat dedicated the Khao Kæo cetiya and the *vihara* there. /

8.7. On the third day of the waning moon of the fourth month in the same year,[9] he conscripted 10,000 laborers to erect a dwelling at Tong Tüm Tòng and go and construct major irrigation canals and repair the Samun dam. Together with the distribution ditches, there were 9,232 ditches. The mouth of the ditches was 2 fathoms wide, and the width of the channel was 4 elbows wide. On the twelfth day of the waning moon of the fifth month[10] the work was completed. On the fourteenth day of the waning of the fifth month,[11] the ruler returned to the capital. In CS 1177, /171/ a *dap kai* year, the ruler noticed that the dam was not strong enough. On the first of the seventh month,[12] he ordered up 10,000 men to reinforce it again from the seventh of the month. On the thirteenth the work was completed, and on the fourteenth day of the waning moon of the seventh month,[13] he returned to the capital.

8.8. In CS 1178, a *lwai cai* year, on the eleventh day of the ninth month,[14] the Cao Paña Cangwang Khwa, his elder brother died. Then, on the ninth day of the tenth month,[15] the Cao Paña Cangwang Sai, also an elder brother, died.

---

[1]Müang La and Müang Pong were to the northeast of Muong Sing in northwestern Laos, now across the border in China. See the map of the Sipsong Panna in *Muang Boran* 15, 3 (July-Sept. 1989): 52.

[2]PTMN f° 3/1 says that it was a *tao san* year, and the day was Saturday the 15th waxing of the 9th month (Monday 25 May). Saturday 23 May 1812.

[3]PTMN f° 3/2 concurs. December 1812.

[4]PTMN f° 3/3 concurs. May 1813.

[5]PTMN f° 3/3 concurs. September 1813.

[6]PTMN f° 3/4 concurs. January 1814.

[7]PTMN f° 3/4 concurs. Sunday 6 March 1814.

[8]PTMN f° 4/1 concurs. Wednesday 4 May 1814.

[9]PTMN f° 4/2 concurs. Thursday 29 December 1814.

[10]PTMN f° 4/3 concurs. Monday 6 February 1815.

[11]8 February 1815.

[12]Friday 29 March 1816.

[13]Friday 27 April 1816.

[14]PTMN f° 5/1 concurs. Thursday 7 June 1816.

[15]PTMN f° 5/1 concurs. Wednesday 4 July 1816.

8.9. In this year an elephant trainer, Nòi Khanta, captured a male white elephant / 3 fathoms, 1 *khüp,* and 6 *niu* high, with tusks 1 *khüp* 3 *niu* long, in the area of Müang Ngim,[1] which was brought to the ruler's pavilion at Ta Khi Lek. On the eleventh day of the fourth month, and the twelfth day of the fourth month,[2] the ruler brought up all his forces, family, and officials to receive the white elephant. / On Tuesday, the thirteenth day of the fourth month,[3] the ruler had his forces form a procession to bring the white elephant into his enclosure at the noon watch.[4] He ordered that the elephant be carefully guarded for presentation.

8.10. In that year, on the eighth day of the sixth month,[5] / the ruler led his forces, princes, and the rulers of Chiang Khong, Chiang Khæng, and Pukha Müang Luang in escorting the white elephant down to be presented to the king in the golden palace in Bangkok.[6] The king was highly pleased, /172/ and rewarded Cao Sumanatewalat with two *chang* of Siamese money [160 baht] and many fine gifts. When the ceremonies were over, the ruler took his leave and headed for home by way of Müang Phichai.

8.11. After the ruler had left for the South, the / elephant trainers captured a female red elephant, which was brought to Nan in the *müang pao* year, 1179, on the thirteenth day of the first ninth month.[7] On the eleventh day of the second ninth month,[8] Cao Paña Lattana and the Cao Latcawong brought the red elephant down to Phichai, where they met the / ruler. The ruler then appointed Paña Lattana, the *hua müang kæo,*[9] and the Cao Latcawong to escort the red elephant down to present to the king in the South. The king was most appreciative towards the ruler [of Nan], on whom he bestowed / generous rewards. The ruler continued his journey homewards, and reached the city on the fourth day of the waning of the tenth month.[10]

8.12. As soon as he had returned, the ruler had a *devata* shrine built in the forest in the region of Müang Ngim where the white elephant had been caught, / as a gesture of propitiation, and he forbade the killing of animals in that area.[11]

---

[1]Not located.

[2]The original would translate "On the eleventh day of the fourth month, the eleventh day of the twelfth month, the twelfth day of the fourth month," which is very confusing. I have changed the passage in translation to accord with PTMN f° 5/4. Sunday-Monday 30-31 December 1816.

[3]PTMN f° 5/4 concurs. Tuesday 1 January 1817.

[4]PTMN f° 6/1.

[5]PTMN f° 6/2 concurs. Sunday 24 February 1817.

[6]The Bangkok court astrologers' record notes the arrival of this white elephant from Nan on Thursday 11 April 1817 (*Chotmaihet hon,* Prachum phongsawadan 4, 103).

[7]PTMN f° 6/4 concurs. Thursday 26 June 1817.

[8]PTMN f° 6/4 says the 10th day of the second 9th month. Thursday 24 July 1817. These two successive references provide good evidence that Nan astrologers added an intercalary *ninth* month, not an eighth or tenth month.

[9]Better, Phraya Lattana is head of that portion (probably administrative rather than geographical) of the principality known as the Kæo division. Such titles are common in the Northern Tai/Lao world. See similar additional references in §§4.26 and 4.28.

[10]Sunday 31 August 1817.

[11]PTMN f° 7/3 also includes this episode.

8.13. In that same year [1179], on Saturday the 10th day of the waning moon of the second ninth month,[1] in the *tut cao* watch, the Nan River flooded the city. Temples and homes were inundated and destroyed. /173/ Cao Sumanatewalat observed that the old city was constricted, and its eastern side had been undermined by the river. Therefore, he ordered his councillors and senior princes to consider a new site for the city. They decided upon Dong Panet Cang, / 36 *sen* north of the old city and 20 *sen* from the river, for a new and larger city of Nan.[2] [At the end of the rainy season,] on the 9th day of the waxing moon of the third month,[3] the ruler called up all the labor and officers, and began the work, first clearing the site. On Friday, the 3rd day of the fourth month,[4] a new palace was begun, continuing to the 2nd day of the fifth month.[5] On Saturday, the 9th day of the fifth month, a Thai *poek san* day, in the / second lunar mansion, called Mahadhana in the Karakataraja,[6] in the *tut cai* watch, the city gate was inaugurated. The enclosure of the city measured 940 *ta* on the east, 728 *ta* on the west, 393 *ta* on the south, and 677 *ta* on the north. The walls (?) were 4 elbows wide and 9 elbows high (?). The four / sides of the city totaled 3038 *ta*,[7] and they were finished in the sixth month.[8] [There, in the new city,] the ruler inaugurated the new year, on Tuesday, the 8th day of the seventh month.[9]

8.14. [A week later,] in this *pœk yi* year 1180, on the full-moon day of the seventh month,[10] the ruler inaugurated the great *vihara* to the south, a major image of the Buddha, and a library for the scriptures, /174/ as a major benefaction. In this same year, the ruler ordered the reconstruction of temples and homes, as before.

8.15. In the *kat mao* year 1181, on Tuesday the 8th day of the ninth month, in the eleventh lunar mansion named Mahadhana,[11] in the midday watch, Cao Sumanatewalat / led his family back to reside in the city.

8.16. In the *kot si* year, 1182, on Saturday the 3rd day of the eighth month,[12] the ruler appointed four *sænluang* as *paña*, as well as the eight *khun* and the twelve *khun calæ*,[13] / to advise him and attend to business in the *sanam*.[14]

---

[1]PTMN f° 7/4 concurs. Thursday 7 August 1817.

[2]PTMN f° 8/1 says the site for the new city was selected on the 4th day of the 3rd month. Friday 12 December 1817.

[3]17 December 1817. PTMN f° 8/3 says the 4th day of the 3rd month (12 December 1817).

[4]PTMN f° 8/4 concurs. Friday 9 January 1818.

[5]PTMN f° 9/1 concurs. Saturday 7 February 1818.

[6]PTMN f° 9/1 concurs. Saturday 14 February 1818.

[7]PTMN f° 9/1-2 gives slightly different measurements: 940 x 728 x 693 x 679; but it agrees on the total, 3038. The figures given in MS1 total 2738, while those in PTMN total 3040; so the latter are much closer to adding to the total both manuscripts give. But what is a *ta*? I can find the term in none of the dictionaries available to me.

[8]March 1818.

[9]PTMN f° 9/2 concurs. That year, the new year began on the 8th waxing of the 5th month (Southern style; 7th month Northern style), which was Monday 13 April 1818.

[10]PTMN f° 9/3 concurs. Monday 20 April 1818.

[11]PTMN f° 9/4 concurs. Monday 31 May 1818; or Tuesday 1 June 1818.

[12]PTMN f° 10/1 concurs. Saturday 15 April 1820.

[13]PTMN f° 10/1 has *khun cârê*. These must be what the Burmese called *sare*, "writers."

[14]As I understand the administration, it was headed by four *sænluang*, who were akin to ministers, assisted by eight *khun* and twelve scribes. The entire group sat as a sort of royal council (*sanam* or *sanam luang*) and attended to both civil administration and judicial matters.

8.17. Later in the year, on the 14th day of the tenth month,[1] a male red elephant was caught and brought to the palace that day and put in the charge of the *sanam luang*. / On the 6th day of the waning moon of the sixth month[2] the ruler appointed the Uparaja and other officers to take the red elephant to be presented to the king in Bangkok.

8.18. On Saturday the 11th day of the waning moon of the first month[3] / the ruler had the officials erect a pole for the tutelary deities in the western part of the city, and a hitching post for white elephants in the center of the *sanam luang*. Two days later[4] he had them erect a pole for the tutelary deities in the north of the city.

8.19. In the same year, the ruler /175/ observed that the great *vihara* of Wat Cæ Hæng was now in a bad state of disrepair. The ruler led the royal family and officers in restoring all the walls of the building, and in regilding the main Buddha image. / The ornamental parasols (*chatra*) at the four corners of the cetiya were rebuilt with hardwood and covered with copper sheeting weighing 120,000,[5] and they were decorated and gilded. A large bell weighing 170,000 / and a smaller one weighing 130,000 were cast, and towers were built for them, to the west and east.[6] On Sunday, the full-moon day of the sixth month,[7] the ruler, together with his chief queen, members of the royal family, and his officials and retainers, both inner and outer, / paid reverence to the Holy Reliquary. Moreover, he presented to the Reliquary three people, a woman with a son and daughter, who were to serve it for the duration of the 5,000 years.[8] / As for the members of the Sangha who were given alms at that time, there were the heads of 165 temples, as well as 379 monks and 749 novices.[9]

8.20. On Friday, the 6th day of the waning moon of the sixth month,[10] there was an earthquake, which broke the tip of of the cetiya of Wat Cæ Hæng.[11] On the 13th day of the waning moon,[12] /176/ the ruler conscripted ten thousand men to repair the Samun dam and fix the canal that conveyed water to the city.

8.21. In the *luang sai* year 1183, on the 5th day of the seventh month,[13] the Sipsong Panna and Chiang Hung sent a delegation with presents consisting of

---

[1]PTMN f° 10/2 concurs. Saturday 24 June 1820.

[2]PTMN f° 10/3 concurs. Saturday 24 March 1821.

[3]PTMN f° 10/4 has Saturday, 10th waning of the 1st month. Thursday 2 November 1820 or Monday 22 October 1821, depending on whether the month is a Keng Tung-style month or a Northern month.

[4]But PTMN f° 10/4 has the 13th waning of the 1st month.

[5]1,000 weights = 1.33 kg.

[6]PTMN f° 11/3 concurs on weights.

[7]PTMN f° 11/4 concurs. Sunday 18 March 1821.

[8]Prasœt Churat's earlier translation stated that "He also had made plaster images of a man, a woman, and a child, to serve the holy cetiya for a duration of 5,000 years." I can find no way to translate the text in this fashion here. PTMN f° 11/4 does not change my reading.

[9]As of 1966, there were 349 Buddhist monasteries in Nan. *Thamniap phrasamanasak læ thamniap wat tangtang thua ratcha'anacak Ph.S. 2509* (Bangkok, 1966).

[10]PTMN f° 12/2 says Saturday, 6th waning of 6th month. Saturday 24 March 1821.

[11]The Bangkok astrologers' diaries record no earthquakes in this or the surrounding years.

[12]PTMN f° 12/3 concurs. Saturday 31 March 1821.

[13]Saturday 7 April 1821.

four ponies, 7,400 in money, three pieces of Burmese silk, 1 bolt (*lam*)[1] of red silk, 1 bolt of *læ* silk, 1 bolt of green *sakin*, 1 bolt of *læ* silk, 6 lengths of red *kien*, and one piece of flowered *kien* [cloth]. The delegation, consisting of Paña Alin, Raja Panya, and Raja Kham Lü, and twenty-three men, had been sent to Cao Sumanatewalat to negotiate the purchase of six male elephants, which they wanted as presents for the new emperor of China.[2] Cao Sumanatewalat hesitated, and sent Mün Nalat with a letter to consult the king of the South [i.e., Siam]. The king replied that, since Peking[3] was friendly with Siam[4] it was quite proper for the ruler of Nan to sell the elephants for this purpose. Cao Sumana then told / his ministers to look around Nan for six male elephants with good ears and tails for sale to Paña Alin at a price of 11,570 *ngœn lang*.

8.22. On Thursday, the 6th day of the waning moon of the ninth month, in the 25th lunar mansion, called Burapharatha,[5] /177/ Cao Sumanatewalat realized that Buddhism [in Nan] had no learned leader or great teacher to lead and teach the Sangha. In order to prevent the decline of Buddhism he resolved to do everything in his power. As of that day, Buddhism / had then existed for 2,364 years, two months, and twenty-one days, and its future was therefore 2,635 years, nine months, and nine days.[6] He appointed the abbot of Wat Paña Wat, named Thipphawongso, / as Sangharâja to advise and instruct the Sangha of Nan.[7] To celebrate the appointment he invited / 123 monks and 86 novices to receive food alms.

8.23. On the 6th day of the waning moon of the third month in the *tao sanga* year 1184,[8] [Cao Sumana] ordered the Cao Latcawong of Chiang Khong to take 300 men and assist Paña Alin / in transporting the six elephants to the North and protect them against enemies and bandits. In devout piety, this year he had a bronze image cast for Wat Sathalot[9] in the middle of the city, on the 3rd day of the waning moon of the fifth month.[10] /178/ The image required 75,000 units of metal.

8.24. In the *ka met* year 1185,[11] [Cao Sumana] ordered his officials to have timber cut and finished for the building of a new royal residence. For the two great central posts, he had people go to fell teak at the Tæn Kæo Mountain in the

---

[1] A *lam* of cloth is a 4-*wa* length (approximately 8 yards or meters).

[2] *cao fa wong*, the term usually used for the emperor of China. This episode does not occur in the PTMN. In China, the Jiaqing Emperor died in 1820, succeeded in 1821 by the Daoguang Emperor.

[3] *müang Phraküng*.

[4] Sri Ayudhiya.

[5] PTMN f° 12/4 says Thursday, 3rd waning of 9th month, a *ruang met* day, omitting the lunar mansion. Thursday 21 June 1821, which was a *ruang met* day. There are no later dates in the PTMN.

[6] This calculation was made with reference to the popular belief that Buddhism would have a life on earth of 5,000 years.

[7] Wat Paña Wat was just outside the city walls to the south, on the road to Wiang Sa.

[8] Wednesday 4 December 1822.

[9] Wat Sathalot is at the far north end of the modern city.

[10] Wednesday 29 January 1823.

[11] AD 1823/24. There is an inscription from Wat Satharot (MNBPS, pp. 282-83) which names the ruler as Sumanathewarat (8 June 1823; J.C. Eade).

area of Müang Som La.[1] On Saturday, the 13th day of the waning moon of the sixth month, a *müang pao* day, 8th lunar mansion,[2] in the *kòng ngai* watch, the pillars were erected. On Friday, the 11th day of the (?) month, 8th lunar mansion,[3] / in the *kòng læng* watch, the ruler took up residence in the new palace.

8.25. In the *kap san* year 1186, on the 4th day of the waning moon of the fifth month,[4] construction began on the main part of the Jewelled Palace, 79 fathoms long and 70 fathoms wide.[5]

8.26. On the 12th day of the sixth month,[6] something strange occurred at Müang Bò: the Mang River suddenly dried up at midday. Then, in the *kòng ngai* watch, it resumed its normal flow.[7]

8.27. On the 12th day of the sixth month,[8] / a letter from the Crown Prince arrived telling of the death of his father the king [Rama II of Siam], and commanding the ruler of Nan to attend the royal funeral obsequies in Bangkok.[9] Cao Sumanatewalat organized tribute and, with his retinue, /179/ left for Bangkok on the 5th day of the waning moon of the sixth month.[10] They arrived in Bangkok on the 14th day of the seventh month.[11] On the 13th day of the waning moon,[12] the ruler was stricken with cholera, and he died in the *kòng læng* watch on Sunday, the 1st day of the eighth month.[13] / The new [Siamese] king arranged for his funeral at Wat Cæng on the 7th day of the waning moon of the ninth month.[14]

8.28. Cao Sumanatewalat was sixty years old when he became ruler of Nan, and he had ruled for fourteen years. At his death, he was / seventy-four years old. He was the eighth ruler of his line, and the fifty-eighth from Cao Khun Fòng.

8.29. When Cao Sumana died it was a new year, 1187. After he had left Nan / for Bangkok, around the New Year,[15] there had been a frightful windstorm which came from the west. It blew down many trees and houses.

---

[1]Not identified.

[2]Saturday 27 March 1824, a *luang lao* day. This date is corrupted. In CS 1185 (AD 1823/24), the only *müang pao* day that fell on a Saturday was the 10th waxing of the 9th month (Southern form, which would be the 11th month in the North, or 10th month Keng Tung-style). No *müang pao* day that year fell in the waning half of any month.

[3]Has to be the last month of the year; Friday 9 April 1824.

[4]Monday 8 February 1825.

[5]This was a very large building indeed, larger than a football field. Do these figures perhaps include the surrounding landscaping?

[6]Tuesday 2 March 1825.

[7]This, of course, could have been caused by something like a landslide interrupting the flow of water for a period of time.

[8]Tuesday 2 March 1825. Noticc the synchronicity of a miracle and a portentous event.

[9]Rama II died on 4 /11 8 in 1186 (Thiphakòrawong, *Phraratchaphongsawadan Krung Rattanakosin ratchakan thi* 2, p. 205): 23 July 1824.

[10]Wednesday 10 March 1825.

[11]Saturday 3 April 1825.

[12]Saturday 17 April 1825.

[13]Monday 19 April 1825.

[14]Wednesday 8 June 1825. Wat Cæng is, of course, Wat Arun, the "Temple of Dawn" opposite the Grand Palace.

[15]Songkran was Wednesday 13 April 1825.

The images of Wat Cang Kham and Tiposot perspired during the storm, and the finial of the cetiya of / Wat Pu Piang [Cæ Hæng] was bent towards the southeast.

CHAPTER NINE

MAHAYOT, ACITTAWONG, AND MAHAWONG, AD 1825–1851

9.1. In that *dap lao* year, 1187, on the 9th day of the waning moon of the ninth month,[1] the king [in Bangkok] appointed the Cao Latcawong, Cao Mahayot, son of Cao Attawalapanño, as ruling prince of Nan. He was presented /180/ with the regalia of office, just like those of his predecessor.

9.2. After having been formally invested as ruling prince of Nan, Cao Luang Mahayot took leave of the king and returned [to Nan]. At first he stayed at the Dòn Cai palace in the old city, and then on the 8th of the waning moon of the eleventh month[2] he / went to live in his old Mangalaniwet Palace. On Saturday, the 4th day of the waning of the sixth month in 1187,[3] in the *tut cai* watch, the princes and officials formally invited him to take / up residence in the main palace in place of its builder, Cao Sumanatewalat.

9.3. In the *lwai set* year 1188, on the 11th day of the waning sixth month,[4] a royal command which had been relayed from province to province / reached Cao Mahayot from Phichai. Explaining that Cao Anu of Vientiane had revolted against the king of Siam, it commanded the prince of Nan to call up a force of 5,000 men and go and help take Vientiane.[5] [Three days later,] on the 14th day of the waning sixth month,[6] a royal commissioner, / Fæng Satan, brought an urgent command ordering Cao Mahayot immediately to proceed to Vientiane, joining forces from Chiang Mai, Lamphun, Lampang, and Phræ.

9.4. On the 4th day of the sixth month,[7] Cao Luang Mahayot appointed the Cao Latcawong as commander of a vanguard of 1,000 men, /181/ ordering him to set up camp at Müang Tòng; and he ordered the Cao Pa Müang Kæo to take 500 men and go by way of the Nam Pat [river] to meet the Lampang, Chiang Mai, and Lamphun forces.[8] As for the ruler, he led a force of 3,500 men out to the Tamnak Dòn Cai on Tuesday, the 13th day of the waning seventh month, in the *kòng læng* watch, in 1188, a *lwai set* year.[9] / On Friday, the 2nd day

---

[1]Friday 10 June 1825.

[2]Tuesday 6 September 1825.

[3]Monday 27 March 1826 .

[4]Friday 23 March 1827.

[5]On the conflict between Cao Anu of Laos and King Rama III, the best introduction in English is Walter F. Vella, *Siam Under Rama III* (Locust Valley, NY, 1957), Ch. 6.

[6]Monday 26 March 1827.

[7]Has to be the seventh month. Saturday 31 March 1827.

[8]The Nam Pat, a river, empties into the Nan River above Uttaradit, and runs up a long valley that leads to the (modern) Laos border. It was a particularly good point for joining forces coming from Chiang Mai, Bangkok, and Nan, as it lay on the easiest route to Vientiane.

[9]Tuesday 24 April 1827. The year has to be 1189, not 1188.

of the eighth month,[1] the prince led his men from Dòn Cai to Müang Tòng, and thence to Müang Pan Pao on the 5th day of the waning ninth month.[2] The [Siamese] Front Palace King, and all the Thai and Lao and provincial armies, all assembled there at Pan Pao, in numbers beyond counting.

9.5. As for Cao Anu of Vientiane, / when his people and army learned of the approach of the massed armies to Vientiane, they fled the city. Cao Anu escaped to Müang Phuan[3] by boat from the Ta Si Da landing.

9.6. The Front Palace King ordered all the provincial armies to cross [the Mekong River] and occupy Vientiane and to / capture the family of Paña Supak Piao and all the people of Vientiane who had escaped to Ban Khæm.[4] These people were captured and brought to the Front Palace King, who sent all of them to Siam. / Müang Nan captured 1,200 families and presented them to the Front Palace King. Phraya Ratchasuphawadi[5] came up [to Vientiane] by way of Prachinburi and Champassak and arrived at Pan Pao on the 8th day of the eleventh month,[6] and the Front Palace King returned to Siam. On the 12th day of the eleventh month,[7] Ratchasuphawadi gave 438 of the captives from Vientiane to the /182/ prince of Nan. The prince of Nan then returned to Nan on the 13th of the waning first month.[8] A large number of Lao from Lomsak, Lœi, Kæn Tao, and Nam Pat poured into Nan asking the protection of the prince of Nan, and the prince / had shelters built for them. People were not yet coming from Luang Prabang.

9.7. The [Siamese] king now felt uneasy because of the common frontier with Müang Phuan, and because Cao Anu was still at large. He therefore sent Phraya Phichai with / 500 men up to Luang Prabang. He also ordered the prince of Nan to gather a force and proceed to Luang Prabang, to await further orders. In the *müang kai* year 1189, on the 8th day of the fourth month,[9] Cao / Luang Mahayot ordered Sæn Sirisongkham to go with sixty men to join Phraya Phichai in Luang Prabang and await the king's orders.

9.8. Phraya Phichairannarit came up to Nan with the king's order to take away Lao families who had taken refuge in Nan. The ruler then called up 144 of his officers and / men to escort these families to Phræ, on the 8th day of the tenth month in 1190, a *pœk cai* year.[10] On the 12th day of the tenth month,[11] Phraya Phichairannarit left Nan, going by way of Phræ. As for the old prince of Chiang Khong, he died in that rainy season, on the 12th day of the waning eleventh month.[12] Mom Nòi /183/ appointed Raja Siricai and Tao Pakancai to carry tribute to Nan [and announce the death of the ruler].

---

[1]Friday 27 April 1827.
[2]Thursday 14 June 1827.
[3]That is, to the Xieng Khouang ("Plain of Jars") region to the northeast.
[4]This place must be in Laos; not identical to the Ban Kæm at Pua.
[5]That is, Caophraya Bòdindecha (Sing Singhaseni).
[6]Tuesday 31 July 1827.
[7]Saturday 4 August 1827.
[8]Thursday 18 October 1827.
[9]Tuesday 25 December 1827.
[10]Thursday 20 June 1828.
[11]Monday 24 June 1828.
[12]Saturday 7 September 1828.

9.9. On the 4th day of the waning twelfth month,[1] Luang Caiyot, a royal commissioner, brought a royal command ordering Nan to take an armed force up to Luang Prabang. On the 13th day of the waning first month,[2] the ruler sent Cao Pa Müang Laca and Paña Sæn / with a force of 650 men to guard Luang Prabang. On the 13th day of the waning second month,[3] he sent Cao Pa Müang Cailaca and the governor of Chiang Khæng with another 650 men; and on the 11th day of the waning second month[4] he sent Sæn Tanancai and Sæn Cittamano with 300 men to Pak Lai to await news / of Vientiane with the governor of Lap Læ.[5]

9.10. Sæn Cittamano went to Vientiane to brief Phraya Ratchasuphawadi and then returned to Sam Mün Müang Füang to sweep up families. Cao Luang Mahayot was informed / that Sæn Cittamano had stationed himself at Sam Mün Nòng Kæo Hat Dia. On the 11th day of the waning fourth month[6] he sent Cao Suliya with 300 men to assist Sæn Cittamano in sweeping up the Vientiane families / who had escaped to Sam Mün Müang Füang and Nòng Kæo Hat Dia. They rounded up 3,000 families and sent them to Phra Lap Læ, and encamped at Pak Lai. Phraya Phichairannarit sent Phra Mahasongkhram to Pak Lai, and he gave 170 prisoners to Cao Suliya and 61 to Sæn Tanancai. /184/

9.11. When Phraya Phichai, who was then in Luang Prabang, learned that Cao Anu was hiding in Müang Phuan, he sent Paña Len and Phra Lap Læ with 170 men to Müang Phuan to search him out. They captured Cao Anu and Nang Khampong on the 12th day of the third month,[7] in the middle of the night, / and took them to Phraya Ratchasuphawadi in Vientiane. Paña Len was given 30 prisoners as a reward.

9.12. In the *kat pao* year 1191, on Saturday the 13th day of the waning twelfth month,[8] / in the *tut cai* watch, Cao Luang Mahayot went with the princes to an audience with the king, and asked him to appoint his nephew, Cao Mahawong Pa Müang Cai, as the Uparaja of the Front Palace. He also requested the appointments of Nai Nan Lammasen, son / of the ruler of Chiang Khong, as ruler of Chiang Khong, and the new rulers of Chiang Khæng and Müang Luang Paña Pukha. He then returned to Nan, and the prince of Chiang Khong returned home.

9.13. Lamasen, the ruler of Chiang Khong, decided to present one of his daughters / to the Latcawong of Chiang Mai. Learning of this, Cao Luang Mahayot deigned to favor him by accompanying this daughter, whose name was Pimpa, to Chiang Mai and to stand in her father's place [in the marriage ceremony], as the rulers of Chiang Khong for the previous two generations had had intimate connections with Nan. This Cao Lamasen, of the third generation, fol-

---

[1]Saturday 28 September 1828.

[2]Wednesday 6 November 1828.

[3]Thursday 5 December 1828.

[4]Tuesday 3 December 1828?

[5]Pak Lai is situated near the "elbow" of the Mekong, where it flows from the north and turns to the east. Lap Læ, now a district center in Uttaradit province, is immediately adjacent to the modern town of Uttaradit, on the north side.

[6]Friday 31 January 1829.

[7]Thursday 19 December 1828.

[8]Saturday 26 September 1829.

lowed them in presenting his daughters /185/ to foreign rulers, just as Paña Siwicai had sent a daughter to the ruler of Vientiane and Paña Aliya had sent one to cement ties of friendship with Luang Prabang.[1]

9.14. After Cao Luang Mahayot had ruled Nan for ten years, in / CS 1197, a *dap met* year,[2] he went to see the king in Siam. He became seriously ill and died there. He was the ninth ruler of his line, and the fifty-ninth from Cao Khun Fòng. /

9.15. In the *lwai san* year, 1198, on Tuesday, the 1st day of the eighth month,[3] in the *tut cai* watch, the Latcawong, Cao Acittawongsa, son of Cao Sumanatewalat, went down to have an audience with the king in Bangkok. He reached there on the 7th day of the third month.[4] / On the 10th day of that month he was appointed ruling prince of Nan.

9.16. After Cao Acittawong had received his appointment as ruler of Nan from the king, he took leave and returned to Nan on the 12th day of the waning sixth month.[5] / He stayed at first in the Tamnak Cai in the old city. On the 12th day of the seventh month[6] he was ordained a novice until the next day, when at the *kòng ngai* watch he performed a *buddhâbhiseka* ceremony. On the 15th there was a solar eclipse.[7] On the 1st day of the waning moon, now in CS 1199, a *muang lao* year,[8] /186/ in the *kòng ngai* watch, he left his dwelling in the old city and went to live in the palace in the new city.

9.17. On the 12th day of the waning seventh month,[9] Cao Acittawongsa went to Cæ Hæng to extend the finial of the Reliquary, which originally Prince Attawalapanño had made 12 / elbows in length. Together with the princes, officials, and Sangha, they took down the finial, which had been bent to the southeast,[10] and fixed it and extended it another 4 elbows for a total height of 16 elbows, and added an additional two / tiers to its umbrella, namely the uppermost and lowest tiers, making a total of eleven. Later, on the 8th day of the ninth month,[11] the prince, together with his family and officials, performed a *buddhâbhiseka* ceremony to make merit, and the next day he returned to the city.[12]

---

[1] I have been unable here to improve on the original translation of Prasœt Churatana.

[2] AD 1835/36. There is an inscription on the base of a wooden Buddha image in Wat Cæ Hæng dated 4 April 1833 (J.C. Eade; MNBPS, pp. 281 85).

[3] Saturday 17 April 1836.

[4] 16 December 1836.

[5] Sunday 3 April 1837.

[6] Monday 18 April 1837.

[7] Thursday 21 April 1837. The Bangkok astrologers' records indeed report a solar eclipse on that day. (*Chotmaihet hon*, p. 109.)

[8] Friday 22 April 1837.

[9] Tuesday 3 May 1837.

[10] In the windstorm mentioned above, §8.29.

[11] Sunday 11 June 1837.

[12] One of the astrologers' notebooks from Bangkok (*Cotmaihet hon chabap Phraya Pramunthanarak*, Bangkok, 1921, p. 52) states that on 3 December 1837, "relics came from Nan." Might these have been taken from Cæ Hæng? Perhaps local people were not told, which would account for there being no mention in the Nan sources. Perhaps it even accounts for the ruler's illness and death?

9.18. When Cao Luang Acittawongsa had gone down to receive his appointment as ruler, he contracted a disease, which gradually became more severe after he returned to rule in Nan and / he extended the finial on the Cæ Hæng Reliquary. After making merit, he improved somewhat; but after he moved back to the city on the 9th of the waning ninth month[1] his condition worsened, and he was swollen from his feet /187/ to his abdomen, and the efforts of physicians were to no avail. On the 12th day of the eleventh month,[2] in the midnight watch, he passed to the next world. Cao Acittawongsa had ruled Nan for just seven months[3] when he died in CS 1200, a *pœk set* year. He is considered the tenth ruler in his line, / and the sixtieth from Cao Khun Fòng. Cao Acittawongsa had two sons, Cao Paña Wang Khwa Dang, and Cao Nan Suya. His second and third wives had no children.

9.19. In the *pœk set* year CS 1200,[4] / after the funeral of Cao Luang Acittawongsa, the Uparaja, Cao Mahawong, a son of Mæ Cao Nang Lœt, went to audience with the king in Bangkok; and the king was pleased to appoint / Cao Mahawong as ruler of Nan. After receiving his letter of appointment, Cao Luang Mahawong took leave of the king and returned.

9.20. Cao Luang Mahawong now noticed / the condition of the temple buildings of his city. They were old and dilapidated and were a disgrace to Buddhism. Therefore he built the *vihara* and reliquary of Wat Sathalot, a *vihara* at Wat Pa Kœt, and repaired the small *vihara* of Wat Cæ Hæng.[5]

9.21. In 1208, /188/ a *lwai sanga* year, on Friday the 11th day of the waning ninth month, a Thai *kot si* day,[6] in the evening watch, with his family and officials he built four cetiya around the main cetiya of Wat Cæ Hæng. He also repaired the *vihara*, the sala, / and a gate by the Nang Yòng sala of the same temple. On the same day, the finial of the cetiya was taken down and repaired and extended. On the 11th day of the tenth month,[7] having taken down the umbrellas and finial, he added to them six silver and six golden lotuses and ten small bells. Three Buddha images also were cast for the temple. Two days later,[8] they performed a *buddhâbhiseka* ceremony as a major merit-making ceremony. Then the ruler and the ruling family and officials and people built the Ta Lò Reliquary. He then built the *vihara* at Wat Cao Cang Phüak.[9] He built the Dòn Nam Reliquary at Pua, and he repaired the *vihara* of Wat Pang Sanuk at Wiang Sa. Besides building and repairing temples, /189/ Cao Luang Mahawong urged his relatives and the people to maintain, improve, and build temples so that they would be better than before.

---

[1]Tuesday 27 June 1837.

[2]Sunday 13 August 1838.

[3]One year and seven months are required by the MS, which I have double-checked.

[4]AD 1838/39.

[5]There is an inscription on the base of a wooden Buddha image at Wat Sathalot dated 21 December 1839 (J.C. Eade; *Müang Nan*, pp. 295-99). Wat Sathalot, Wat Pa Kœt, and Wat Panet all are in the same sub-district, on the north end of the modern city of Nan.

[6]Friday 19 June 1846, which was a *kot si* day—but was the 10th waning of the month.

[7]Saturday 4 July 1846.

[8]Monday 6 July 1846.

[9]In the northern section of the modern city. See city map.

9.22. Cao Paña Nan Mahawong was the son of Mæ Cao Nang Lœt and Cao Mahapom / of Müang Thœng. Mæ Cao Nang Lœt was a daughter of Mæ Cao Nang Tep, who was a daughter of Cao Luang Tin Mahawong by his Chiang Mai wife.

9.23. Cao Luang Mahawong's wife was Mæ Cao Nang Yòt. / Before he became ruler, he was Cao Müang Cai, and then became the Prince of the Front Palace before succeeding to the throne. He had three sons: Cao Nòi In Ban, who was Latcabut and then became the Puri;[1] / Cao Kham Khuang, who was Cao Wang Khwa; and Cao Nòi Nò Müang. By his second wife there were two children, Cao Pimmasan and Cao Tui.

9.24. Cao Luang Mahawong ruled / Nan for thirteen years before dying in Nan in the *luang kai* year, CS 1213. He is considered the eleventh ruler of his line, and the sixty-first from Cao Khun Fòng.

---

[1]The full title, which must be on the ladder of succession in Nan, is given in §10.1.

CHAPTER TEN

ANANTA AND SULIYAPHONG, AD 1851-1894

10.1. In 1214, /190/ on the 11th of the waning sixth month,[1] the Cao Bulilat Hua Müang Kæo, eldest son [of Cao Luang Mahayot], named Cao Anantayot, went down to an audience with the king in Bangkok. The king then was pleased to appoint him ruling prince of Nan, with the name Cao / Paña Mongkhonwalayot. He presented the ruler with the regalia of office, consisting of a tunic with gold strip binding, a garment cloth with gold edges, a golden headdress, golden spittoon, golden goblet, golden betel-nut chewing set, a first-quality gun, a sword with a golden scabbard, two silver vessels, and / two spears. Having completed his business, the prince took leave of the king and returned to Nan in the ninth month of CS 1215.[2]

10.2. As soon as he had arrived, Cao Paña Mongkhonwalayot received / an urgent command from the king ordering him to send a force of men to the Sipsong Panna and Chiang Hung immediately, as a Bangkok army and armies from Phræ, Lampang, Lamphun, and Chiang Mai were on the way to take Keng Tung. So, in the second month of that *ka pao* year, CS 1215,[3] Cao Mongkhonwalayot conscripted a force and led it up to the Sipsong Panna. The Bangkok main force, led by Prince /191/ Krommaluang Wongsa[thiratsanit],[4] came up by way of Chiang Mai, [where it joined] the Chiang Mai force commanded by Cao Mahapom and continued on to Keng Tung, while the Nan army came down from Chiang Hung. Cao Mahapom commanded the vanguard.[5]

10.3. When the Nan army reached the Sipsong Panna, the defenders did not dare to fight with the ruler of Nan, and together they came to pledge their loyalty to the king in Bangkok. /

10.4. After the surrender of the Sipsong Panna and Chiang Hung, the prince had the country thoroughly scouted. Then the prince of Nan despatched the Uparaja of Chiang Hung to take a force to / Prince [Wongsathiratsanit], commander of the Bangkok army, at Keng Tung; but he was too late: the Prince and Mahapom had failed to take the city, and had withdrawn. The Uparaja of Chiang Hung caught up with the main army along its line of march, and came

[1]Saturday 6 March 1853.

[2]May 1853.

[3]November 1853.

[4](1808-1870), son of King Rama II and younger brother of Rama III and Mongkut.

[5]The Keng Tung wars are treated extensively in Chaophraya Thiphakòrawong's chronicle of King Mongkut's reign, translated by Chadin Flood as *The Dynastic Chronicles, Bangkok Era, The Fourth Reign* (Tokyo, 1965), I, 95 ff. Documents concerning the wars are in *Cotmaihet rüang thap Chiang Tung* (Bangkok, 1916).

back with the / Prince. When Prince [Wongsa]'s army reached Nan, they encamped at Na Lin, southeast of the northern city. As for the ruler of Nan, he withdrew from the Sipsong Panna and joined the Prince at Na Lin.

10.5. When Prince Krommaluang Wongsa arrived in Nan, he conscripted /192/ men from Luang Prabang, Lom [Sak], Lœi, and all the Lao; and from Nan, Phræ, Lampang, Lamphun, and Chiang Mai, and marched this army to Keng Tung again. The ruler of Nan followed the Prince, in the second month of CS 1216.[1] The / Siamese army engaged the forces of Keng Tung, but they were unable to take the city, as the defending force was too strong. They therefore had to retreat. The prince of Nan was following Prince Krommaluang Wongsa all the time in order to protect his life from the rear. The ruler of Nan withdrew from Keng Tung and arrived back in the ninth month of CS 1217, a *dap mao* year.[2]

10.6. As soon as he had returned, Cao Mongkhonwalayot went down to an audience with the / king in Bangkok and asked his permission to restore the old city. The king was pleased to grant this permission. The work of restoration was begun the same year. The ruler called up all the labor of the town / to clear the undergrowth in the old city. On Tuesday, the 13th of the eighth month,[3] in the watch near noon, all the ruling family and officials began the main city gate and the walls of the city.[4]

10.7. That year, the ruler /193/ appointed his two sons, Cao Nan Mahapom and Cao Suya, to lead a party of princes from the Sipsong Panna, Chiang Hung, Müang Luang Pukha, Müang La, and Müang Pong down to Bangkok to formally present tribute to the king. / The two brothers spent the rainy season there in 1218.[5] At that time, the king was pleased to appoint Cao Nan Mahapom, the elder brother, as Cao Paña Maha Uparaja of the Front Palace, and Cao Suya, the younger, / as Cao Paña Latcawongsa. All their business completed, the brothers then led their retainers and state guests in taking leave of the king and returning to Nan.

10.8. In the second month of the year 1218,[6] / the ruler of Nan, Mongkhonwalayot, took his princes, officers, and retainers down to Bangkok for an audience with the king. The king promoted Cao / Mongkhonwalayot to be Cao Anantawòralittidet Kunlacettamahantacaiya Bòrommahalatcawongsa Cao Nakhòn Müang Nan. He was presented with the regalia of office: a [gold] food-carrying set, a golden crown, a five-tiered throne, a six-tiered white parasol,[7] /194/ two swords with gold scabbards, four richly-adorned lances, two first-quality guns, a golden cuspidor, a golden ewer, a betel set on a tray with all the paraphernalia in gold and two golden handles, a golden *mapatti* (?) in two rows

---

[1]October-November 1854.

[2]16 May-13 June 1855.

[3]Has to be the 10th month (Northern): Tuesday 15 July 1856.

[4]Careful inspection of the city map (above) shows an ovoid city plan to the north-northeast of the walled city.

[5]June-October 1856.

[6]November 1856.

[7]This is very significant: that the king of Siam enjoyed a seven-tiered parasol and the king of Nan a six-tiered parasol makes a statement about their relative status.

with figures of horses in gold, a raised silver offering tray, and a golden tobacco container.[1]

10.9. In that same year, 1218, a *lwai si* year, / on Sunday, the twelfth day of the fifth month,[2] after the Lord of Life[3] had gone down to be appointed, he led his forces in a successful invasion of Chiang Khæng and brought back to Nan many families.[4]

10.10. In the *müang sai* year, CS 1219,[5] / the ruler commanded all the officers and councillors of the country to build the Golden Pavilion and the Bejewelled Palace. Cao Anantawòralittidet Kunlacettamahantacaiya Bòrommahalatcawongsa , the Great Lord of Life, then reigned in the city of Nan. The country was then serene and peaceful; its fame was suffused with his majesty, which extended abroad. Those who wished to trade, traded; and / thieves were nowhere to be found.[6]

10.11. Upon ascending the throne, [the king] appointed Paña Luang Casænlacacai Aphaiyanantawarapanyawisuttimongkhon as prime minister to lead his Council, and appointed the four *paña* and eight *sænluang* and *sænnòi*, altogether thirty-two in number, to comprise /195/ the Council (*sanam luang*). He also appointed the *sula-aiyakan* and the servants and pages. The country [now] was much more orderly than before.

10.12. He then observed and reflected upon the infirm state of the Religion of the Buddha, which had to be improved and reformed. Moreover, in piety / he desired to have the Holy Teachings copied; that is, all the Pali and *nipâta* and *nikâya* and *niyâya*, in order that the religion of the Gotama should flourish in the future.

10.13. Having reflected thusly, at first he constructed the *vihara* of [Wat] Cang Kham; then / the [Wat] Ku Kham *vihara* ; then he built the *vihara* of Wat Ming Müang; then the *vihara* of Wat Na Pang; then the Khing Dæng Reliquary; then / the Phai Müang *vihara* and Còm Tòng Reliquary of Müang Pong;[7] then the Nòng Bua Reliquary of Müang Cai Pom; then the *vihara* of Wat Dòn Cai of Müang Sisaket;[8] then the great *vihara* of Wat Phumin; then the reliquary at Wat Paña Phu; then the Còm Chon Reliquary of Müang Thœng; then the Phu Tung Reliquary of Müang /196/ In; then the Sop Wæn Reliquary of Müang Chiang

---

[1]This list is very difficult to translate; all the more so because it differs somewhat from that in the published version (Kaona ed., p. 502)

[2]Sunday 8 February 1857 has to be the day intended, though it was the 14th of the waxing moon.

[3]*cao chiwit*.

[4]As noted above, Chiang Khæng is difficult to locate. The reason apparently is that the town itself moved a number of times. By the early 1890s it was located near what we know as Muong Sing, in northwestern Laos. See James McCarthy, *Surveying and Exploring*, p. 151, who indicates that Chiang Khæng was "only a few days' march" to the west of Muong Sing.

[5]AD 1857/58.

[6]A curious echo of the language of the Ramkhamhæng inscription. Late nineteenth-century travelers confirm the low incidence of crime in Nan. See, for example, *Report by Mr. C. E. W. Stringer of a Journey to the Laos State of Nan, Siam* (London, 1888; Parliament, Papers by Command, C.-5321), p. 6.

[7]There is a Ban Müang Pong 28 km. due northwest from Tha Wang Pha.

[8]Müang Sisaket was between Wiang Sa and Na Nòi, in the mountains.

Kham; then the Beng Sakat Reliquary of Müang Pua;[1] then the scripture library southeast of the Bejewelled Palace; then / the *vihara* of Wat Muang Tai; then the *vihara* of Wat Suan Tan and an uposotha there; then the Dòn Khao Kæo *vihara* and the *vihara* at the foot of Dòi Khao Kæo, and the *chatra* and a finial / atop the Khao Kæo Reliquary; then the *vihara* of Wat Montian; then the *vihara* of Wat Pan Ton; then a *chatra* and finial atop the Cæ Hæng Reliquary; then / the *vihara* of Wat Hua Khuang and the uposotha of Wat Cang Kham; [twenty-two meritorious works in all].[2]

10.14. Furthermore, from the very beginning he never ceased to be filled with the essence of the teachings of the Dhamma. Here we will speak of his sponsoring of the [copying of the] Scriptures.

10.15. In the year CS 1217,[3] from his Privy Purse he disbursed funds for the copying of all the scriptures, as enumerated below; namely: (See Appendix 1) ... /199/ altogether 80 chapters. The total honoraria for the members of the / Sangha who copied texts was 19,100 *thòk*.

10.16. In the *kot san* year, CS 1222, on the 3rd day of the second month,[4] the ruler announced to the princes, officials, and people that they would construct the great *mondop* / at the Sanam Luang as a four-faced building with white drapings. (?) This meritorious work would be accompanied by daily chanting, from the 3rd day of the second month until the 1st waning of the third month,[5] / when it would be completed. By the time they were finished, they had listened to [the chanting of] 423 chapters. Cao Anantawòralittidet ..., the Great Lord of Life of Nan, having so strengthened the Dhamma, / thus had the Dhamma listened to [in this fashion] for the first time.

10.17. In the *luang lao* year, 1223,[6] Cao Ananta disbursed funds from his Privy Purse for the copying of the scriptures, as enumerated below, namely: (See Appendix 1) ... These he had copied from the *luang lao* year, CS 1223, until now. Altogether there were 72 works, in 459 fascicles. Counting /203/ miscellaneous works, the total was 532 fascicles.[7]

---

[1]The Beng Sakat Reliquary is the chief religious center of Pua.

[2]If all these religious constructions could be plotted on a map they would geographically define this political and religious community.

[3]AD 1855/56.

[4]Wednesday 18 October 1860. There is an inscription on a wooden manuscript chest at Wat Dòn Cai in Wiang Sa district, dated 6 March 1860 (J.C. Eade; *Müang Nan*, pp. 300-303).

[5]From Wednesday 18 October until Thursday 30 November 1860.

[6]AD 1861/62.

[7]There is a very interesting set of laws of this period, dated according to the text CS 1202 (AD 1840/41), "Kotmai phracao Nan [Laws of the Kings of Nan]," in *Kotmai phra cao Nan [læ] Tamnan phra cao Hai* (Chiang Mai: Sun Songsœm læ Süksa Watthanatham Lan Na, Witthayalai Khru Chiang Mai, 1980; 'Ekkasan lamdap thi 4), pp. [1-20]. The date would appear to be later: one passage (page [16]) bears a date of CS 1223 [AD 1861/62], which seems reasonable in the light of other provisions dealing with foreign traders. Most of the laws deal with subjects such as cattle theft, damage to irrigation works by stray animals, etc. One interesting provision (p. 14) forbids "provincial" people, such as those from Müang Len, Chiang Khæng, Müang Luang, Müang Phukha, Chiang Lap, and Müang La, from moving to and living in other *müang* within the domains of Nan.

10.18. In the first month of CS 1224,[1] [Cao Ananta] ordered the princes, nobles, officers, and people to work together to add five spires to the great four-faced *mondop* at the Sanam Luang, and invited them to provide / the necessary materials. On Friday, the 2nd day of the second month,[2] he led the princes, officials, and people in a *buddhâbhiseka* ceremony and a great celebration. It was not until the 1st day of the waning second month[3] / that it was completed. On this occasion when [the ruler] worshipped with offerings there were 189 fascicles presented, each ornamented with shell inlays on the wooden covers, including 5 *bat dok* in 62 fascicles. The monks who received food offerings on this second occasion / came from all over the domains of Nan.

10.19. In the *ka kai* year CS 1225,[4] the ruler expended funds from his Privy Purse to hire the further copying of the scriptures, as enumerated below, namely: (See Appendix 1). ... This copying was accomplished over eight years, from CS 1225 to CS 1232.[5] Altogether, the ruler /210/ during this third period had 189 texts copied, or a total of 1,251 fascicles.[6]

10.20. In the latter half of the first month of that year,[7] the ruler again invited the princes, officials, and people to erect the great, four-sided *mondop*, eight fathoms high and draped in / white cloth, at the Sanam Luang and provide it with all the requisite offerings, which they did. On the 3rd day of the second month,[8] the ruler conducted a *buddhâbhiseka* ceremony to inaugurate the chanting of the Dhamma and making of merit, which began that day and continued / until the 1st day of the waning second month,[9] when it was completed—a very great ceremony indeed.

10.21. Measured by the number of chapters recited, this time there were 316; or by the cost, it ran to 2 *thæp* of rupees.[10] The Uparaja sponsored 50 chapters, / the Cao Latcawong 10, Cao Suliya 5, and the Cao Latcabut 5. In addition, the faith of the princes and officials was expressed in 1 or 2 chapters each. The monks whom the ruler invited for alms offerings this time / numbered 389, to whom the ruler gave food offerings amounting to 870,000 of rice, 27,500 of *khao pan kon* (?), and 100,000 of milk rice. In addition, on this third occasion he offered monks of Phræ 1,037,000 of rice.

10.22. In CS / 1236, a *kap set* year, on the 3rd day of the waning tenth month,[11] [Cao Ananta] expended funds from the Privy Purse to hire the copying of the scriptures, as enumerated below, namely: (See Appendix 1) ... altogether 10 fascicles, copied in CS / 1236.

---

[1] 24 September–22 October AD 1862.

[2] Friday 24 October 1862.

[3] Friday 7 November 1862.

[4] AD 1863/64.

[5] AD 1870/71.

[6] There are three wooden Buddha images from CS 1231 (18 November 1869) in the National Museum in Nan (J.C. Eade; *Müang Nan*, pp. 306-11).

[7] 11-24 October 1870.

[8] Thursday 27 October 1870.

[9] Wednesday 9 November 1870.

[10] McFarland (p. 392) defines *thæp* as "a coin used in the north," and *ngœn thæp* as "rupee." Clearly this was not just a question of 2 rupees. This is the first explicit mention of the use of Indian rupees in the text.

[11] Wednesday 1 July 1874.

10.23. The main *vihara* of Wat Phuminthalaca in the middle of the town of Nan was constructed from Friday, the 6th day of the sixth month, a *dap mao* day, in the *muang mao* year, CS 1229, in the 25th lunar mansion, /212/ called Pubbhatra.[1] Construction took eight years, until CS 1236, a *kap set* year,[2] when it was completed.

10.24. In that year, in the second month,[3] the ruler encouraged the princes, officials, councillors, and people of communities throughout the domain to support, by their offerings of all kinds, the promulgation of the written teachings [of Buddhism], as in other countries like Lampang, Lamphun, Chiang Mai, Phayao, Chiang Rai, and Luang Prabang. /

10.25. In the fifth month,[4] he had the great four-sided *mondop*, draped with white cloth, erected on the Sanam Luang, as before. On the first day of the / sixth month[5] he held a *buddhâbhiseka* ceremony to make merit, inaugurating the chanting of the Dhamma, from that day until the 8th,[6] breaking [for rain?] from the 9th to the 12th. On the 13th and 14th,[7] all the / towns and villages brought offerings and fireworks into the precincts of Wat Phumin to inaugurate the temple. After circumambulating the temple, every village and town brought presents to the ruler at his residence at the Sanam Luang. /213/ After performing a *buddhâbhiseka* ceremony to inaugurate Wat Phumin on the full-moon day of the sixth month[8] and lustrating [the image] on the next day, all the villages and towns took their rockets to the field at the foot of Dòi Pu Piang Cæ Hæng, / where they fired them off for three days. The dedication of Wat Phumin at this time was a very great occasion.

10.26. On the occasion of the inauguration of Wat Phumin, [Can Ananta] commissioned and presented 99 texts, or, counted / as fascicles, 1,036. The ruler invited 537 monks to accept alms at this time, as well as 47 novices from outside the domain and countless local novices. As for the offerings that were presented, they included / white rice, 24,804,500;[9] chili peppers, 340,000; tobacco, 64,500; *pun* (eaten with betel), 40,000; pickled fish, 30,000; catfish roe, 60,000; dried fish, 350,000; dried betel, 30,000; ginger, 24,000; / onions, 20,000; fermented tea leaves, 340,000; areca nuts, 6,500; betel, 380,000; gunpowder [for fireworks], 650,000; tin, 40,000; gunpowder distributed within(?), 100,000; and sulphur, 30,000. Altogether, the cost of gunpowder amounted to 350,000 *ngœn thæp;*

---

[1] There were no *dap mao* days on Fridays during that yẹar. The closest *dap mao* day would seem to be 5 6/ 3 (30 January 1868).

It is on the basis of this paragraph, and §§10.25-27 below, that it is usually stated that the murals of Wat Phumin were painted at this time. Elsewhere (*Temple Murals as an Historical Source: The Case of Wat Phumin, Nan,* Bangkok, forthcoming) I have argued for a date of 1894 for the murals.

[2] AD 1874/75.

[3] 9 November-8 December 1874.

[4] February 1875.

[5] Sunday 7 March 1875.

[6] Sunday 14 March 1875.

[7] Friday-Saturday, 19-20 March 1875.

[8] Sunday 21 March 1875.

[9] The unit of measure is the *mün* (10,000), equal to 10 liters; so this quantity is equal to 24,804.5 liters.

/214/ and rupees, which he gave to those in the procession, totaled 485 *thæp* and 3,400 rupees.

10.27. In the building and renovation of Wat Phumin, the following were offered: iron, 30,000; copper, 6,100; gemstones, 332,000; / gold leaf, 54,700; lac [as an adhesive for gold leaf], 35 *hai*, 16 *bòk*; *hang* sap, 28 *hò* / *satai* juice [for stucco], 20 *hai*; sugar juice [for making cement], 10,650,000; lime, 24,340,000; and on carpenters and their maintenance 5 *chang* and 300 *thæp* were expended. This was the fourth building and copying work that the ruler accomplished.

10.28. In the *kap kai* year CS 1237,[1] the ruler disbursed from the Privy Purse to hire the further copying of the scriptures, / as enumerated below, namely: (See Appendix 1) .... [f° 215/5] These were copied over five years, from the *dap kai* year 1237 until the *kat mao* year CS 1241,[2] for a total of 34 works, /216/ or 434 fascicles. The total cost of hiring the monks to copy the scriptures during this time amounted to 645 *salüng*, or 182 *thæp* 3 *salüng*. [3]

10.29. In the *kat mao* year, CS 1241, in the second month,[4] the ruler issued an order inviting the princely family, / officials and councillors, and the people to erect the large, four-sided *mondop*, draped with white cloth, on the Sanam Luang, replete with the requisite offerings. On the 8th day of the second month,[5] / the ruler led a *buddhâbhiseka* ceremony to inaugurate the chanting of the scriptures. From that day until the 1st of the waning moon,[6] the chanting continued until finished. During the chanting of the scriptures the earth quaked, on the 8th day of the second month.[7] It quaked from the north. This great ceremony was the fifth such.

10.30. In the *kot si* year, CS 1242,[8] the ruler disbursed from the Privy Purse to hire the further copying of the scriptures, as / enumerated below, namely: (See Appendix 1) ... [f° 219/2] These texts were copied from the *kot si* year CS 1242 to the *ka met* year CS 1245,[9] and included 61 titles, or 271 fascicles; and the cost of hiring monks to write them was 56 *thæp*.

10.31. When the copying was completed, / in CS 1245, the ruler had a library constructed, as a *mondok*, decorated with stone facing and adorned with gems and gold leaf. The walls were painted with beautiful figures of the seated Buddha. It was surrounded by walls atop which there were two demons and two lions on the east side at the north, opposite the southeast corner of the royal palace.

10.32. When it was completed that year, in the second month,[10] the ruler issued a command inviting / the princely family, officials and councillors, and

---

[1] AD 1875/76.

[2] AD 1879/80.

[3] This figure suggests a bit over 3.5 *salüng* per *thæp*.

[4] 16 October-14 November 1879.

[5] Thursday 23 October 1879.

[6] Friday 31 October 1879.

[7] Thursday 23 October 1879. The Bangkok astrologers' notebooks end before this date, so the earthquake cannot be confirmed from the usual sources.

[8] AD 1880/81.

[9] AD 1883/84

[10] November 1883.

people to join in presenting offerings and erecting a large four-sided *mondop* at the Sanam Luang.

10.33. On the 7th day of the second month,[1] the ruler accompanied the princes, /220/ officials and councillors, and people in carrying in procession the scriptures to the royal *mondok* at the Sanam Luang, to the tune of music. The next day, they had a *buddhâbhiseka* ceremony to open the chanting of the scriptures, which / continued to the 1st day of the waning second month.[2] When this had finished, the ruler led a procession which carried the scriptures to the new *mondok*. On this sixth occasion, the ruler dedicated the scriptures and the new library.

10.34. Later, on the 1st day of the ninth month, / a Sunday, a Thai *dap kai* day, in CS 1246, a *kap san* year,[3] the ruler made an offering of a male elephant, 10,000 of beeswax, and 9,000 [units of] iron from the Müang Sa mines to Pa Maha Kuba Cao Jeyyasamka of Wat Luang Caisatan in the middle of Phayao town.

10.35. In that year, the ruler disbursed funds from the Privy Purse to hire the copying of the scriptures, as enumerated below; namely: (See Appendix 1) ... [f° 221/2] These the ruler had copied between CS 1246 and CS 1248,[4] including 24 titles and / 202 fascicles.

10.36. In that year, [Cao Ananta] restored the ordination hall at Wat Cang Kham, which was completed the same year. In the second month,[5] he issued a command inviting the royal / princes, officials and councillors, and the public to erect the large *mondop* at the Sanam Luang and properly equip it with utensils and offerings, as usual. On the 7th day of the second month,[6] he invited the scriptures / to come to the *mondok luang* at the Sanam Luang, and he prepared the way with music. The next day, the chanting of the scriptures began, continuing to the 14th. On the full-moon day,[7] the ruler led a *buddhâbhiseka* ceremony in /222/ the ordination hall of Wat Cang Kham, and listened to the six chapters of the Buddhâbhiseka text. They concluded the next day. This inauguration of the scriptures and dedication of the ordination hall marked another great festival, the seventh. On this occasion, / 38 titles were copied, comprising 292 fascicles.

10.37. Cao Anantawòlalittidet Kulacettamahantacheyyanantapuli Mahalatcawongsa, Lord of Nan, since first receiving royal appointment, / had first been Cao Pakicailaca, then was Cao Paña Lattana Hua Müang Kæo. Not long after, he became Cao Paña Bulilattana. Then he became Cao Paña Mongkhonwalayot, Lord / of Nan; and then not very much later he was Cao Anantawòlalittidet Kunlacettamahantaceyya Bòlommahalatcawongsathibòdi, Great Lord of Life and Lord of Nan, his fifth appointment. When he began his rule / as Lord of Nan, he was 46 years old; and he became Cao Ananta when he was

---

[1]Tuesday 6 November 1883.
[2]Thursday 15 November 1883.
[3]Sunday 26 May 1884, a *dap kai* day.
[4]AD 1886/87.
[5]November 1886.
[6]Wednesday 3 November 1886.
[7]Thursday 11 November 1886.

51. In his reign, Buddhism flourished and the country greatly prospered, more than before.

10.38. His /223/ first wife[1] was named Mæ Cao Sunantaket, and bore him four sons and one daughter. Her first son was Cao Nan Mahapom, who was named Cao Paña Maha Uparaja Hò Na and died soon thereafter. Her second son was Cao Suya. He / was the Cao Paña Latcawongsa, and then became Cao Maha Uparaja Hò Na in place of his elder brother. He succeeded his father as ruler. Her third son was Cao San. He was the Cao Suliyawongsa, / soon became Cao Latcawongsa, and then became Cao Maha Uparaja Hò Na. He is deceased. Her fourth son was Cao Bunlangsi. He was the Cao Latcabut, and / then died. Her only daughters were Cao Mòk Kæo and Cao Khamtip.

10.39. His second wife was named Mæ Cao Khot Kæo. She had one son, Cao Nòi Pom. This son was the Cao Latcabut, and became the Cao Latcawong. He then became Cao Maha Uparaja Hò Na. Her daughter was Cao Yòt Manola.

10.40. His third wife was Mæ Cao Khampiu. She had no children.

10.41. His fourth wife was Mæ Cao Buakhieo, a woman of Phræ. She had a daughter named Nai Piu.[2] /224/

10.42. His fifth wife was Mæ Cao Wæn. She had two daughters, Cao Kæolaima and [Cao] Butsaba, and one son, Cao Nòi Bunsawan.

10.43. His sixth wife was Mæ Cao Ammala, who was also his niece. She had one son, Cao Nai Fa Luan Müang In, and one daughter, Cao Khankham.

10.44. His seventh wife was Mæ Cao Balika, a woman of Chiang Khong. She had seven sons and one daughter. Her first son was Cao Nòi Bua Lom. He was the Cao Bulilat briefly, and then died. / Her second son was Cao Nòi Bua Lieo. Her third son was Cao Po Yang Kham Khieo. He was a monk, and has died. Her fourth son was Cao Nòi Bua Long Pong Fa Buntanawong. Her fifth son was Cao Nòi Mòk Mung Müang. Her sixth son was Cao Nan Lattana Hüang Langsi. Her seventh son was Cao Nòi Suttana. Her daughter was Cao Kieo.

10.45. His eighth wife was Mæ Cao Sukhanta, who had one son and three daughters. Her daughters were Cao Kiang Kham, Cao Müan, and Sao Di; and her son was Cao Nòi Anulotlangsi.

10.46. His ninth wife was Mæ Cao Wæn, a Lü[3] woman from Müang Kussawadi. She had no children.

10.47. His tenth wife was Nang Kæo, a woman of an official family who was a niece/granddaughter of Luang Montri. She had a son, Cao Nan Mahawong, and a daughter, Nai[4] Bok.

10.48. His eleventh wife /225/ was Nang Khampæng, a commoner of Ban Na Pang. She had one son and one daughter. Her son was Cao Nòi Non. Her daughter was Nai[5] Bua Fæng.

10.49. He also had a son, Cao Nan Mahawong, by Nang Cai.

10.50. Altogether, he had 17 sons, or 18 including the one by Nang Cai, and 12 daughters. /

---

[1]Different word used for wife here.

[2]Sic.

[3]The Tai Lü are the Thai group indigenous to the Sipsong Panna.

[4]Sic.

[5]Sic.

10.51. Cao Anantawòlalittidet Kunlacettha Mahantaceyyananta Bulommahalatcawongsa, the Great Lord of Life, reigned for thirty-nine years, and died at the age of eighty-six, going to the next world in the *luang mao* year, CS / 1253, on Friday, the 7th day of the waning eighth month, a Thai *dap mao* day.[1] At that time, the Cao Maha Uparaja appointed princes and elders to go to an audience with the king in Bangkok to report the death of Cao Ananta. /

10.52. In the *tao si* year, CS 1255,[2] a command was issued by [a committee] including the Cao Maha Uparaja Hò Na as head; Phraya Suntharanurak, the [Siamese] commissioner for Nan; the Cao Latcawong, / and the councillors and officials ordering the people to cut wood for the funerary pyre. That same year, a command of the Cao Maha Uparaja, as head; the Cao Latcawongsa; Phraya Suntharanurak, the Commissioner for the domain; the princes, /226/ councillors, and officials together convened all the carpenters to build a large funerary pavilion on the Victory Field at Wat Hua Wiang.[3] [The Uparaja] appointed Paña Luang Casæn Latcai to take charge of and supervise all the carpenters / in building the funerary pavilion and pyre. [The pavilion] was to be cruciform, with a decorated central spire, and painted in various colors, with neat ornamental parasols. There was to be a / *sala* on all four surrounding sides, decorated with *kha hum* and pure white cloth. The four entrance gates were to be hung with lanterns.

10.53. On the 6th day of the eighth month in CS 1255,[4] / the late ruler's remains were taken from the Golden Pavilion, the royal residence, and bathed, while music played and drums were beaten. The images of thirty-two *devaputta* were at the head of the procession which took the body of the prince / to the funerary pavilion. With it emplaced there, entertainments were staged and all the grateful people performed merit-making acts dedicated to the deceased. On the 14th day of the eighth month,[5] the /227/ remains of the ruler were consigned to the flames.

10.54. On the 1st day of the waning eighth month,[6] the Cao Maha Uparaja Suwanna of the Golden Pavilion as head and the Cao Latcawongsa presiding, the princely family, officials, and councillors together / invited the royal ashes down from the funeral pyre and, accompanied by music, they were placed in the great *vihara* of [Wat] Cang Kham, where they were reverenced and a merit-making ceremony was conducted. On the 3rd day of the waning eighth month, at the third hour,[7] the ashes of the late ruler were enshrined in a crypt northwest of the reliquary at [Wat] Cang Kham.[8]

---

[1] Friday 29 May 1891, a *dap mao* day.

[2] AD 1893/94.

[3] There is a Wat Hua Wiang Tai immediately to the north of the old city walls. See city map.

[4] Friday 21 April 1893.

[5] Saturday 29 April 1893.

[6] Monday 1 May 1893.

[7] Wednesday 3 May 1893. Note that the time of day is no longer expressed in terms of what watch it is. Note also the complete absense of any comments regarding the Paknam Affair and the loss of most of Nan's territory in mid-1893.

[8] Where they remain to the present day.

10.55. In that same year, / on the 9th day of the waning third month,[1] the Cao Maha Uparaja Hò Na went down to an audience with the king in Bangkok to present tribute. On that occasion, His Majesty King Chulalongkorn was pleased to appoint the Cao Maha Uparaja Hò Na, the son of Cao Anantawòlalittidet, as ruler of Nan, with the title Cao Suriyaphongsa Phrittidet /228/ Kulachetthamahantacheyyanantha Burommaharatchawongsathibòdi, Ruling Prince of Nan. The king presented him with the regalia of rank, namely, a gold betel tray with gold implements, a gold cuspidor, a gold ewer, gold-decorated vestments, and various articles of clothing. His business at court concluded, the ruler took leave of the king and returned.

10.56. In the *kap sanga* year, 1256, on the 8th day of the ninth month,[2] the ruler returned. On the 4th day of the second month,[3] the / princely family, officers, and councillors together performed a *buddhâbhiseka* ceremony and ritually bathed him (?), and then collectively invited [Cao Suliyaphong] to take up residence in the Golden Pavilion, in the place of his father. As for Cao Anantawalalittidet, / when he went to the next world he was considered to have been the 12th of his line, the 60th[4] from Cao Khun Fòng to rule the domain.

10.57. When Cao Suliyaphong Phalittidet Kulacettamahantaceyya / Bulommahalatcawongsa had begun his reign, he had six great officials, namely, Interior, Justice, Military, Palace, Finance, and Agriculture. The country was more than ever a vassal state.(?)

10.58. When Cao Suliyaphong Phalittidet, the ruler of Nan, was still the Cao Latcawongsa—the date cannot be recalled—he had a dream, in which he saw Suliya, the Sun, appear out of / the cumulus clouds above, to the east, and yield forth a heavenly radiance over the entire universe.

10.59. Not long afterwards, His Majesty Anantawòlalittidet, his father the Great Lord of Life, / out of his graciousness said that henceforth the Cao Latcawongsa would be charged with the renovation of the Pu Piang Cæ Hæng Reliquary, that it would become more splendid than ever before. / From that time forward, the Cao Latcawongsa—namely, Cao Suliyaphong Phalittidet—took most seriously and literally the gracious words of the ruler, the Great Lord of Life.

[End of the published text.]

---

[1] Monday 1 January 1894.
[2] Monday 11 June 1894.
[3] Thursday 1 November 1894.
[4] Actually, the 62nd.

CHAPTER ELEVEN

EPILOGUE

11.1. Not long afterwards, in CS / 1241, the great *vihara* at Wat Cæ Hæng was constructed.[1] When [Cao Suliyaphong] was the Cao Latcawong, he had the gallery (*salabât*)[2] built around the Great Reliquary and the great *vihara*. The total cost of building the gallery was 2,456 baht. The exterior and interior of the gallery /230/cost 438; the cost of landscaping the area in front of the gallery was 182 baht 50 satang; the cost of cutting the wood slats for the roof tiles and of expanding the gallery was 105 baht; / the cost of making the arched entrance and making the frames for the doors was 500 baht; and the base of the walls of the gallery was 300 baht. To stucco around the base of the gallery cost / another 41 baht 75 satang. To hire sawyers to saw the wood of the gallery cost 738 baht 75 satang. Hiring the wood done for the doors of the gallery cost / 26 baht; and it cost another 150 baht to cut additional wood. It was 35 baht to [further] clear the ground in front of the gallery. The 7,312,240 bricks used to construct the walls around the gallery / cost 3,536 rupees and 3 salüng—in baht, 1617 baht 70 satang. The 160,570 clay tiles to cover the gallery cost 1,255 baht. Cement from Müang Ngæng [was procured] in the amount of 137 million, /231/ 66 hundred-thousands, 2 ten-thousands (?); amounting to 10 million, 3 hundred-thousands, 8 ten-thousands; and the total lime was 15 million, 6 hundred-thousands, 5 ten-thousands; costing in *siang* and *phai* money, 61x[3] baht. The cost of preparing the earth and razing the buildings in front of Wat Cæ Hæng on the west side and carting away the rubble he paid for in baht; / altogether for a total of 4,853 baht. Hiring *Sæn* Suliya Salaphan to construct two nagas cost 2,400 baht. Hiring Maung Kong[4] to build a wall around the Holy Reliquary on all four sides and two lion statues / cost 1,835 rupees, equivalent to 1,126 baht 25 satang. To repair the Great Vihara, and the gallery there that was dilapidated, a total of 386 baht. For the stairway to the sala, / to buy and move wood and hire the carpenters to make the sala for Cæ Hæng was a total of 1,122 baht. This was all the cost of

[1]AD 1879/80. This text is clearly different from what precedes it. The hand is different; the numerals used now are the regular secular figures; and there are four lines per folio, rather than five. Spellings also differ from those employed earlier in the text.

[2]This particular word has caused me a great deal of difficulty. A book on the architecture of Phayao and Nan (*Sathapattayakam Phayao læ Nan*, Chiang Mai, Social Research Institute, Chiang Mai University, 1989, p. 169) has a full architectural plan of Wat Cæ Hæng on which the *salabat* is clearly marked: it is the long gallery of many rooms that completely surrounds the enclosure that includes the cetiya, the *vihara*, and the ordination hall. It measures roughly 144 x 68 meters—a very large structure indeed!

[3]The third digit is illegible.

[4]The name is obviously Burmese.

building in the vicinity of the Cæ Hæng Reliquary. Altogether the total was 18,671 baht 75 satang in money. /232/

11.2. In CS 12...,[1] the inauguration of the Cæ Hæng Reliquary was completed with a grand fête, and Caokhun Phra Jayânandamuni, head of the Pamok Sect and Patriarch [of the principality] himself / set up many fireworks for the festivities from Pin Nòi to the city of Nan; and the fireworks' fuse was a hundred fathoms long. / All the abbots of temples from all over the province (*cangwat*) of Nan were presented with food alms at the Great Reliquary. In the middle of the night there was a procession to listen to sermons, and the / firing of fireworks [of various sorts]. The festivities continued for three days, with sermons and fireworks each day, as was the custom of the principality.[2]

11.3. This Book of the 15 Great Dynasties, that is, this chronicle of Nan, Cao Uttarakankoson had me—Phrakhru Nandasamanâcâriyawongsâ, patriarch of the Pamok Sect of Nan Province—arrange to have inscribed in order to / further the future of the ruling family. I am convinced that Cao Uttarakankoson is a person of great merit and wisdom, / with intelligence and expertise, which is of great importance in the lineage of Cao Latcañattiwongsa. He is a person committed to the Five Precepts and the Eight Precepts; a person of great Buddhist faith, as is shown by his / many generous benefactions for the building of religious edifices. For example, in RS 123[3] he built the vihara of Wat Panet, in RS 132[4] he built the vihara of Wat Na Lüang Nòk, in RS 134[5] /234/ he built the *vihara* of Wat Muang Na Phat, and in RS 138[6] he built the ordination hall of Wat Panet. He is responsible for many other generous benefactions of which I am not aware.

11.4. Among the sons and nephews of the lineage of Cao Latcañattiwongsa, which has almost died out, / this Cao Uttarakankosonis a man of ideas, wisdom, expertise, and energy. He is a man of rank and accomplishment / who is respected by all the princes and officials and the people. This Cao Uttarakankoson is a major prince in the Wiang Nüa district[7] at the present time. I have placed his biography / here in order that his descendants might find it exemplary. This is the truth as I know it. In fact, I am beholden to none. /235/ He has given me nothing beyond the cost of palm leaves and the costs of copying this work and the costs of food, so I should be in no one's debt, motivated only by respect.

11.5. Cao Uttarakankoson, / nâi Nòi Mahacai,[8] was born in RS 83,[9] the son of Cao Nòi Sammana. His mother was named Cao Bun Nam. [He was] born

---

[1]There is a blank space here approximately two inches long.

[2]Roughly six-inch blank to end of line and end of page. Here begins a long duplication. With but minor differences, ff° 233-236 are duplicated on ff° 237-240, with the exception of the final paragraph, which occurs only at the very end of the text. In both cases, both sides of two palm leaves are involved.

[3]AD 1904/05.

[4]AD 1913/14.

[5]AD 1915/16.

[6]AD 1919/20.

[7]The word used is *tambon*. It might refer to the extensive populated area immediately abutting the city of Nan on the north.

[8]Nòi Mahachai apparently is his given name, while Uttarakankoson is a conferred title.

[9]AD 1864/65.

in Ban Chiang Khong Wiang Luk Nüa.[1] His wife was named Cao Bualalâ. Cao Nòi Sammana / was the son of Cao Latcañattiwongsa, that is, Cao Si Sòng Müang. Cao Latcañattiwongsa was the son of Cao Nòi; and Cao Nòi was the son of Cao Yattakankoson.

11.6. Cao Uttarakankoson was ordained as a novice / at Wat Panet in RS 116,[2] and entered government service as a public prosecutor in the city of Nan. In RS 120[3] he was given the title of Phaya Uttarakankoson. In RS 127[4] he received royal appointment /236/ raising his rank to Cao Uttarakankoson. In RS 130[5] His Majesty was pleased to appoint him a *ròng ammat tho*. He received such royal decorations as the Fifth Class of the Order of the Crown of Siam / and the Fifth Class of the Order of the White Elephant. These should suffice to demonstrate his goodness and the favor in which he was held by the ruling family. This book was completed on 5 August / BE 2461, a *lwai sanga* year; second of the waxing moon in the twelfth month in CS 1280.[6]

11.7. This Book of the 15 Great Dynasties,[7] that is, this chronicle of Nan, Cao Uttarakankoson had me—Phrakhru Nandasamanâcâriyawongsâ, patriarch of the Pamok Sect of Nan Province—arrange to have inscribed / in order to further the future of the ruling family. But I am convinced that Cao Uttarakankoson is a person of great merit and wisdom, / with intelligence and expertise, which is of great importance in the lineage of Cao Latcañattiwongsa. He is a person committed to the 5 Precepts and the 8 Precepts; a person of great Buddhist faith, as is shown by his / many generous benefactions for the building of religious edifices. In RS 123[8] he erected the *vihara* of Wat Panet, and in RS 132[9] he erected the *vihara* of Wat Lüang Nòk. In RS 124[10] he erected the *vihara* [of Wat] Muang Na Pang and /238/ in RS 135[11] he erected the ordination hall of Wat Panet. He also performed many other works of merit of which I am not aware.

11.8. Among the sons and nephews of Cao Latcañattiwongsa, a lineage which has almost died out, this Cao Uttarakankoson / is a man of ideas, wisdom, expertise, and energy. He is a man of rank and accomplishment who is respected by all the princes and officials / and the people. This Cao Uttarakankoson is a major prince and leader in the Wiang Nüa district[12] at the present time. I have placed his biography here in order that his descendants might / find it ex-

---

[1]This might simply be a descriptive reference to the neighborhood to the north of the fortified area within the city walls.

[2]AD 1897/98.

[3]AD 1901/02.

[4]AD 1908/09.

[5]AD 1911/12.

[6]End of folio. 5 August 1918. There has to be an error here: BE 2461 was a *pœk sanga* year, not a *rawai sanga* year. The nearest *rawai sanga* year was twelve years earlier, in 1906/07. That this date is misread is confirmed by repetitions of the calendrical data elsewhere in this chapter.

[7]Here begins the duplication of ff° 233-236.

[8]AD 1904/05.

[9]AD 1913/14.

[10]Surely a mistake for RS 134, AD 1915/16.

[11]AD 1916/17.

[12]The word used is *tambon*. It might refer to the extensive populated area immediately abutting the city of Nan on the north.

emplary. This is the truth as I know it. In fact, I am beholden to none. He has given me nothing beyond the cost of palm leaves and the costs of copying this work and the costs of food, / so I should be in no one's debt, motivated only by respect.

11.9. Cao Uttarakankoson, nâi Nòi Mahachai, was born in RS 83,[1] the son of Cao Nòi Sammana. His mother / was named Cao Bun Nam. [He was] born in Ban Chiang Khong Wiang Luk Nüa. His wife was named Cao Bualalâ. Cao Nòi Sammana was the son of Cao Latcañattiwongsa, that is, Cao Si Sòng Müang. Cao Latcañattiwongsa was / the son of Cao Nòi; and Cao Nòi was the son of Cao Yattakankoson.

11.10. Cao Uttarakankoson was ordained as a novice at Wat Panet in RS 116[2] and entered government service as a public prosecutor / in the city of Nan. In RS 120[3] [His Majesty the King] was pleased to confer on him letters patent as Phraya Uttarakankoson in RS 127,[4] and he was subsequently raised to the rank of Cao Uttarakankoson in /240/ RS 130,[5] when [His Majesty was] pleased to bestow upon him the rank of *ròng 'ammat tho*. He received the decorations of the Fifth Class of the Order of the Crown of Siam and the Fifth Class of the Order of the White Elephant, among others, which attest to the favor in which he was held / by the ruling family. This book was completed for the sixth time (?) on the 9th of August in BE 2461, a *pœk sanga* year, on Saturday, the second waxing of the eleventh month[6] Cao Uttarâkânkosala sponsored it.[7] /

11.11. In CS 1280, a *pœk sanga* year, on a *kot cai* day,[8] the piety of Cao Uttarakankoson took the lead to join with members of the royal line including Cao Bualilâ and all the royal sons, daughters, nephews, and nieces / together to construct this local chronicle, that the Religion might endure for 5,000 years. Cao Uttarakankoson, who lives in Ban Panet, Wiang Nüa district, of Nan province, has copied this chronicle.

End of the manuscript.

---

[1] AD 1864/65.

[2] AD 1897/98.

[3] AD 1901/02.

[4] AD 1908/09.

[5] AD 1911/12.

[6] Friday, 9 August 1918; or Saturday 10 August 1918. Notice that f° 236 says the twelfth month, while f° 240 says the eleventh month. Here I suspect we have an example of the conflict between two different dating systems, the so-called Keng Tung style and the Northern style of counting months.

[7] The duplicated passages end here.

[8] Wednesday, 14 August 1918.

APPENDIX 1

THE COPYING OF BUDDHIST TEXTS

In the final chapter of the translation, numerous references are made to the copying of Buddhist texts by the pious King Anantaworarit. This is a very long list, of more than 700 titles; and it seems that the most useful way to present this interesting information is to arrange it alphabetically by title. In the list that follows, the title is followed by the number of bundles (*phuk*) and the CS year in which the text was copied.

The works listed below are primarily Buddhist texts, either in translation or in Pali. Some information as to the contents of some can be gained from standard works on Pali literature: see, for example, K. R. Norman, *Pali Literature, Including the Canonical Literature in Prakrit and Sanskrit of All the Hinayana Schools of Buddhism* (Wiesbaden: Harrassowitz, 1983); *A History of Indian Literature*, ed. Jan Gonda (VII, fasc. 2). As an example of what might be done with a list like this, see Oskar von Hinüber, "Remarks on a List of Books Sent to Ceylon from Siam in the 18th Century," *Journal of the Pali Text Society* 12 (1988): 175-83. Relatively few of the works listed here appear in the standard sources. Most are at least listed in the consolidated catalogue of palm-leaf manuscripts microfilmed by the Social Research Institute of Chiang Mai University: *Raichü nangsü boran Lan Na: ekkasan maikhrofim khòng Sathaban Wicai Sangkhom Mahawitthayalai Chiang Mai pi 2521-2533* [Catalogue of palm-leaf texts on microfilm at the Social Research Institute, Chiang Mai University 1978-1990] (Chiang Mai: Sathaban Wicai Sangkhom, 1991).

The critical reader should note that spelling follows that in the Nan Chronicle, and is not necessarily "correct" Pali (in particular). I have tentatively identified some of the texts, using the abbreviations J for Jâtaka tales and PJ for the Paññâsajâtaka

50 jāti	10	1223
50 jāti	10	1225
7 gambhīrā	7	1223
7 gambhīra	1 kaṇḍha	1242
84,000 kaṇḍha	1	1217
84,000 kaṇḍha	1	1225
84,000 kaṇḍha	1	1242
Abhayarāja	8	1225
Abhidhamma čhǭng	1	1217
Abhidhamma čhǭng	10	1225
Abhidhammacoda	6	1242
Abhidhammasaṅgaha	5	1225
Abhidhammasaṅginī	11	1217
Abhidhammasaṅgiṇī	11	1225
Aggaraṭṭhadhamma	9	1236
Alina (?Alinacitta, J 156)	1	1223
Anāgatavaṃsa	5	1225
Anulokasāsanā	1	1225
Aṅguttaranikāya	13	1217
Aṅguttaranikāya	13	1225
Aṅguttaranikāya	5	1242
Arabimma	2	1225
Aruṇavatī	4	1217
Asivisasūtta	1	1225
Asivisasūtta vijānasūtta	2	1242
Asītinipāta	6	1225

Asītinipāta, mat 80		1217
Asokarāja nibbāna	1	1225
Athāpāla	2	1242
Attha uparipaṇṇāsa	11	1225
Atthasaṅkhāraloka	1	1237
Atītabuddhavaṃsa	15	1225
Aṭṭhakathā ekanipāta	10	1223
Aṭṭhaṅgika	1	1217
Ānisaṅgha prathīp	1	1217
Ānisaṃsa	1	1223
Ānisaṃsa	1	1225
Ānisaṃsa 5000 thuan	1	1242
Ānisaṃsa bǫk fai	1	1237
Ānisaṃsa bǫk fai	1	1242
Ānisaṃsa dhammasavana	1	1223
Ānisaṃsa khamson	1	1223
Ānisaṃsa khāo 20 met	1	1242
Ānisaṃsa khāo 20 met	1	1242
Ānisaṃsa klǫng chai	1	1242
Ānisaṃsa parivāra	1	1223
Ānisaṃsa phī tāi	1	1225
Ānisaṃsa phračhao	1	1242
Ānisaṃsa piṭaka	1	1242
Ānisaṃsa sap thān	5	1237
Ānisaṃsa sap thān	5	1242
Ānisaṃsa visuddhimagga	10	1246
Bakula (PJ 50)	1	1223
Balasaṅkhayā	9	1223
Bantakī	8	1225
Bavilati	4	1225
Bhabhakumāra	2	1237
Bhayavināsa upātasanti	3	1225
Bhuridatta (J 543)	5	1217
Bimbā khanun ngiu	5	1225
Bodhipakkhiyadhamma	4	1223
Bojjhaṅga thang 7	2	1236
Borāṇasaṅgaha	14	1223
Brahmajālasūtta	12	1223
Bua hom	5	1223
Bua lom	4	1225
Buddhaghosathera	5	1217
Buddhamanta	1	1223
Buddhanibbāna	1	1225
Buddhanibbāna	15	1225
Buddhanibbāna	12	1242
Buddhanidāna	4	1223
Buddhanidāna	1	1225
Buddhapāramī	4	1242
Buddhapāramī	5	1242
Buddhasenā	4	1223
Buddhavaṁsa	7	1223
Buddhavaṃsa	9	1225
Buddhābhiseka	3	1225
Buddhābhiseka	3	1225
Buddhābhiseka	2	1225
Buddhābhiseka	5	1237
Buddhābhiseka	2	1242
Buddhābhiseka	4	1246
Buddhābhiseka	5	1242
Buddhābhiseka bāramī	6	1225
Buddhānussatikammaṭhāna	5	1236
Buddhāpadāna	1	1225
Cakkavatti khan khak	3	1225
Cakkavāḷadīpanī	10	1225
Cakkhāvudha and Sihanāda	2	1223
Campā 4 ton	4	1225
Campā 4 ton mat 3	13	1225
Candabāṇija	1	1236
Candagādha	6	1217
Candakinarī (J 485)	1	1223
Candakumāra	2	1217
Candakumāra	4	1242
Candasuriya	1	1217
Candasūtta	3	1242
Cariyāpiṭaka	20	1225
Cattāḷīsanipāta, mat 40		1217
Catukkanipāta aṅguttaranikāya	3	1225
Cāmadevī	5	1225
Cetiyabhedā	4	1223
Chang phong	4	1223
Chāng sathan	1	1242
Culanīpanda	1	1217
Cundasuriya	1	1223
Cūḷadhammapāla (J 358)	7	1225
Cūḷamaṇīsuddhodhirā	2	1225
Cūḷavagga	11	1217
Cūḷavagga	5	1242
Cūḷavagga	14	1242
Cūḷavibhaṅga	9	1237
Cūḷavibhaṅ[ga] Buddhaguṇa 10 duang	10	1223
Cūḷavipāka	1	1236
Cūḷavipāka	1	1242
Dabbamallaputtanibāna	1	1225
Dakkhiṇāvibhaṅgasūtta	1	1225
Dalidadaka	1	1225

Dasajāti	1	1217
Dasajāti	1	1217
Dasajāti	13	1225
Dasapañhā	1	1242
Dasavatthu	8	1225
Dasavatthu	8	1225
Devadantasūtta	8	1225
Devadukka	5	1217
Devasīsahaṅsa kham	1	1236
Devatā thām pañhā	1	1237
Devatā thām pañhā	1	1237
Dhammacakka	1	1217
Dhammacakka ton	1	1225
Dhammadāyāda	3	1223
Dhammadāyāda chai prākān	3	1225
Dhammadhajagga	1	1217
Dhammadhajagga	1	1223
Dhammaraṅsī	1	1236
Dhammasavana (or Dhamma suan)	1	1242
Dhammasukho	1	1217
Dhammavedī thang Pāḷi	7	1225
Dhātukathā	6	1217
Dhātuvibhaṅga	11	1223
Dikā Abhidhamma	9	1217
Dinarājajātha	1	1225
Dīghanikāya	11	1217
Dīghanikāya	7	1242
Dīghanikāyadosa	1	1225
Duggatakumāra	1	1223
Duggatasūtra	9	1223
Dukkakumāra	3	1236
Dukkanipāta	10	1225
Dukkasikkhāvinicchaya	3	1225
Dullabhā	1	1236
Dusakumāravijayasūtta	1	1237
Ekanipāta aṅguttaranikāya	2	1223
Ekādasanipāta, mat 11		1217
Etadagga	13	1223
Etadagga aṅguttaranikāya	11	1225
Gambhīra	7	1246
Girimānanda	1	1217
Girimānanda khrǫng vipassanā	3	1225
Gonanda	1	1242
Gonasūtta	14	1225
Govinda	1	1223
Gurudhamma	12	1225
Gurusāsati	1	1236
Jambūpati	8	1223
Janaka	2	1217
Janaka	5	1242
Janasanda	3	1217
Javanahaṅsajātaka(J 476)	1	1242
Kaccāyanathera	12	1223
Kammavācā	4	1225
Kammavācā	4	1225
Kammavācā	4	1242
Kamphra roi khot	1	1225
Kamphrao wua thong	4	1223
Kaṅkhāvīttaraṇī	7	1217
Kaṇḍha 1	12	1217
Kapana	6	1225
Kapina	1	1242
Karuṇa	95	1225
Kasapathera	1	1225
Kathāvatthu	7	1217
Kathāvatthu	6	1242
Kathāvatthu	5	1242
Kaṭhinavinicchaya	1	1225
Kayavirati	1	1236
Kāmadhamma	1	1242
Kāmaṇīcanda	5	1225
Khandha thang 5	1	1242
Khānavuttibuññakiriyā supinasāmaṇera	3	1225
Khuddakanikāya	17	1217
Kusalanisayadhurapuṇṇa-ganthī	1	1236
Kusarāja (J 531)	2	1223
Kwāng dam Mandātu-rāja (J 258)	9	1225
Lohanajivahā	14	1225
Lokacakkhu	5	1223
Lokako	5	1217
Lokanaya	11	1223
Lokapaññati	1	1217
Lokasathāsadivohāra	?	1242
Lokavidū	4	1223
Lokavinaya	15	1225
Madhurasa	2	1223
Madhurasa	10	1225
Madhurasa, ch. 1	6	1223
Madhurasasavāhinī	10	1223
Madhurasavāhini	11	1225
Madhurasavāhini	10	1225
Mahā Ananda nibbāna	1	1225

Mahābuddhaguṇa	1	1217
Mahāluya	2	1223
Mahāmūlanibbāna	1	1242
Mahānibbāna	1	1225
Mahānibbāna luang	10	1237
Mahānibbānasūtta	13	1225
Mahāpadhānasūtta	11	1225
Mahāpaṭṭhāna	8	1217
Mahāpaṭṭhāna	17	1242
Mahāsamayasūtta	1	1246
Mahāvagga	11	1217
Mahāvagga	9	1223
Mahāvagganidāna	8	1225
Mahāvagga......	?	1225
Mahāvaṃsa lūang	13	1217
Mahāvaṃsa lūang	21	1225
Mahāves chabap fā khāo (J 547)[1]	15	1236
Mahāves chabap Kamphaeng channai	16	1225
Mahāves chabap khǫ mư̄ lek	16	1236
Mahāves chabap Müang Song	16	1225
Mahāves chabap Phra Hin Pu	16	1225
Mahāves chabap Phra Yot Soi	16	1225
Mahāves chabap phrāo phan lam	15	1236
Mahāves chabap Phu Kam	16	1225
Mahāvessantarajātaka, chabap hai lao	13	1225
Mahāvipāka	1	1242
Mahāvipāka	4	1242
Mahāvipāka	4	1242
Mahosatha	9	1217
Mahosatha	13	1237
Mahosatha	13	1242
Majjhimanikāya	16	1217
Majjhimapaṇṇāsa	7	1225
Manoratha	13	1242
Maṅgalabhedā	7	1223
Maṅgaladīpanī	13	1225
Maṅgaladīpanī	1 kaṇḍha	1242
Maṅgalapañhā	6	1217
Maṅgalapañhā	8	1223
Maṅgalasūtta	12	1225
Maṇīpadīpa	16	1225
Matasūtta	1	1225
Mālai prōt lōk	1	1242
Mālā	2	1225
Metteyyasūtta	3	1225
Metteyyasūtta	4	1246
Metteyyavaṁsa	6	1225
Milindapañhā	15	1225
Milindapañhā	16	1237
Moggallānanibāna	1	1236
Moggallātheranibbāna	1	1225
Mudutādevatā	1	1237
Mūla ṛkṣa	2	1225
Mūla ton thayya, mat 1	5	1217
Mūladhammacakka	5	1223
Mūlaḍikāsūtra	3	1223
Mūlaḍīkāsūtra	1	1225
Mūlaḍīkāsūttasuññasūtta-kāḷīdhātu	3	1225
Mūlakammaṭhāna	2	1225
Mūlakammaṭhāna	2	1225
Mūlakamṭhāna	1	1217
Mūlamūlī	2	1242
Mūlanibbānasūtra	1	1217
Mūlasikkhā	2	1223
Na-anuññātasabbasūtta	1	1242
Nandasena	6	1225
Naratanattihāra	5	1223
Nākittasūtra	1	1225
Nāmasabda Cūḷavagga	14	1242
Nāmataddhita	7	1217
Nārada	3	1217
Nārada	3	1246
Nātha abhidhamma	15	1223
Nemirāja	2	1217
Nemirāja (J 541)	4	1242
Nidānavaggasaṅyuttanikāya	12	1225
Nikāya thang 5 phūk 1, 4, 5	3	1246
Nisaya	12	1225
Nisaya 50 jāti mat 3	10	1225
Nisaya 50 jāti mat 4	?	1225
Nisaya Aṅguttaranikāya	9	1223
Nisaya Bimbātherī	7	1225
Nisaya Buddhamantra	2	1223
Nisaya Dāmocana	7	1225
Nisaya Dhammapada mat 11	10	1225
Nisaya Kathanāpaṭṭhāna	4	1225
Nisaya Madhurajambū	15	1225
Nisaya Mahāpaṭṭhāna	4	1225
Nisaya Majjhimanikāya mat 1	14	1225

[1]The *Mahavessantarajataka*.

Nisaya Majjhimanikāya mat 2	10	1225
Nisaya Mūlapuggaḷikā paṭṭhāna	14	1225
Nisaya Porāṇaḍikā	13	1225
Nisaya Saccasaṃkhepa	8	1225
Nisaya Saddabhedacintā	13	1225
Nisaya Samantapāsādikā	14	1225
Nisaya Sīlavaggadīghanikāya	17	1225
Nisaya Vinicchaya	16	1225
Nisaya Vuttodapa Pāḷi	16	1225
Nisayacatukkanipāta	15	1225
Nisayaḍikāsatipaṭṭhāna	15	1225
Niyyādhammo	7	1225
Om lom tom kham	2	1223
Ovādānusāsanī	1	1217
Ovādāvicaraṇa	1	1236
Padumakumāra (J 261)	1	1225
Pakiṇṇaka	5	1225
Pañcanipāta, mat 4, 5, 6, 9	4	1217
Pañcavuḍha	1	1237
Pañhā phrayā pasasenadi	1	1242
Pañhā Phrayā Passenadi	1	1242
Pañhā rājasuga	1	1223
Paññābala	2	1223
Paññāsajāti	10	1223
Paññāsanipāta, mat 50	1	1217
Paṇidhāna	1	1242
Paṇṇāsanipāta	12	1225
Paṇṇāsanipāta	3	1225
Paramatthavibhusanī	12	1225
Paramatthavibhūsanī	12	1223
Parābhava	2	1223
Parājikakaṇḍha	20	1217
Parāyanavagga attadantā	6	1225
Parivāra	11	1217
Parivāra	11	1217
Paṭhama	1	1223
Paṭhamabhāṇavāra	1	1223
Paṭhamamūlamūlā	5	1225
Pācittiya (?PJ 39)	11	1217
Pāḷi Atthamadāvagga-saṁyuttanikāya	12	1225
Pāḷi Atthapañca-aṅguttara-nikāya	14	1225
Pāḷi Atthadukkanipāta aṅguttaranikāya	15	1225
Pāḷi Atthakathā khandhavagga saṅyuttanikāya	4	1225
Pāḷi Atthakathā mahāvagga saṅyuttanikāya	8	1225
Pāḷi Atthakathā pañca aṅguttaranikāya	14	1237
Pāḷi Atthakathā paṇṇāsa majjhimanikāya	12	1225
Pāḷi Atthamahāvagga saṅyuttanikāya	8	1237
Pāḷi Atthamahāvagga Saṅyuttanikāya	1	1242
Pāḷi Cattāḷīsanipāta	4	1225
Pāḷi Catukkanipāta	8	1236
Pāḷi Cūḷavagga mat 1	11	1237
Pāḷi Dhammapada	14	1225
Pāḷi Dhātukathā	5	1237
Pāḷi Dhātukathā pakaraṇa	4	1242
Pāḷi Kaccāyanāsandhi	1	1225
Pāḷi Kaccāyanātathakāraka	1	1225
Pāḷi Kaccāyanātathataddhita	3	1225
Pāḷi Kathāvatthupakaraṇa	7	1242
Pāḷi Mahāpaṭṭhāna	11	1237
Pāḷi Mahāpaṭṭhāna mat 2	11	1236
Pāḷi Mahāvagga	9	1225
Pāḷi Nārājadhātavaṅsa	1	1225
Pāḷi Nātha-atthakathā abhidhamma	15	1225
Pāḷi Nidānasaṃyuttanikāya	12	1225
Pāḷi Paṇṇāsanipāta	3	1225
Pāḷi Phra Sihiṅga	1	1225
Pāḷi Phra Ves	9	1225
Pāḷi Puggalapaññati	6	1242
Pāḷi sabda thang 8	8	1242
Pāḷi saddā thang 8	8	1242
Pāḷi Saṅgiṇī pakaraṇa	10	1242
Pāḷi Saṭṭhīnipāta	1	1225
Pāḷi Suñña	18	1225
Pāḷi Vibhaṅga	17	1225
Pāḷi Vibhaṅga Aṅguttara-nikāya	13	1242
Pāḷi Vibhaṅga pakaraṇa	17	1242
Pāḷi Yamaka	8	1242
Pāḷi Yamaka mat 1	13	1237
Pāḷi Yojanā	15	1223
Pāramī	1	1242
Pāramī phọkhā kæo	1	1237
Pāramī phọkhā kæo	1	1242
Pātimokkha	1	1225
Pāṭha	14	1225

Pāṭhamat I	10	1217
Pāṭhamat II	12	1217
Pāṭhamat III	12	1217
Pāṭhamat IV	12	1217
Pāṭhamat V	12	1217
Pāṭhamat VII	7	1217
Pāṭhamat VIII	9	1217
Pāṭhamat IX	9	1217
Pekhaṇasūtta	1	1225
Petavatthu	18	1225
Petavatthu	17	1225
Phra Jīva	4	1223
Phra Kǣo phra čhan hua lān bư̄a het khao kan	36	1225
Phra Ves [Vessantara]	13	1225
Phra Ves chabap cariyā	16	1246
Phra Ves chabap chiang sǣn	16	1242
Phra Ves chabap chiang thǭng	16	1237
Phra Ves chabap hing kǣo	16	1246
Phra Ves chabap kamphǣng 1000 chan	16	1242
Phra Ves chabap kālakhǭt	16	1237
Phra Ves chabap khā pān	16	1246
Phra Ves chabap lāi hin	16	1237
Phra Ves chabap mangtharā	16	1242
Phra Ves chabap mangtharā	16	1246
Phra Ves chabap mangthā	16	1237
Phra Ves chabap muk mun sai mūn	16	1237
Phra Ves chabap muk mun sai mūn	16	1246
Phra Ves chabap muk mun sāi mūn	16	1242
Phra Ves chabap mư̄ang hān	16	1242
Phra Ves chabap Nān kao	16	1237
Phra Ves chabap pā chāng	16	1246
Phra Ves chabap pā hiang rǣng phī	16	1237
Phra Ves chabap pā kī	16	1246
Phra Ves chabap phra rǭi	16	1237
Phra Ves chabap phǣndin wai	16	1237
Phra Ves chabap plā chāng	16	1242
Phra Ves chabap plā phai čhǣ	16	1237
Phra Ves chabap Sīharasa	16	1237
Phra Ves chabap thao nang rung	16	1246
Phra Ves chabap thā pǣn	16	1246
Phra Ves chabap thǣn kǣo	16	1237
Phra Ves chabap thǣn kǣo	[16]	1246
Phra Ves chabap vaṃsa	16	1225
Phra Ves chabap wing wǭn	16	1246
Phra Ves chabap wongkot	16	1225
Phra Ves hing kǣo wingwǭn	16	1242
Phra Vesapa tǭn kwāng	16	1225
Phracao liap lok	9	1217
Piṭaka	4	1225
Piṭaka	4	1237
Piṭaka cariyā	1	1225
Piṭaka cariyā	10	1242
Piṭaka nong khwāi	4	1225
Piṭaka thang 3	3	1242
Piṭaka thang 3	4	1246
Piṭaka thang 3 ruam	4	1225
Piṭaka thang 6	6	1242
Porāṇa	8	1225
Porāṇasaṅgaha	10	1225
Puggalabaññati	6	1217
Puggalapaññati	6	1242
Puṇṇanāga	1	1223
Ratanasūtra	1	1217
Rathavanītasūtta	9	1225
Rathavīnītasūtta	10	1225
Raṭṭhadīpanī	4	1225
Raṭṭhapāramī	2	1242
Rāhulasūtta	1	1225
Rāhulovādasūtta	1	1236
Rājābhiseka cao Jālīkaṇhā	1	1225
Rāmakian	7	1223
Rāyaṅū	7	1223
Rūpasiddhi	13	1223
Sabba sǭn	1	1242
Sabbapuṇṇapadasaṅgaha	5	1225
Sabbasūttamanta thang 5	7	1225
Sabbasūttasaṅgaha	15	1225
Sabbī	1	1225
Sabda Abhidhammasaṅgaha	9	1225
Sabda Abhidhammasaṅgaha	?	1225
Sabda Akkharaganthī	3	1225
Sabda Ākhayāta	4	1242
Sabda Cūḷavagga	17	1237
Sabda Karasadda	2	1242
Sabda Khuddakasikkhā	5	1225
Sabda Nipuṇṇapadasaṅgaha	11	1225
Sabda Parivāra	9	1237

Sabda Paṭhama	22	1225
Sabda Pācitūya	10	1237
Sabda Pāramī	12	1237
Sabda Pāramī	12	1242
Sabda Pātimokkha	9	1237
Sabda Pātimokkha	9	1242
Sabda Samanta 1	9	1225
Sabda Samantapāsādikā mat 7	8	1225
Sabda Samantasaṅghādisesa	10	1225
Sabda Sammatā	12	1225
Sabda Subodhālaṅkāra	2	1225
Sabda Taddhita 3 kaṇḍha, Sabda Sūtta 3, Sabda Kāraka 3	17	1242
Sabodona(?), or Saphao dona	1	1242
Sabtanāma, mat 1	13	1217
Sabtapaṭisaṅkhāyo	1	1223
Sabtapāṭha	5	1225
Sabtasamanta	12	1217
Saccadhamma	1	1217
Sadāvimalā	2	1242
Saddavimala	1	1217
Saddhammoparāyana	8	1223
Sakaravatthu	5	1217
Sakkavaratāna	7	1225
Salākavirijā	1	1242
Saḷāyatanavagga saṅyutta-nikāya	18	1225
Samantapāsādikā	16	1217
Samaya	9	1217
Samudaghosa (PJ 1)	1	1217
Samudaghosa	8	1225
Samudaghosa	8	1237
Samudaghosa	8	1242
Samudaghosa	12	1242
Saṁyuttanikāya	11	1217
Saṃ rūam dhātu	4	1242
Saṃsāravaṭasūtta	11	1242
Saṅkhapatta (PJ 41)	2	1217
Saṅkhayāloka	4	1237
Saṅkhāvaḍhana	5	1242
Saṅyutta	6	1242
Saṅyuttanikāya	11	1242
Sapda muat Vagga	15	1225
Saradamānaba	1	1223
Saradamānaba	1	1242
Saradamānaba	1	1242
Sarup Dasapāramī	6	1223

Sarupa Vinayagambhīra atthapadaṇī	9	1242
Sarupa Vinayagambhīra raṭṭhadīpanī	9	1237
Satipaṭṭhāna	4	1223
Satipaṭṭhāna	4	1223
Satiyasaṅkīr......	?	1225
Sattanipāta	10	1225
Sattatinipāta, mat 70		1217
Saṭṭhīnipāta	3	1225
Saṭṭhīnipāta	3	1225
Savathakumāra	4	1242
Sādhinarājamūlakittikā	2	1237
Sālākavirijāsūtta	1	1242
Sāmaññaphala	9	1223
Sāmaññaphalasūtta	7	1225
Sārasaṅgaha	14	1225
Sāriputtanibāna	1	1225
Seṭhī piang mǫ	1	1236
Seṭhi thang 5	5	1223
Seṭhī thang 5	5	1225
Seṭhī thang 5	5	1242
Seṭhī thang 5	5	1246
Sihanāda (PJ 52)	2	1217
Silakathā	1	1242
Sinchai rācha	17	1225
Siṅgālasūtra	9	1217
Siṅgālasūtra	9	1223
Siṅhapakaraṇa	10	1223
Sirimahāmāyā	5	1223
Sirimahāmāyā	6	1225
Sirimānanda	1	1217
Sirinanda	3	1223
Sirinda	3	1223
Sirisuddhodana	5	1225
Sīlajāṭaka	1	1217
Sīlakathā ruam	1 kaṇḍha	1242
Sīlakhandhavagga dīghanikāya	11	1223
Socandakumāra	5	1236
Sodakiṇī	1	1237
Sodantajātaka (J 532)	1	1237
Sodasanī	5	1242
Sodassanī	5	1237
Sodatarasa	1	1223
Sodattakī	6	1225
Sodattakī	6	1225
Sodattapekakhaṇasūtta sutta-saṅgaha	3	1225

Srīvijayyantahaṃsa	10	1225
Subrahmamokkha	10	1223
Suddhasukkarī	4	1223
Suddhābhojana	2	1225
Suddhābhojanā	2	1223
Sudhana (PJ 2)	9	1223
Sudhana	9	1225
Sudhanū (PJ 3)	2	1223
Sumaṇaseraṭhi amittabandhu	11	1225
Sunanda asaṅkheyya	5	1225
Sunandavohāravammikasūtta	4	1225
Surisa	1	1217
Surupavinisaya gambhīra 1 (PJ 26)	9	1225
Sutantasaṅgaha	13	1225
Suttasaṅgaha	10	1225
Suttasaṅgahalokavidū	1	1225
Suttasoma	8	1223
Suttasoma	6	1225
Suvaṇṇa hen kham	7	1237
Suvaṇṇa hen kham	1	1242
Suvaṇṇa hen kham	1	1242
Suvaṇṇa Hoi saṅkha	6	1223
Suvaṇṇajambū	12	1246
Suvaṇṇajambū	12	1246
Suvaṇṇajivahā	6	1225
Suvaṇṇajivahā	4	1246
Suvaṇṇamegha	5	1223
Suvaṇṇamokkha	10	1217
Suvaṇṇamorā	1	1225
Suvaṇṇasāma	2	1217
Suvaṇṇhaṃsa kham (J 136)	6	1242
Suvaṇṇa khāng kham	3	1242
Suvaṇṇasāma (J 540)	4	1242
Sūtta manta thang 5	1	1242
Sư̄a tāi sư̄a nǭn lokavatthu	2	1225
Tamnān Lawǣk	1	1225
Tamnān Phra Dhamma	2	1242
Tamnān phrabāt phrathāt	11	1225
Tamnān Phrayā Chư̄ang	11	1225
Temīya (?J 538)	3	1217
Temīya	4	1242
Tepadumakumāra	4	1223
Terasanipāta, mat 13		1217
Tesakuṇā	7	1225
Theyyabrahma	8	1223
Tikkanipāta	15	1225
Tikkanipāta	15	1225
Tikkanipāta	15	1225
Tilakkhaṇa	5	1217
Tilakkhaṇa yot dhammapada	5	1225
Tilokadīpa	5	1237
Tiṁsanipāta, mat 30		1217
Traipidok thang 6 khamphī	6	1217
Tǣng khieo	4	1246
Ṭīkā Abhidhamma	9	1225
Ṭīkā	1	1223
Ṭīkā Bāhuṁ	1	1225
Ṭīkā Buddhā	5	1223
Ṭīkā Dhammacakka	1	1223
Ṭīkā Mahāsamaya	4	1223
Ṭīkā Malai	12	1223
Ṭīkā Mālā	1	1223
Ṭīkā Mūlapaṇṇāsa majjhimanikāya	10	1236
Ṭīkā Namo	3	1223
Ṭīkā Nipāta	16	1225
Ṭīkā Paramatthanisaya	13	1223
Ṭīkā Saṅgaha	16	1223
Udāharaṇa sabda thang 8	8	1225
Udenarāja	9	1223
Ulakadhātu	6	1225
Uṇhisavijaiya	1	1223
Upagutta	10	1223
Upāsandi	1	1242
Upāsanti	2	1223
Ussābārasamaga plai	7	1223
Ussābārasamaga ton	8	1223
Vakkharanamo	1	1225
Valayuttadevanda	6	1225
Vantujana	6	1225
Vaṇṇavaṇṇanabrāhmaṇa (PJ 49)	5	1217
Vataṅgulī (PJ 20)	1	1217
Vattaṅgulī	1	1225
Vārāsijaya	1	1237
Vedamūlaganthī	4	1237
Vessantara nok khao	2	1223
Vessantaracariyapiṭaka	15	1217
Vibhaṅga	18	1217
Vibhaṅga	10	1242
Videvandakumārajātaka	1	1223
Vidhūra (J 545)	5	1217
Vijānasūtta	2	1225
Vilimaṅsaṅ	10	1225
Vimānavatthu	9	1225

Vimānavatthu	7	1225
Vimānavatthu	6	1225
Vinaya	9	1225
Vinaya ruam	11	1225
Vinaya thang 5	5	1242
Vinaya thang 5	1 kaṇḍha	1242
Vinayadhammacakka	8	1223
Vinayasaṅgaha	12	1223
Vinicchaya Cūḷavagga	12	1225
Visākhā	8	1225
Visuddhimagga	15	1225
Visuddhimagga	16	1225
Visuddhimagga mat 1	8	1225
Visuddhimagga mat 2	11	1225
Visuddhimagga mat 3	8	1223
Visuddhimagga mat 3	13	1225
Vitti-anīṭikā mahāvagga	9	1225
Vīsati ovāda	7	1223
Vīsatinipāta	8	1225
Vohāra Abhidhamma	9	1237
Vohāra Aṅguttaranikāya	8	1237
Vohārabhayanivāsa	6	1236
Vohārabhayavināsa	13	1236
Vohāradhātuvibhaṅga	11	1223
Vohāradibamanta	7	1236
Vohārapadhānasūtta	9	1225
Vohāravinaya thang 5 kaṇḍha	5	1223
Vohārayānī	2	1217
Vuttodaiya	4	1223
Ya-unñatabbasūtta	1	1242
Yamaka	9	1217
Yamaka mat 2	10	1236
Yasanadharā	6	1223
Yasanadharā	1	1223
Yasanadharā	7	1225
Yasatīti	11	1225
Yojanā abhidhammasaṅgaha	8	1225
Yojanāsaddā	19	1225
Yojanāsammohavinodanī	16	1225
Yokappako	5	1225
Yǭt Traipidok	1	1217
Yǭt Traipidok	1	1242

APPENDIX 2

DAILY WATCHES OR HOURS

0600-0730	tut cao
0730-0900	kòng ngai
0900-1030	tæ tiang
1030-1200	tiang
1200-1330	tut cai
1330-1500	kòng kham
1500-1630	tæ kham
1630-1800	kham
1800-1930	tut dük
1930-2100	kòng dük
2100-2230	tæ dük
2230-2400	dük
2400-0130	tut rung
0130-0300	kòng rung
0300-0430	tæ rung
0430-0600	rung

Nan Puangkham Tuikhieo, "Wiang bôrân—yan cârük cæng hua rin, kânbæng welâ samai bôrân," in *Kamphæng müang Chiang Mai, anusòn nüang nai phithi pœt læ chalòng Pratu Tha Phæ* (Chiang Mai, 1986), p. 107.

APPENDIX 3

A NOTE ON CHRONOLOGY

Thai chronology is a difficult subject, and hardly an exact science. The note that follows attempts to explain the calendar, and to outline the steps that have been taken to check the dates in the chronicles and to convert them to the Western calendar.

The traditional Thai calendar was luni-solar; that is, the days of the month were counted by the phases of the moon, but the years were figured according to the movements of the sun in the heavens. The solar new year, called *songkan* in the North, usually occurred towards the end of March up to and including 1582, and thereafter in the first half of April, on the day when the sun entered into the constellation of Aries. That particular day might occur anytime between the sixth day of the fifth lunar month and the fifth day of the sixth lunar month, and the first day of the new year was *not* the first day of the month.

Northern Thai months were not numbered the same as their counterparts in Siam. Most sources state that Northern lunar months are numbered two higher than Siamese months—e.g., the 9th Northern month is the Siamese 7th month, and so forth—but this is not strictly correct. Ample epigraphic evidence, as well as the evidence of many Nan chronicles, demonstrates that, at some times, people in Nan numbered their lunar months *one* in advance of the Siamese months, so that the Nan 9th month might be the Siamese 8th month.

This phenomenon becomes clear when we notice frequent Nan references to the *second ninth month*. Now, in order to keep the lunar and solar calendars synchronized, calendrists throughout this part of the world—following Indian chronological manuals—added leap-days and leap-months to the lunar year. Though ordinarily odd-numbered months would have 29 days, and even-numbered months 30, at regular intervals the 7th Siamese month (9th Northern month) would have 30 days instead of 29. Similarly, sometimes they would add an extra 8th month (Siamese) or 10th month (Northern). The Nan Chronicle frequently makes mention of a second *ninth* month.[1] Following the work of J.C Eade, I have termed this form of reckoning "Keng Tung style."

Weekdays were named as in the West, i.e., Sunday, Monday, ... Saturday, with the first weekday being Sunday and the seventh Saturday. (And Wednesday in Thailand was also Wednesday in the West.)

Another calendrical complication comes with a second form of denominating days and years which, presumably, is older than the use of the

[1]The nicest example of this occurs in the chronicle at CS 973, 13th waxing of the second 9th month. Note that the PTMN f° 143, dates this in the second *10th* month, i.e., Northern Style.

seven weekday names. By this system, days and years were given two names following ten- and twelve-day cycles, using the same names for both days and years.[2] This yielded a cycle of sixty days: the combination *kat kai*, for example, would occur every sixty days, and for years every sixty years. The two cycles are as follows:

Decimal Cycle	Duodecimal Cycle
pœk	san
kat	lao
kot	set
luang	kai
tao	cai
ka	pao
kap	yi
dap	mao
lwai	si
müang	sai
	sanga
	met

The first problem to arise when confronting the dates of the Nan Chronicle is that, in the earlier portions, there are discrepancies between the year number, expressed in the Culasakarâja Era (CS; +638 = AD), and the cyclical year. In all such cases, I have adopted the cyclical year designations as correct, and the CS figures as erroneous. I have felt justified in doing so because it is clear in such passages that the source of the dates are the chronicles of the Chæ Hæng Reliquary, which give cyclical years without CS numerals; and because the chronicler so often has, for example, paired a CS year ending in 0 with a decimal cyclical year which can never be paired with a CS year divisible by ten:[3] CS years ending in 0 are always *pœk* years.

The best, i.e, the fullest, dates in the chronicles are those that provide a weekday, both Sunday-Saturday style and Northern Thai cyclic-day style; a day in the lunar month, a year in both cyclic style and in the CS era, and a day in the 27-day cycle of lunar mansions *(rœk,* Northern Thai *lœk)*. An excellent example is the date for the accession of Cao Paña Læ Mum, who "in the *kat pao* year CS 1011 ... On Sunday, the full-moon day of the eighth month, a *ka lao* day, in the watch near noon, in the fifteenth lunar mansion ... took his place in the audience hall." All that data can readily be checked. The CS year 1011 was indeed a *kat pao* year. The full-moon day of the eighth month (Northern; sixth Siamese month), however, was on a Monday; but the preceding day, the 14th of the waxing moon, was a Sunday and a *ka lao* day. The fifteenth lunar mansion began in mid-morning on that day, which was April 25, AD 1649.

---

[2]See Roger Billard, "Les cycles chronographiques chinois dans les inscriptions thaïs," *Bulletin de l'École français d'Extrême-Orient* 51 (1963): 416 ff.

[3]See David K. Wyatt, "The Chronology of Nan History, A.D. 1320-1598," *Journal of the Siam Society* 64, 2 (July 1976): 202-6.

How can such details be so exactly checked? I have used two computer programs to do the checking. The first is based on the calendrical data presented in Eade's *Southeast Asian Ephemeris*.[4] It can generate complete monthly calendars for any month, showing also weekdays, cyclical days, and AD equivalents. For the lunar mansions (*rœk*) and planetary positions, I have used a computer program written by J. C. Eade. Both programs we expect to polish and make available to interested parties in the near future.

Finally, in measuring time, Southeast Asian chroniclers generally count years in current, rather than elapsed fashion. That is, from 1987 to 1992 is six years, not five.

---

[4]J. C. Eade, *Southeast Asian Ephemeris: Solar and Planetary Positions, AD 638-2000* (Ithaca, 1989).

BIBLIOGRAPHY

Manuscripts

Phün wongsa caonai ton sawœi latcasombat nai müang Pua læ müang Nan. MS. Wat Dòn Kæo, *tambon* Nai Wiang, *amphœ* Müang, Nan; SRI 82.107.05.044, 130 ff°.

Phün wongsa mahakasat tang lai tangtæ Paña Samantalat phon ma læ phün wongsa caonai ton sawœi latcasombat nai müang Pua læ müang Nan. MS. Wat Panet, *tambon* Wiang Nüa, *amphœ* Müang, Nan; SRI 82.107.05.043, 240 ff°.

Prawat müang Nan læ Tamlâ yâ. MS. Wat Muang Tüt, *tambon* Muang Tüt, *amphœ* Müang, Nan; SRI 82.107.05.047, 39 ff°.

Prawat tang müang Nan. MS., SRI 82.107.05.045, 182 ff°. Transcription: SRI, by "Buntha—Caran" and checked by Buntha Sriphimchai; dated 19 November 2525 (1982).

Takun cao latcawong Mahapom. MS. Wat Mongkhon, *tambon* Nai Wiang *khet* 2, *amphœ* Müang, Nan; SRI 82.107.05.052, 9 ff°; originally dated 1850; copy dated 1879.

Tamnan Cæ Hæng. MS. Wat Sæn Fang, *tambon* Chang Mòi, *amphœ* Müang, Chiang Mai; SRI 78.020.01L.038; 19 ff°.

Tamnan müang Nan. MS. Wat Tan Cum, Nan; copied by Noi Inta Müangpom, 1972. Davis fl-47. Lanna Thai Manuscripts from the Richard Davis Collection, Australian National University; Microfiche #24.

Tamnan Pathat Cæ Hæng. MS. Wat Phaya Phu, Nan, dated 1928; copied by *nân* Kua Lüalit, 1972. Davis fl-38; Lanna Thai Manuscripts from the Richard Davis Collection, Australian National University; Microfiche #3.

Tamnan Pathat Cæ Hæng. MS. Wat Tan Cum, undated. 21p. Davis Ms. fl-49; Lanna Thai Manuscripts from the Richard Davis Collection, Australian National University; Microfiche #12.

Tamnan Pathat Cao Cæ Hæng. MS. Wat Muang Tüt, Nan, dated BE 2481 [AD 1938]. 13 double pages. Davis Ms. fl-?; Lanna Thai Manuscripts from the Richard Davis Collection, Australian National University; Microfiche #8.

Books and Articles

"Anacak lak kham (kotmai müang Nan)," in Saratsawadi Òngsakun, *Lakthan prawattisat Lan Na* (Chiang Mai, 1991), pp. 56-100 and photocopy of text in appendix.

Aroonrut Wichienkeeo, "Phraratchakatha müang Nan R.S. 111," *Ruam botkhwam prawattisat* 2 (January 1981): 34-49.

Billard, Roger. "Les cycles chronographiques chinois dans les inscriptions thaïs," *Bulletin de l'École français d'Extrême-Orient* 51 (1963): 416 ff.

Charnvit Kasetsiri, *The Rise of Ayudhya: A History of Siam in the Fourteenth and Fifteenth Centuries*. Kuala Lumpur, 1976.

Chiang Mai University. Social Research Institute. *Raichü nangsü boran Lan Na: ekkasan maikhrofim khòng Sathaban Wicai Sangkhom Mahawitthayalai Chiang Mai pi 2521-2533* (Catalogue of palm-leaf texts on microfilm at the Social Research Institute, Chiang Mai University 1978-1990). Chiang Mai: Sathaban Wicai Sangkhom, 1991.

Cœdès, G. "Documents sur l'histoire religieuse et politique du Laos occidental," *Bulletin de l'École français d'Extrême-Orient* 25, fasc. 1-2 (1925): 1-202.

Cotmaihet hon chabap Phraya Pramunthanarak. Bangkok, 1921.

Cotmaihet rüang thap Chiang Tung. Bangkok, 1916.

Davis, Richard B. *Muang Metaphysics*. Bangkok: Pandora, 1984.

Eade, J. C. *Southeast Asian Ephemeris: Solar and Planetary Positions, AD 638-2000*. Ithaca: Cornell Southeast Asia Program, 1989.

Griswold, A. B., and Prasert na Nagara. "A Fifteenth-Century Siamese Historical Poem," in *Southeast Asian History and Historiography: Essays Presented to D.G.E. Hall*. Ithaca: Cornell University Press, 1975.

Griswold, A. B., and Prasert na Nagara. "The Epigraphy of Mahâdharmarâjâ I of Sukhodaya (Epigraphic and Historical Studies, No. 11)," *Journal of the Siam Society* 60, pt. 1 (Jan. 1973), 71-82, and 60, pt. 2 (July 1973), 91-128; or *Epigraphic and Historical Studies* (Bangkok, 1992), pp. 425-570.

Griswold, A. B., and Prasert na Nagara. "The Pact Between Sukhodaya and Nân (Epigraphic and Historical Studies, No. 3)," *Journal of the Siam Society* 57, pt. 1 (Jan. 1969): 57-108.

Griswold, A. B., and Prasert na Nagara. *Towards a History of Sukhodaya Art*. Bangkok: Fine Arts Dept., 1967.

Harvey, G.E. *History of Burma*. London, 1925; reprinted London: Frank Cass, 1967.

Hundius, Harald. "The Colophons of Thirty Pâli Manuscripts from Northern Thailand," *Journal of the Pali Text Society* XIV (1990): 1-173.

Hundius, Harald. *Phonologie und Schrift des Nordthai*. Stuttgart: Franz Steiner, 1990. (Abhandlungen für die Kunde des Morgenlandes, Bd. XLVIII, 3.)

"Intercourse between Burma and Siam," *Selected Articles from the Siam Society Journal* 6 (Bangkok, 1959).

Kachorn Sukhabanij, "The Thai Beach-Head States in the 11th-12th Centuries," *Sinlapakòn* I, 3-4 (Sept.-Nov. 1957).

Khamman Vongkotrattana, *Cao. Phongsavadan sat lao*. Vientiane: National Library, 1973.

"Kotmai phracao Nan [Laws of the Kings of Nan]," transcribed by Singkha Wannasai, in *Kotmai phra cao Nan [læ] Tamnan phra cao Hai*. Chiang Mai: Sun Songsœm læ Süksa Watthanatham Lan Na, Witthayalai Khru Chiang Mai, 1980. (Ekkasan lamdap thi 4.)

le Boulanger, Paul. *Histoire du Laos français*. Paris: Plon, 1931.

le May, Reginald. *An Asian Arcady: The Land and People of Northern Siam.* Cambridge, 1926.

[Luang Prasœt Chronicle of Ayudhya] "Translation of Events in Ayuddhya 686-966," *Journal of the Siam Society* 6, 3 (1909): 1-21; reprinted in *Selected Articles from the Siam Society Journal* (Bangkok: The Siam Society, 1954), I, 38-64.

McCarthy, James, *Surveying and Exploring in Siam.* London: John Murray, 1900.

McCarthy, James. *An Englishman's Siamese Journals, 1890-1893.* Bangkok, 1983.

McFarland, George Bradley. *Thai-English Dictionary.* Stanford: Stanford University Press, 1944

Muang Nan. Bangkok: Fine Arts Dept., 1987.

Müang Nan: borankhadi prawatsat læ sinlapa. Bangkok: Fine Arts Dept., 1987.

Norman, K. R. *Pali Literature, Including the Canonical Literature in Prakrit and Sanskrit of All the Hinayana Schools of Buddhism.* Wiesbaden: Harrassowitz, 1983. (*A History of Indian Literature,* ed. Jan Gonda, vol. VII, fasc. 2.)

Notton, Camille, tr., "Chronique de Xieng Mai," *Annales du Siam,* III. Paris, 1932.

Paññasami. *The History of the Buddha's Religion,* tr. B. C. Law. London, 1952.

Phama rop Thai. Chiang Mai: Sathaban Wicai Sangkhom, 1989.

Phra Ratchawisutthisophon et al., *Müang Phayao.* Bangkok, 1984.

Phün na müang Nan læ khâo thâng müang Nan, ed. Aroonrut Wichienkeeo. Chiang Mai: Sûn Watthanatham Cangwat Chiang Mai, Witthayâlai Khru Chiang Mai, 1985. (Ekkasan lamdap thi 9.) MS., SRI 82.107.05.049, 42 ff°.

Prachakitkoracak, *Phraya. Phongsawadan Yonok.* Bangkok, 1973.

Prachum phongsawadan. 79 vols. Bangkok: var. pub., 1914-1965. Reprints: 14 vols., Bangkok: Samnakphim Kaona, 1963-1974; 50 vols., Bangkok: Khurusapha, 1963-1970.

Prasert na Nagara. "Samphanthaphap rawang ratchawong Phra Ruang kap ratchawong Nan [Relations between the dynasties of Phra Ruang and Nan]," in his *Ngan carük læ prawattisat* (Bangkok, 1991), 156-58.

Raingan khwamkaona kandamnœn ngan süksa wicai anurak læ phatthana Wat Phra Phai Luang. Bangkok, 1986.

Rank, Otto. *The Myth of the Birth of the Hero and Other Writings.* New York: Vintage Books, 1959.

Ratanapañña Thera, *The Sheaf of Garlands of the Epochs of the Conqueror, being a translation of* Jinakâlamâlîpakaranam, tr. N. A. Jayawickrama. London: Luzac for the Pali Text Society, 1968.

Râtchasomphan, *Sænluang. The Nan Chronicle,* tr. Prasœt Churatana. Ithaca: Cornell University Southeast Asia Program, 1966. (Data Paper, no. 59.)

Râtchasomphan, *Sænluang. Râtchawongpakon, phongsâwadân müang Nan.* Bangkok?: Crem. Phracao Suriyaphongphrittadet, 1918. (*Prachum phongsawadan,* 10.)

Reinhorn, Marc. *Dictionnaire laotien-français.* Paris, 1970.

Sanguan Chotisukkharat, *Nangsü phün müang Chiang Mai*. Chiang Mai, 1972.

Sanguan Chotisukkharat, *Tamnan müang nüa*. Chiang Mai, 1955-56, vol. I (2nd ed.) p. 44.

Sathapattayakam Phayao læ Nan. Chiang Mai: Social Research Institute, Chiang Mai University, 1989.

Sila Viravong, *Maha. History of Laos*. New York: Paragon Book Reprint Corp., 1964.

Singwætlòm sinlapakam cangwat Nan. Nan: Nuai Anurak Singwætlòm Sinlapakam Thòngthin, 1990.

Somcit Rüangkhana, *Namchom borannawatthusathan nai amphœ Chiang Sæn cangwat Chiang Rai*. Bangkok, 1970.

Stringer, C. E. W. *Report by Mr. C. E. W. Stringer of a Journey to the Laos State of Nan, Siam*. London, 1888. *Parliament. Papers by Command*, C.-5321.

Taillard, Christian. *Le Laos: stratégies d'un Etat-tampon*. Montpellier, 1989.

Tamnan Phrathat Cæ Hæng. Bangkok: crem. Cao Mahaphrom Surathada (Mahaphrom na Nan), 1931.

Tamnan phün müang Chiang Mai, ed. Sanguan Chotisukkharat. Bangkok: Samnak Nayok Ratthamontri, 1971.

Tamnan sip ha ratchawong. 3 vols. Chiang Mai: Sathaban Wicai Sangkhom, 1981-1990.

Tamnân Pathât cao Pû Piang Cæ Hæng. Chiang Mai, 1923.

Tamnân Phrathât Cæ Hæng, chabap Phrasamuha Phrom læ wannakam khamson Khrao Ham, ed. Somcet Wimonkasem. Nan: Sun Watthanatham Cangwat Nan, 1983.

Thamniap phrasamanasak læ thamniap wat tangtang thua ratcha'anacak Ph.S. 2509. Bangkok, 1966.

Thawi Swangpanyangkun. *Sakkarat thiap hon Thai*. Chiang Mai: Author, 1988.

Thiphakorawong, *Caophraya*. *Phraratchaphongsawadan Krung Rattanakosin ratchakan thi* 2. Bangkok: Khurusapha, 1961.

Thiphakorawong, *Caophraya*. *The Dynastic Chronicles, Bangkok Era, The Fourth Reign*, tr. Chadin Flood. Tokyo, 1965.

Thiphakòrawong, *Caophraya*. *The Dynastic Chronicles, Bangkok Era, The First Reign*, tr. Thadeus and Chadin Flood. Tokyo, 1978.

Thongthaem Nartchamnong. "Thinthan khòng chao Tai nai Sipsòng Phanna = The Land of the Tais (Dai) in Sipsong Panna," *Muang Boran* 15, 3 (July-Sept. 1989): 51-65.

Udom Roongruangsri, *Photcanânukrom Lân Nâ-Thai, chabap Mæfâ Luang*. 2 vols. Chiang Mai and Bangkok: Mûnnithi Mæfâ Luang and Thanâkhân Thai Phânit, 1991.

Vella, Walter F. *Siam Under Rama III*. Locust Valley, NY: J. J. Augustin, 1957.

Vliet, Jeremias van. *The Short History of the Kings of Siam*, tr. Leonard Andaya. Bangkok: The Siam Society, 1975.

Walailak Songsiri, "Chum chon boran thi Ban Bò Luang," *Muang Boran* 17, 3 (July-Sept. 1991): 55-61.

Wat Phumin and Wat Nong Bua. Bangkok: Muang Boran, 1986.

Wells, Kenneth E. *Thai Buddhism: its rites and activities*. Bangkok, 1960.

Wenk, Klaus. *The Restoration of Thailand Under Rama I 1782-1809*. Tucson: University of Arizona Press, 1968.

Wood, W. A. R. *A History of Siam*. London, 1926; reprint Bangkok: Chalermnit, 1959.

Wyatt, David K. "Assault by Ghosts: Politics and Religion in Nan in the 18th Century," *Crossroads* 4, 2 (1989): 63-70.

Wyatt, David K. "Chronicle Traditions in Thai Historiography," in *Southeast Asian History and Historiography: Essays Presented to D. G. E. Hall*, ed. C. D. Cowan and O. W. Wolters (Ithaca: Cornell University Press, 1976), pp. 107-22.

Wyatt, David K. "Siam and Laos, 1767-1827," *Journal of Southeast Asian History* 4, 2 (Sept. 1963): 19-21.

Wyatt, David K. "The Chronology of Nan History, A.D. 1320-1598," *Journal of the Siam Society* 64, 2 (July 1976): 202-6.

Wyatt, David K.*Temple Murals as an Historical Source: The Case of Wat Phumin, Nan*. Bangkok: Chulalongkorn University Press, 1993.

INDEX

www.ingramcontent.com/pod-product-compliance
Ingram Content Group UK Ltd.
Pitfield, Milton Keynes, MK11 3LW, UK
UKHW010028310125
454458UK00009B/533

9 780877 2771